THE CURSE
OF ICARUS

The health factor in air travel

F. S. KAHN

London and New York

First published 1990
by Routledge
11 New Fetter Lane, London EC4P 4EE

Simultaneously published in the USA and Canada
by Routledge
a division of Routledge, Chapman and Hall, Inc.
29 West 35th Street, New York, NY 10001

Phototypeset in 10pt Baskerville by
Mews Photosetting, Beckenham, Kent
Printed and bound in Great Britain by
Biddles Ltd, Guildford and King's Lynn

British Library Cataloguing in Publication Data

Kahn, F.S.
The curse of Icarus.
I. Title
613.6'8

Library of Congress Cataloging in Publication Data

Kahn, F.S. 1941–
The curse of Icarus : the health factor in air travel / F.S. Kahn.
p. cm.
1. Air travel – Health aspects. 2. Aeronautics – Health aspects.
I. Title.
RC1077.K34   1990
616.9'80213–dc20
90-8443
CIP

ISBN 0-415-04882-6

TO MY PARENTS

CONTENTS

ILLUSTRATIONS

TABLES

FIGURE

PREFACE

This book is revolutionary inasmuch as it will change for ever the way people think about air travel. From now on, everyone will be aware of how and why this mode of transport can affect their health. Such a realization is bound to shock and even stun the public because flying is taken so much for granted today. However, I am sure that for some time many of us have known intuitively that aviation, like other technologies, has a downside. And to deliver a further blow, a branch of medicine has existed for over 50 years which not only recognizes the medical hazards of the flight environment but is actively engaged in the maintenance of the health and fitness of airline and military pilots.

Two questions must therefore be asked. Why has no information so far been disclosed? And why have the passive flyers, the fare-paying passengers, been denied medical facilities that are a standard feature for active flyers? The same answer applies to both: *to safeguard the vested interests of the airlines and the travel industry*. They know, and have known all along, that if the public got wind of any adverse effects they might 'cease to patronize the airlines. The inevitable dissemination of such information would unquestionably discourage potential passengers. . . . This question is not academic, but reflects a very lively fear in the minds of those concerned with airline operation' (Edgerton 1936). This spectre was raised by an American official when aviation was in its infancy and has loomed ever since.

The time has come to spill the beans and let consumers decide for themselves whether they want to fly or not. Indeed, in our democratic societies that is the bottom line and no institution or industry should be allowed to prevent us from exercising this freedom.

The work has taken more than three years to write and the facts and figures presented are well substantiated, as one would expect from a primer on aviation or aerospace medicine. However, I have two things to confess. The first is that I was once barred from a library and the second is that I was fortunate to win the confidence of many top experts. One of these, an American professor of medicine, revealed that some airline lobbyists had vetoed his appointment as chairman of the important Committee on Airliner Cabin Air Quality because of his outspoken views. Another, a British doctor, told of how his talk on medical problems in air travel, which was to be given to the 1979 conference of the Association of British Travel Agents (ABTA), was cancelled at the last moment.

I must warn readers that there is no short cut to aviation medicine even in this popularized version. If you want to know the how, the why, the where, the what, and the who of health risks in flying, you must understand at least some basics of the specialism: the atmosphere – its physical laws and composition; the psychological aspects – the fear of flying; the physiological features – oxygen want, over-breathing, gas expansion, and jet lag; and the heart of the matter, the Greek myth that sums it all up. But it is worth the effort because most of the material is new, and also fascinating.

The first step to the reality of flying is that it is not comparable with other forms of surface transport. The reason is that the latter occur in a natural environment, usually at sea-level, while the former occurs in the artificial environment of an aircraft cabin that is pressurized to an altitude of between 6,000 and 8,000 ft. Therefore, it would be more accurate to compare flying with mountaineering. For within minutes, each male and female, child or octogenarian, irrespective of physical condition, reaches the height of a minor peak in the Alps. And it is not pure, thin Alpine air that they breathe. In fact, it is polluted and the concentrations of the pollutants in some cases contravene the regulations permitted for indoor environments on the ground (CACAQ 1986).

An important feature of the book is the two health checklists which enable passengers to determine instantly which diseases are contra-indicative to flight and what preventive measures can be taken (Chapter 12). Or if they are fit, what circumstances or minor ailments may cause them to have problems. Another useful addition is the issue of legal rights of air travellers with regard to medical incidents under the Warsaw Convention of the Air Law. It is an area which is still unexplored by lawyers.

And now for the final blow: the extent of the health risk. As there is a dearth of statistics – they are supplied by the airlines themselves – I asked for comments from two prominent specialists, Dr Geoffrey Bennett, Chief Medical Officer of the Civil Aviation Authority in the UK and, in the USA, Dr Stanley R. Mohler, Professor and Vice-Chairman of the Department of Community Medicine, and Director of Aerospace Medicine, Wright State University, Dayton, Ohio. *Their estimate is that 10 per cent of the average passenger load are not totally fit.* At Heathrow Airport, where passenger traffic is some 35 million per annum, this represents 3.5 million, while in the USA, where 28 per cent of the population fly at least once a year, it amounts to 2.8 per cent of all Americans. That demonstrates just how big the health factor in air travel is.

ACKNOWLEDGEMENTS

It gives me great pleasure to thank Air Commodore J. Ernsting, OBE, Commandant of RAF Institute of Aviation Medicine, Professor D.M. Denison, National Heart and Lung Institute, Group Captain D.H. Glaister, Whittingham Professor of Aviation Medicine, and Dr F.J. Mills, Regional Medical Director of Janssen Pharmaceutical Ltd, for the many useful suggestions about the manuscript.

I am also indebted to Dr. G. Bennett, CMO, Civil Aviation Authority, Professor Sir David Weatherall, Nuffield Department of Clinical Medicine, Professor P. Sleight, Department of Cardiovascular Medicine of Oxford University, and Wing Commander R.M. Harding, RAF Institute of Aviation Medicine, for their advice.

In addition, I would like to thank members of the Royal Aeronautical Society and the many interviewees for their time and effort; Gill Davies and the staff of Routledge for all their hard work; and Diana Burfield for her encouragement.

Also to Random House and Faber & Faber Ltd for permission to reprint excerpts from 'The Journal of an Airman' from *The English Auden: Poems, Essays and Dramatic Writings 1927–1939* by W.H. Auden, and Harcourt Brace Jovanovich and Faber & Faber Ltd for permission to reprint excerpts from 'Burnt Norton' from *Four Quartets* by T.S. Eliot.

Chapter One

THE BARRIER OF SILENCE: UNSUCCESSFUL ATTEMPTS AT DISCLOSURE

There was a time when people thought that it would never be possible to fly faster than the speed of sound, or, as it is termed, Mach 1. The reason was simple. Whenever anyone had tried, the controls would freeze and the aircraft would go into a shudder. Such was the resistance of the shock waves that it gave rise to the belief in the existence of an invisible wall of air which would smash any craft that ran into it. Indeed, several test pilots had lost their lives in attempts. One of them, Geoffrey de Havilland, Jnr, was blown to pieces when his tailless experimental aircraft, the 'Swallow', reached Mach 0.94 on a dive, and as a result the British programme (carried out by the de Havilland company) was cancelled. The sound barrier appeared to be invincible.

Several months after de Havilland's death, Chuck Yeager, on 14 October 1947, flew supersonic in the rocket-powered X-1. The 24-year-old USAF captain had been able to control the violent shakes through a special stabilizer, and he described the 20-second trip at Mach 1.07 – 700 m.p.h. – in his inimitable way: 'it was as smooth as a baby's bottom: Grandma could be sitting up there sipping lemonade' (Yeager and Janos 1985: 130). But there was another aspect to his attainment which he mentions in his autobiography *Yeager*.

> After all the anticipation to achieve this moment, it really was a let-down. It took a damned instrument meter to tell me what I'd done. There should've been a bump on the road, something to let you know you had just punched a nice clean hole through the sonic barrier. . . . Later on, I realized that this mission had to end in a let-down, because the real barrier wasn't in the sky, but in our knowledge and experience of supersonic flight.
>
> (Yeager and Janos 1985: 130)

I quote the example because it can serve as an analogy for a situation that exists in civil aviation today: the misconception that air travel is like any form of surface transport. And whenever there is an air disaster, airlines reinforce this impression when they produce statistics to demonstrate that flying is still safer in comparison to travelling by train or in motor vehicles on land. Some doctors add to the misapprehension when they measure a heart patient's ability to fly, e.g. by whether they can walk 50–80 metres or halfway up a flight of stairs (Wright 1983). Perhaps, they might have reservations if they knew that the regulation had a nautical origin – a walk up the gangway was a ship's doctor's test. (Dr Peter Chapman, who has a penchant for such items, showed me an entry in the 1939 Imperial Airways booklet, by Colonel F.B. Mackie, in which American Lines is given credit for the rule.)

What has happened is that due to the general ignorance and inexperience of the hostile atmosphere, and the airline industry's implementation of the 'Edgerton Agreement' (Edgerton 1936) to suppress medical information, a barrier of silence has arisen. Whoever speaks out now will encounter disbelief and may even be subject to ridicule. 'That's impossible' is a common response from air travellers whose quick mental check confirms that they have experienced no signs other than those they would consider to be innocuous – stress, discomfort, inconvenience, and jet lag. If the speaker persists, they will encounter, at some time or other, the erroneous argument about safety. 'There's less chance of me being killed in the air than when I cross the road.' Or another that cuts the speaker down to size: 'If there were any problems, we would have been told.' There is also the remark that goes to the heart of the matter. 'Won't this stop people from flying?' But if anything, the speaker emerges from these exchanges with a reputation less than intact. It is not difficult for them to be labelled a sensationalist, scaremonger, or as someone not to be trusted. In effect, the silence not only halts discussion on the subject but introduces an element of absurdity which reflects on those who initiate the discussion. However, emphasis should be put on the fact that there never can be a meaningful dialogue in the absence of a context, i.e. a knowledge of aviation medicine. Here, then, is a defensive structure, a deterrent, or what amounts to a wall.

The question to be asked is whether any attempts have been made on the barrier of science. The answer is yes, several. If the people making such attempts are to be categorized, it would be an easy task for the majority are members of the medical profession. 'Doctors with a conscience' may be an apt description. One of the first ran a banner, 'Illness in the clouds', before his peers that appeared in the *British Medical Journal* (Anon. 1975) as an editorial. For the readers, it affords a glimpse of the harm that can be done by the pressure environment of an aircraft. The article announces a new area of public health which will grow in the future. Concern is shown at the high numbers of passengers using London's Heathrow Airport – some 21 million between 1973/4 – and the introduction of the profitable wide-bodied Boeing 747 that will ensure this trend continues.

An airport, the writer points out, is a stressful place with interminable procedures (and long walks to departure gates undertaken with hand luggage) that 'may cause anxiety before the passenger has even boarded'. Once in the air there is an additional hazard to face as each person is exposed to altitudes of between 5,000 and 7,000 ft through cabin pressurization. 'Healthy people have no difficulty in adapting their circulation to the resulting mild degree of hypoxia, but anyone with cardio-respiratory disease may become distressed' (Anon. 1975). If there is a particular group that is susceptible to medical problems, it is the elderly and middle-aged for they are 'prone to ischaemic heart disease and cerebrovascular disease both of which may be adversely affected by hypoxia' (Anon. 1975). In all, it is apparent that the atmosphere of an aircraft cabin is detrimental to the vital organs – the heart, the lungs, and the brain – of an unhealthy passenger. What is significant is that a direct association between air travel and these illnesses was established by Dr Peter H. Beighton and Dr Peter R. Richards in their 1968 study (Beighton and Richards 1968). Over a period of 3 years, 1963–5, they investigated forty-two patients who had collapsed during or immediately after a routine flight and been admitted to the Hillingdon, a large general hospital near Heathrow.

The editorial next quotes from a survey of 377 medical incidents that occurred on flights with a long-haul carrier (BOAC). The highest proportion, 25 per cent, were of a neurological nature, and this was followed by 11 per cent for heart disease and 7 per cent for respiratory conditions. A 20-year analysis of the causes of death on board was also given.

Of 90 deaths from natural causes in passengers from 1947 to 1967 on B.O.A.C. flights 34 were due to myocardial infarction, 6 to heart failure, 7 to cerebrovascular accidents, 13 to cancer, 3 to leukaemia,

3 to renal failure, 2 to pulmonary embolism, and 2 to cirrhosis of the liver. The remaining 20 deaths were due to other causes; 47 of the deaths were in notified invalid passengers.

(Anon. 1975)

The fact that people could die on an aircraft because of the abnormal environment would appear to have been well concealed – and may have come as a revelation to the medical profession, for the source of the statistics was an MD thesis (Richards 1970). The same author did a further survey of 615 passengers in 1973 (Richards 1973). However, the figures reported by airlines must be treated with caution as little is known about their origin. If the editorial makes a contribution, it is in the exposure of three salient points. The first is that there is a link between travel by plane – both on the ground and in flight – and illness. The second is that there are specific diseases that are aggravated by air travel, and the third is that this problem should be faced.

Here, then, was a somewhat timid attempt – the identity of the writer was concealed – to arouse the interest of the medical establishment, and there were few takers. In fact, the leading article only generated two letters in the correspondence column of the *British Medical Journal*. The first, which was written by Dr Richard Fairhurst (who would later become the Chairman of the British Aeromedical Practitioners Association), made the observation that the medical certificate of fitness for air travel (MEDIF) should not be taken as a protection against illness in-flight. The fact that 47 of the 90 deaths that occurred were of notified invalids proved the point (Fairhurst 1975). The other response came from a doctor in South Africa who advised 'passengers with marginal cardiorespiratory reserve' to check on the altitude of their transit and final destinations. He mentioned the case of an angina pectoris patient 'who was symptom-free in Cape Town at sea-level, but who suffered severe angina at rest after travelling to Johannesburg, which is above 5,000 ft'. The situation is common enough when holidays are taken in mountain resorts (Lee 1975).

Perhaps, the indifference shown by the doctors to 'Illness in the clouds' is due in part to what would appear to be the small numbers of passengers at risk, to the fact that the problem is not perceived to require immediate attention but as something to be dealt with in the future, and to the false impression created that aviation medicine is a mere extension of general practice. However, the editorial was not a complete failure as there was one group that benefited – the pilots. Nine months later, the Royal College of Physicians set up a working party to consider cardiovascular disease associated with flying. The aspects to be studied were reported in the *British Medical Journal*:

> guidelines for the acceptance of candidates for training as airline pilots and recommendations regarding the cardiovascular fitness of serving pilots; health education of pilots; the electrocardiogram and effort testing in the assessment of cardiovascular fitness for pilots and the place of coronary arteriography; problems relating to the reissue of flying licences after cardiovascular illness.
>
> (WPCFAP 1975)[1]

The second assault on the barrier of silence was to come from across the Atlantic. The American Medical Association (AMA) fielded four members of its Air Emergency Task Force to search for conditions that would render passengers unfit for air travel. The result, 'Medical aspects of transportation aboard commercial aircraft' (AMACEMS 1982), is a series of guidelines for physicians. The approach is considered and logical and, although unsupported by statistics and references, it does much to broaden the scope of the task. Here for once is a general review of most of the conditions that in theory may be at increased risk in the air.

A simple explanation is given, i.e. the low partial pressure of oxygen (PO$_2$): there is the aircraft that operates at a pressure differential to the outside atmosphere.

> Assuming a flight at 35,000 ft. where the atmospheric pressure is only 3.40 psi, the cabin compressor adds another 8.6 psi. The ambient pressure is 3.4 psi plus 8.6 psi, or 12.0 psi, which is the atmospheric pressure at 5,500 ft. above sea level. Similarly, the cabin pressure at 40,000 ft. is 2.72 psi plus 8.6 psi, a psi of 11.32, equivalent to an altitude of 7,500 ft.
>
> (AMACEMS 1982: 1007)

This in turn has repercussions in our lungs.

> The alveolar PO$_2$ of a person with normal lungs is 107 mmHg at sea level, where the atmopheric PO$_2$ is 159 mmHg. However, at the 5,000 ft. level simulated by pressurized aircraft actually flying at 35,000 ft., the atmospheric PO$_2$ has dropped to 130 mmHg and the alveolar PO$_2$ to 76 mmHg; at a simulated cabin pressure of

8,000 ft., the atmospheric PO_2 is 116 mmHg, and the alveolar PO_2 level is only 59 mmHg.

(AMACEMS 1982: 1007)

The reduction in oxygen pressure can have adverse effects on specific illnesses for which the authors have included their recommendations.

All patients with chronic cardiovascular or pulmonary problems such as cystic fibrosis, chronic emphysema, cyanotic congenital heart disease, chronic asthma, coronary insufficiency, or fibrotic pulmonary conditions should have supplemental oxygen at all times during flight at levels above 22,500 ft.

(AMACEMS 1982: 1007)

They suggest further that the arterial PO_2 should be measured before air travel and should be above 50 mmHg.

It may surprise readers that the guidelines recommend that such passengers should be tested before they can fly, particularly at a time when there are no health restrictions in civil aviation. But perhaps this augurs well for the future when regulations will be necessary. Take the case of asthma, a common complaint, which some may argue does not warrant inclusion in this category. There was a well-publicized incident reported by *The Times* and the *Daily Telegraph*, among other newspapers, on 29 April 1987, of a 12-year-old girl who had an asthmatic attack on board a British Airways 747 flight and lost consciousness; because she did not respond to the oxygen and an inhalant from the medical kit, the aircraft had to be diverted (Elliott 1987; Rais 1987). (Chronic bronchitis, which was omitted from the AMA list, should be included – I know of at least one instance where a sufferer experienced post-flight problems.)

Other cardiovascular categories mentioned are myocardial infarction (within 4 weeks), cerebrovascular accident (within 2 weeks), severe hypertension, decompensated cardiovascular disease, or any condition which restricts cardiac reserve; while pneumothorax, congential pulmonary cysts or a vital capacity less than 50 per cent are added to the broncho-pulmonary section.

Contraindications to air travel are shown to range wide and also comprise pregnancy (beyond 240 days or if there is danger of miscarriage), gastrointestinal, neuropsychiatric, hematologic, eye, ear, nose, and throat conditions. To give specific instances, these cover abdominal surgery within 10 to 14 days, ulcers, or inflammation of

6

the stomach and intestinal tract; epilepsy – unless well controlled –
recent skull fracture, brain tumours, or a history of unpredictable or
violent behaviour; anaemia, where the haemoglobin concentration is
less than 8.5 g/dL or the red cell count is less than 3 million/mm^3 in
adults, sickle-cell disease, haemophilia, or aeroembolism within 12
hours of last scuba dive; recent eye surgery, acute sinusitis, acute otitis
media, or cases where the jaws are permanently wired.

The obvious result of prolonged immobilization is also mentioned:
swollen feet and ankles caused when the blood pools. However,
passengers with cardiac insufficiency or thrombic or venous disease
may well suffer from a pulmonary embolism. Indeed, such cases have
been reported in the *British Medical Journal* (Collins *et al.* 1979). Three
of these were aged 68–70 years while one was a man in his mid-40s.
There is the recommendation, too, that people with varicose veins
should wear support hose.

If any comment is to be made on the second assault on the barrier
of silence, it could be said that the impact was similar to that of the
first. Three letters were elicited and appeared in the *Journal of the
American Medical Association*. The first (Roper 1982) drew attention to
the fact that recent eye surgery is not a bar to air travel unless 'intra-
ocular air is present'. The second (Klemes 1982) recounted a medical
emergency on board in which a psychiatrist had attended a passenger
who had lost consciousness and raised the spectre of a malpractice suit.
(There is the anecdote of the doctor who saved a person's life but was
later sued because he broke their ribs in the process.) The third (Whaley
1982) introduced another element, the aircrew, for whom such problems can be critical as they can end a career. The writer, Dr William
H. Whaley, also made an important point, the fact that the guidelines
constituted all that was known as aviation medicine. Indeed, this was
the first occasion that the specialism was mentioned.

If there is a weakness in the endeavour, it may lie in that omission
and that none of the Air Emergency Task Force members appeared
to be a specialist in this field. As a result, readers may be inclined
to dismiss them as armchair experts. But what surprised me was that
no reference was made to an earlier article by a committee of the
Aerospace Medical Association that was similar in content and
appeared in *Aerospace Medicine* (formerly known as the *Journal of Aviation Medicine*) in May 1961 (CMCAMA 1961).

The third challenge, which could be described as the most ambitious
of all so far, has much to recommend it for there is an association with

the Institute of Aviation Medicine, Farnborough, as well as approbation from other authorities. Again the platform was provided by the *British Medical Journal*.

The story begins with a young Turk, F. John Mills, who was on a 5-year short service commission with the RAF. He got a first in Physiology at Cambridge and as he lacked funds for clinical studies, his professor, Sir Bryan Matthews, suggested the services. (Perhaps the old pioneer chuckled over the thought that they might have gained a candidate for a lifetime of research.) Mills completed his training at the Middlesex, and on his second posting arrived at Farnborough. Towards the end of his stint, 'Pushy' Mills – for that was the tag given him by his colleagues – found an unusual opportunity. He attended the annual conference of the British Medical Association (BMA), which that year was held in Brighton, as a member of the Armed Forces Committee, and there he met Stephen Lock, editor of the *British Medical Journal*. 'It was just a very brief meeting', Mills recalled,

> and we got talking. He'd been in the Air Force [for his National Service] and asked me what I did. I explained that I worked at the Institute of Aviation Medicine, and he said 'Sounds very interesting'. 'Well', I said, 'why don't we have a series of articles on aviation medicine?'

> (Mills 1986)

The proposal met with a favourable response and when he was next up in London for an Armed Forces Committee meeting, Mills called on the editor. On this occasion, he mentioned that because of a Ph.D. commitment, he would require a co-author. The person he had in mind was an able colleague, Richard Harding, who was also a flight lieutenant with a diploma in Aviation Medicine. The editor agreed and asked him to submit an outline that would be offered to what was termed the 'editorial hanging committee'.

From Stephen Lock's point of view, the choice of Mills and Harding made good sense. Their credentials had been affirmed by the established authorities and there was a need for an in-depth treatment of the subject as he had found that the current textbook was out of date. When I enquired why he had not preferred to engage senior specialists for the task, he replied, 'You've got to be looking for the authorities of tomorrow rather than of today, and because on the whole young people write far better than older men.'

What Mills achieved in his short career in aviation medicine – he was to leave the RAF 12 months later for a position in industry – was without precedent. Together with his competent colleague he was able to bring to the attention of the medical world 'this relatively new and evolving aspect of medicine' (to quote the editor's preface) which before had been the exclusive preserve of the military. And above all, they had been allocated sufficient space in the *British Medical Journal* – it would amount to twenty-one articles – to maximize the situation.

The provision of an essential guide for the medical profession may seem straightforward, but when seen in perspective it was indeed a formidable assignment. Stephen Lock, in the 1983 preface to the collected series, perceives and defines the problem.

> In 1980 no fewer than 300 million passengers travelled by air and, despite the slowdown in economic growth, their number is likely to continue to increase every year. Such statistics are of concern to the doctor for he may become implicated in at least three ways: to be asked by patients whether they are fit enough to travel by air; as a traveller himself to be asked to attend a medical emergency in flight; and, in a specialist capacity, to advise on specific aspects of aviation medicine such as hygiene, psychology or physiology. Few texts, however, have brought all these considerations together, but this has now been done in a series of articles by Squadron Leaders John Mills and Richard Harding.
>
> (Harding and Mills 1983)

The question the two challengers faced was, how should they start? It was obvious. At the sharp end: the medical emergencies in the air. The first issue they focused on was life-threatening situations in-flight and the likelihood of a doctor being present on these occasions – this varied from 40 to 90 per cent. Of those who were involved, it was found that they were critical of the medical emergency facilities, 'the lack of diagnostic and therapeutic equipment aboard' (Harding and Mills 1983: 7), the failure of airlines to screen passengers for their fitness to fly, and the ingratitude demonstrated by the airlines when they responded to requests for medical assistance. Mention was also made of the fact that, in the USA, dissatisfaction with this state of affairs had caused a group of citizens and doctors to sue the Federal Aviation Administration (FAA) in order to force commercial airlines to carry additional drugs and medical equipment on all their flights.

The incidence of these emergencies appeared to be low and needed to be interpreted with care because of the number of variables and the different systems of collation employed by the airlines. The rates of attack for passengers of British Airways (BA) and Qantas were similar in one year, i.e. one in 13,000, while for those who had notified the airlines, BA and Air France in this instance, of their disabilities, it increased to one in 350. The length of the flight tended to influence the chance of an incident for a 'long flight may be expected to produce more medical problems because of the greater exposure to factors ranging from immobility and hypoxia to the effects of duty free alcohol' (Harding and Mills 1983: 8).

The causes of medical problems varied. In the case of BA, the most common was associated with the central nervous system, followed by 16 per cent stress and anxiety, 15 per cent the cardiovascular system, 12 per cent the alimentary canal, and 10 per cent the respiratory system. These causes could be contrasted with those in the case of American Airlines where heart attack (real or suspected) and chest pain accounted for 31 per cent, fainting for 20 per cent, and breathing difficulties for 19 per cent of their unscheduled landings from 1964 to 1968 on domestic routes. Most of these diagnoses were based on reports of the cabin crew as doctors rarely appeared to be on board at the time. Cardiovascular disease is singled out as the main cause of serious illness in-flight and is based on studies of deaths on BOAC from 1947 to 1967 and on Qantas from 1975 to 1979.

The legal aspect of emergency care on aircraft is complex, and as there is the additional risk of litigation this has resulted in the reluctance of doctors to attend medical problems on board. In the USA and in most British Commonwealth countries, no legal obligation exists to help a stranger, whereas in most European countries it is a criminal offence not to render assistance. Other factors to be considered include the nationality of the airline, and the airspace of the country in which the emergency occurs. For example, a British doctor's medical insurance does not cover the USA. Last, but not least, is the fact that doctors may hesitate to offer help as the problem may lie outside their specialism. This is a sound reason because the lack of experience appears to be no defence in allegations of negligence.

The other aspect of the treatment of illness in the air is the availability of equipment and drugs for the purpose. Civil aviation regulations require all airlines to have a basic first-aid kit, a portable oxygen set, and an emergency oxygen supply. Some airlines, like BA, carry an upgraded first-aid kit. However, the decision to provide a supplementary kit for the sole use of doctors is left to the individual airline.

Five European airlines, Air France, Alitalia, Iberia, Lufthansa, and Sabena, do equip their aircraft with doctors' kits that are sealed and kept in locked compartments. Air France, too, has used them on all long-haul flights since 1975 because they are 'unquestionably useful to sick persons' (Harding and Mills 1983: 13). It would appear that such an addition could decrease the number of aircraft diversions, and could prove invaluable on transoceanic routes where unscheduled stops could take several hours to effect. There is also the case for the introduction of biotelemetry whereby a ground-based cardiologist, for example, could monitor an arrhythmia in a passenger at high altitude and at a distance of thousands of miles. However, this would be precluded by airlines not only because of the considerable investment but also because it requires cabin attendants to be trained to paramedic standards.

A feature, too, that would appear to be ruled out because of the economics of the airline industry is the installation of a special medical compartment on aircraft for ill passengers. Nevertheless, Air Afrique and UTA have made provision for treatment areas on long-haul aircraft. In the case of cardiac arrests there might be insufficient time to move a patient to this area and resuscitation would have to be undertaken on the spot. Therefore it would be useful if cardiopulmonary resuscitation could be taught to flight attendants 'in view of the difficulties imposed by aircraft' (Harding and Mills 1983: 14).

The last topic to be covered was the prevention of medical emergencies. But not much could be said because little research had been done. 'Possibly airlines do not make enough effort to screen passengers for their fitness to fly' (Harding and Mills 1983: 14). However, if attempts were made, the situation seemed impossible because of the incredible numbers involved. At the time Heathrow handled some 30 million air travellers annually. It was also the authors' opinion that a system should be established whereby those at risk would be identified. In 1976, the medical service of BA had reviewed 26,000 applications from passengers to assess their fitness to fly. It was obvious that any increases in these cases would require additional investment for the airlines in terms of facilities and medical staff.

To cap the initial exposure, Mills and Harding took a bold step and submitted seven recommendations. Some would find them controversial and indeed a disclaimer was printed at the end in which it was stated that the views were the authors' 'and do not necessarily reflect those of British Airways, British Caledonian or the Royal Air Force'. Others would welcome them as it would enable the specialism to come of age and extend into the public sector where the need was the greatest.

1 All airlines should have at least one doctor trained in aviation medicine on their staff.
2 Air travellers should be made more aware of the medical hazards in the air. Since the current system of screening was not satisfactory, it was suggested that a more effective method be adopted. 'Thus a warning to passengers about the health hazards of air travel should be printed on airline tickets in the same way that attention is given to the carriage of certain prohibited goods. To avoid adverse consumer reactions to those airlines which undertake such action voluntarily (and may be assumed incorrectly by the passenger to be unsafe), all airlines should be obliged to comply with this recommendation' (Harding and Mills 1983: 16–17).
3 Doctors, too, should be made aware of the medical problems patients face when they travel by air. Some airlines with medical departments encourage this approach and doctors should avail themselves of the opportunity.
4 There should be an improvement in the provision of statistics on in-flight medical emergencies. The Aerospace Medical Association has already made proposals to remedy the dearth of statistics and these should be accompanied by an internationally recognized protocol for reporting incidents.
5 The proposed standard of emergency facilities should be submitted to the medical profession for open debate.
6 Consideration of the legal implications of Good Samaritan acts should be given on an international basis, as well as medical insurance cover for doctors who provide assistance.
7 All airlines should consider the provision of at least one paramedic on long-haul flights. As it is envisaged that wide-bodied aircraft would be introduced accommodating up to 800 passengers, this could become a necessity; also indeed special treatment areas.

Nine other subjects followed, each dealt with in the same terse, informative style that assists quick assimilation:

1 Fitness to travel by air.
2 Problems of altitude.
3 Acceleration.

4 Function of the special senses in flight.
5 Aviation psychology (by Roger Green of the RAF Institute of Aviation Medicine).
6 Medical aspects of airline operations.
7 Is the crew fit to fly?
8 Special forms of flight.
9 Legal aspects of in-flight emergencies by Dr P.J.C. Chapman of British Caledonian Airways).

There was also a 'valediction', that perhaps should have appeared some time later when a proper assessment of the series could be made. However, here the authors expressed hope that their recommendations would stimulate discussion among doctors, airlines, and government. 'Although many interesting comments have been forthcoming from our peers, a constructive response from organizations such as International Air Transport Association and International Civil Aviation Organization is still awaited' (Harding and Mills 1983: 137). In addition, they expected the British Medical Association to debate some of the points raised at an anual representative meeting but the opportunity was declined.

When I spoke to Richard Harding about the articles, he was pleased to mention that something had been done by the Board of Science and Education at the BMA. They had set up a working party on 'air transportation of the sick and injured' in the summer of 1984 to provide guidance for doctors, nurses, and other personnel who acted as escorts on air ambulance services. The report was issued in May 1985 and it is obvious from the title that no important issues listed in the authors' recommendations were addressed. It was a case of what a Civil Aviation Authority official would describe as 'We ought to be seen to be trying to do something'.

But how does this attempt compare with the previous ones and their own high expectations? In terms of correspondence, they were more successful as four times as many letters appeared in the *British Medical Journal* – some thirteen in fact. Of these, several were critical, in particular those from the gliding enthusiasts who took exception to comments made in the brief section, and few expressed approval. One letter is of interest as it reveals another condition, bullous lung disease, that can be affected by pressure changes in flight. Dr El-Ansary (1983) wrote,

I am sure that a large number of patients with chronic bronchitis and emphysema travel by air each year, and, as about a third of patients with emphysema have bullas [or blisters – a reference to Crofton Douglas Respiratory Disease, 1981 is given] . . . I suspect that the number of people with bullous lung disease who travel each year far outweighs those who have pneumothorax . . . recent middle ear surgery, or . . . recent air encephalography.

(El-Ansary 1983)

The authors replied, 'Problems may be expected, however, only if the bullas are not communicating and probably only then if the aircraft should suffer a rapid decompression at high altitude.'

John Mills recalled the response from the medical profession when I talked to him some 3 years later. There were between 30 and 40 personal letters, in addition to those published in the correspondence columns. 'But I know that the *BMJ* were inundated with letters after the article on Medical Emergencies in the air, particularly because of the legal aspects.' If the authors did not receive general acclaim, there was some consolation in the compliments received from individuals. 'I got a couple of phone calls from one particular woman who'd been trying to get something done about this for years through the annual representative meeting of the BMA and was delighted with that chapter' (Mills 1986). The person turned out to be Dr Jean Lawrie, who had written to the *British Medical Journal* in 1981 (Lawrie 1981) about the medical responsibilities of airlines and had been concerned ever since.

Before we parted, we discussed the overall effect of the articles on aviation medicine. Mills admitted that they had expected 'those recommendations, which we felt could really have an impact immediately on the situation', to be taken seriously. 'The odd thing that has come out of the book, in terms of education, is lectures given to postgraduate medical centres about whether patients are fit to fly – they all seem to be interested in it.' And a last word, perhaps tempered by recent commercial experience, is that 'doctors only respond to pressure from patients'. We are left to conclude that a lack of public interest may have contributed to the vulnerability of such a bid.

There appears to be a seesaw movement of challengers across the Atlantic, for the next attempt was to be launched from the USA. A *tour de force* is the most apt description, as it was backed by a budget of no less than $500,000. The principal proponents involved had, on this occasion, no connection with the medical profession, although a cross-section of experts would follow in their wake. It was an alliance of a US Senator, Daniel K. Inouye (Hawaii), and a union, the Association of Flight Attendants (AFA).

Although airline pilots are required to submit biannual medical certificates to the FAA to demonstrate their fitness to carry out their duties, no such health provision applies to other members of the aircrew. In a measure to counter the absence of a monitorial system, albeit in the most desultory fashion, flight attendants' unions from time to time sponsor mail questionnaire surveys on health-related subjects. One of these, which was conducted by the AFA from January 1977 to April 1982 on poor cabin air quality, was submitted to the Subcommittee on Aviation of the US Senate Committee on Commerce, Science, and Transportation. In spite of the deficiencies of the report – the information collected was selective and fragmentary – it drew attention to an area that hitherto had been neglected and as a consequence jeopardized the health and safety of all who travelled by air.

The Senate Committee recorded 'the fact that in an airliner cabin environment, an efficiently operating air-conditioning system is not merely a convenience or a luxury, but rather an essential "life support system"' and Senator Inouye introduced a Bill to initiate a study on the subject. At the hearing, which was held on 9 November 1983, it was obvious that the views of the industry and experts were polarized (Association of Flight Attendants 1982). The first witness, Mr Craig Beard, FAA Director of Airworthiness, was opposed to the Bill because of the 'adequacy of airliner cabin ventilation systems' (Inouye 1983: 261–18.1). The second witness, Mr John E. Ralph, a senior vice-president of operations and technical support at the Air Transport Association, expressed his approval of the 'adequacy of the industry and the F.A.A. regulations related to cabin air quality and safety' (Inouye 1983: 261–18.2).

On the other hand, Lisa Yates who represented both the Union of Flight Attendants and the Association of Professional Flight Attendants; Janis Bumgarner, a director of air safety of the AFA, and C. Macdonald Denmark, a flight attendant of United Airlines, all supported the Bill. They also voiced 'concerns about respiratory and other problems of flight attendants and passengers related to cabin air quality' (Inouye 1983: 261–18.3). Three other witnesses, including experts Dr Michael B. Gregg, a deputy director of an epidemiology programme, and Dr Thomas Stock of the University of Texas School of Public Health, made statements in support of the Bill and discussed the 'potential for health problems related to air quality and crowding in aircraft cabins' (Inouye 1983: 261-18.4).

The Bill was passed the next year and became known as Public Law 98-466. It directed the Department of Transportation to commission the National Academy of Sciences to undertake a study on air quality aboard commercial carriers and allocated a budget for the purpose. Thus *The Airliner Cabin Environment* report originated (see p. 123). The resources it harnessed in terms of manpower (over 100 people were involved in some way or other in the compilation), institutions, and cost are quite remarkable, and preclude any comparison with earlier challenges.

But what can be said of its achievements? Without doubt Senator Inouye and his supporters were vindicated by the findings. The first recommendation – there were twenty-one – was 'that the health effects associated with air travel should be within the purview of a federal agency' (CACAQ 1986: 3). The need arose because 'under current statutes and administrative orders, no federal office has direct responsibility' for that area (CACAQ 1986: 2). This was borne out by the fact that, in the air, standards set for the environment on the ground either did not exist, were lax, or were contravened. As criteria for cabin ventilation rates, environmental conditions, and air contaminants have not been established and adequate data on such factors are unavailable it was recommended that the FAA institute a programme for

> systematic measurement, by unbiased independent groups, of concentrations of carbon monoxide, respirable suspended particles, microbial aerosols, and ozone and the measurement of actual ventilation rates, cabin pressures, and cosmic radiation on a representative sample of routine commercial flights.
>
> (CACAQ 1986: 11)

The committee also found that the FAA's standard on carbon dioxide concentration was double that permitted for indoor environments while the cabin ozone concentrations did not always comply with Department of Transportation regulations (CACAQ 1986: 4-5).

There were the anticipated observations of the health risks to passengers whose medical conditions were vulnerable to pressure changes and low pressure. However, the onus to warn the public was put on the medical profession as a whole who, further, should supply information on these problems to outlets for air tickets (CACAQ 1986: 167). The most obvious candidates, the airlines and the federal authority, were not mentioned. At times the impression is given that the task is too much of a hot potato and there is an attempt to back-pedal or pass the buck.

> As scientists and engineers, we cannot determine whether FAA alone can address the questions we raise, nor can we easily say whether they are questions of health, safety, or comfort. The legislative branch . . . and the executive branch . . . must sort out responsibilities in appropriate ways.
>
> (CACAQ 1986: viii)

On the other hand, there was an issue that won their unanimous approval – the one that followed a safe and well-trodden path. They advocated a smoking ban on all commercial flights within the USA.

The overall response to the findings would appear to be muted in comparison to the resources available. There was a perfunctory review of the 318-page report in the January 1987 issue of *Aviation, Space and Envionmental Medicine* where other aspects were highlighted: air quality was important because 28 per cent of Americans fly at least once a year and some 70,000 flight attendants work in the cabin environment; even new aircraft recirculate 50 per cent of cabin air and may also have deficient filters; and the restriction of duty hours for pregnant crew members because of the poor air quality and the additive effect of cosmic radiation (Anon. 1987). But the *Journal of the American Medical Association* did not even discuss it. In the general media coverage, the significant conclusions were obscured by the banner headlines, e.g. 'ban smoking on all passenger airlines'.

Although the National Research Council Committee without doubt widened the field of health in the air, they lacked the cutting edge to breach the barrier of silence. That distinction might have been achieved by a counterpart from the Aerospace Medical Association by virtue of their longstanding experience and expertise. It is unfortunate that not one member of their association was on the committee; it is no small consolation that the 1961 report on medical criteria for passenger flying is quoted in the references, though the work of Mills and Harding is omitted (AMA 1961: 369–82). When I contacted Dr Stanley R. Mohler, Professor and Vice-Chairman of the Department of Community Medicine, and Director of Aerospace Medicine, at Wright State University in Dayton, Ohio, he explained the situation:

I was approached in regard to whether or not I would be interested in being Chairman of the group. I answered in the affirmative but certain airline lobbyists, knowing my views, kicked up a ruckus. I did, however, have behind the scenes consultations and believe the report is excellent.

(Mohler 1987)

Here is an indication that the issue might become stuck in a political thicket. But once the oath of silence becomes public knowledge, the outcry will be such that comparison to the thunderous sound of supersonic flight will not be far off.

Chapter Two

DAEDALUS AND ICARUS: THE RELEVANCE OF A GREEK MYTH TODAY

The first events of flight to fire the imagination of mankind were not those undertaken by two pairs of brothers, the Montgolfiers in 1783 with their smoke-filled balloon or the Wrights with their crude, mechanical contrivance in 1903. They occurred several thousand years before.

The earliest tale of flying recalls the journey of the Sumerian shepherd, Etana, who flew off on the back of an eagle in search of the herb that was the source of life. The infertility of his flocks had prompted the quest but, when he was near his destination, he fell from his mount to the earth (Breasted 1926: 142–3).

The other myth, with which we are more familiar, concerns a father and son, and has greater suspense because, in essence, it is an escape story. Part of the rich and complex corpus of Greek mythology encompassed in Robert Graves's two volumes (Graves 1974)), the account is worth reiteration as perhaps the moral is still relevant today.

Daedalus, the cunning one, was a master craftsman who was taught the art by none other than the goddess of wisdom, Athene. He was a member of the Erechtheid royal house in Athens and had a workshop to which his sister's son, Talos, 'the sufferer', was apprenticed. But it would appear that the nephew was more talented than the uncle, for when he was only 12, he cut a stick in half with a snake's jawbone (some say, a fish's spine) and reproduced it in iron, to invent the saw. He had other inventions to his credit – the potter's wheel and the pair of compasses. Soon he enjoyed a great reputation in the city, not unlike his uncle. As Daedalus himself had laid claim to have forged the first saw this could have been sufficient to provoke his envy and anger. However, there was another factor that caused him to take an irretrievable step – the suspicion of an incestuous relationship

19

between the mother, Polycaste, Daedalus' sister, and the son. One day, Daedalus lured Talos onto the roof of Athene's temple at the Acropolis and, while the latter was distracted by the view, he pushed him over the edge to his death. When the murder was discovered Polycaste hanged herself and Daedalus fled (some say, was banished) from Athens. An aspect that should not be overlooked is that the souls of both Talos and Polycaste turned into partridges and took off.

In the meantime, Daedalus arrived in Crete where he was welcomed by King Minos and Queen Pasiphae. With his main rival out of the way, he again excelled in his craft. He delighted them with his animated dolls and was soon taken into the queen's confidence. She had developed an unnatural passion for a white bull – a condition which Poseidon had induced to avenge an insult from King Minos – and sought his advice. He built her a model of a wooden cow, hollowed out, and placed it in the same field as the bull. Later, the queen gave birth to the Minotaur, a monster with a human body and bull's head, and an appetite for human flesh.

King Minos, to avoid a scandal over the queen and her hybrid offspring, consulted Daedalus about the construction of an enclosure for them, which an oracle had ordained to be sited at Knossos. Here is the origin of the Labyrinth – the maze from which it was impossible to extricate oneself –at whose centre was concealed the fearsome Minotaur. (Sir Arthur Evans suggested that the Minoan palace he discovered, with its complex of halls, corridors, room and ante-rooms, was the Labyrinth – such a term was derived from *labrys* or doubled-headed axe, a familiar symbol of Cretan sovereignty. '. . . the maze at Cnossus had a separate existence from the palace; it was a true maze in the Hampton Court sense, and seems to have been marked out in mosaic on a pavement . . .' (Graves 1974: vol. 1, 297).)

Daedalus, who was now married to the slave-girl Naucrate and had a son called Icarus, led a peaceful life on the island. But he longed to return to Greece. However, as King Minos had learnt of his complicity in the queen's shameless act, he ordered that the craftsman be imprisoned in the Labyrinth and never be allowed to leave Crete. Such restriction on someone as talented as Daedalus, who had the reputation of a versatile creative artist, was bound to be seen as a challenge. 'Now, now is the time', he told himself,

to deploy all your skill and craft. Minos rules earth, rules ocean:

no escape by sea or land. All that remains is the sky. So, through the sky we'll seek our passage – God in high heaven, forgive such a project! I do not aspire to touch your starry dwellings: this is the only way I have to escape, My Master. Were there a way by Styx, through Stygian waters, we'd swim to freedom. I must devise new laws for human nature.

(Ovid 1982: 192)

Seen in the context of Greek myths, here was an unprecedented development. Up to this point, it would appear that the only way a mortal could fly was after death, as a soul, as in the metamorphosis of both Talos and Polycaste. What Daedalus now proposed was to emulate the sky-gods. Based on our knowledge of these immortal beings, it would seem that such a desire might not have been impossible to achieve, but probably only at a price. While Athene might have intervened on Daedalus' behalf, another god or goddess may have decided to take the side of the others.

When Pasiphae freed him from the Labyrinth, he set to work on aeronautical designs. He studied birds and how they fly. In the end, he was able to perfect out of feathers, wax, and thread a pair of wings each for himself and Icarus. His young son, however, was unaware of either the father's achievement or the dangerous trip ahead. Instead, he was content to be at his father's side and on occasions disrupted the work while he played with the wax or blew the feathers into the wind.

Daedalus now tested the wings and found that he could hover as well as fly. He attached a pair to Icarus and instructed him in their use. Before the moment of take-off, the father with tears in his eyes, cautioned the son.

I warn you, Icarus, you must follow a course midway between earth and heaven, in case the sun should scorch your feathers if you go too high, or the water make them heavy if you are too low. Fly halfway between the two. And pay no attention to the stars, to Bootes, or Helice or Orion with his drawn sword: take me as your guide, and follow me!

(Ovid 1986: 184)

They flew off from a hilltop and Icarus, after a few fearful seconds, gained enough confidence to follow his father through the air. A fisherman who happened to spot them dropped his rod in surprise. They passed over the Cycladic islands of Naxos, Paros, and Delos, and caught sight of Lebynthos and Calymne on their right. But Icarus, encouraged by the success of the flight, became rash and increased his altitude. As he moved away from his father, he was overcome by joy – an emotion that often affects flyers – and perhaps he also imagined he was a sky-god.

When Daedalus looked over his shoulder, there was no sign of his son. What he saw instead were feathers scattered over the sea like a wreath. The heat had melted the wax of the wings and Icarus had fallen to his death. That was apparent. Daedalus waited for the body to surface and decided to bury it on an island nearby. While he dug the grave, he was aware of a presence – a partridge perched on an oak tree. Sometimes it would flap its wings and crow with glee. The soul of his sister had been appeased.

If we are to look for a moral, what is to to be? That the impossible can be achieved? Ovid's comments would suggest such an answer. 'So Minos failed to clip the wings of a mortal . . .' (Ovid 1982: 193). However, the modern version proposed by the OED in the definition of Icarian includes a rider: 'applied to ambitious acts which end in ruin'. Perhaps we should settle for something prosaic: *although man may fly, his terrestrial body still limits him.*

THE HOSTILE NOTHINGNESS: THE COMPOSITION OF THE ATMOSPHERE AND THE LAWS OF PHYSICS THAT APPLY TO IT

What is it up there that is hostile to terrestrial man and yet protects his life on Earth? To begin to answer that question, we have to picture our planet as a rock in space covered by several layers of chiffon composed of gas and vapour molecules. The appositeness of this analogy soon becomes apparent when we discover that the atmosphere comes in different weights and that its mixture of molecules occurs in the same proportion whatever the weight.

The heaviest layer is found at sea-level where it exerts a pressure of 14.7 p.s.i. (pounds per square inch) or 760 mmHg (millimetres of mercury). The higher we ascend, the lighter the layer until there is virtually no pressure at about 68,000 ft. It is at this point that we stand on the physiological threshold of space as defined by the pioneer of the field, Dr Hubertus Strughold (DeHart 1985). But we have over-shot the mark. What has to be established is that the human body is so constructed that it functions best under the heaviest weight of air. For the pressure here is the right amount required to effect a gaseous exchange in the lungs whereby fresh oxygen is forced into the bloodstream to replace the carbon dioxide that is expelled.

The canary in the cage and the mountain goat, the ibex, breathe in the same mixture of air as we do. If we think in terms of molecules, there are 700 times more oxygen than carbon dioxide and almost four times more nitrogen than oxygen. There are water molecules also, more of which we breathe out than breathe in. Whether we scoop up sea or mountain air the percentage by volume remains the same: 20.9 of oxygen, 0.03 of carbon dioxide, 78 of nitrogen, and less than 1 of inert gases. At each breath, a maximum of oxygen enters, a maximum of carbon dioxide exists and equal amounts of nitrogen enter and exit. The last gas, although inert, prevents lung collapse (Glaister 1969).

23

With carbon dioxide about 150 times more is exhaled than inhaled as it is a by-product of our cells (Eckstein 1970).

When we move upwards towards the lighter layers of nothingness to reach the threshold of space, strange conditions prevail. The air becomes less dense, or thinner, and will have an effect on us similar to being suffocated by a pillow. The temperature drops to the equivalent of twice the cold of an arctic winter, while the lack of moisture, only a couple of molecules per million, causes the air to be drier than a desert. Also an incessant rain of radiation falls, invisible and destructive, and its action on oxygen creates another hazard, ozone. In all, this is bad news for the canary, the ibex, and people, for life cannot exist in the upper layers unprotected.

But if the human body has not been free to move about this environment, our mind certainly has. Each layer has been named and the space it occupies defined. There is the atmosphere and its opposite, the exosphere. The beginning, middle, and end of the atmosphere are populated with molecules, in the main unseen, that are attracted by the Earth's gravitational force until the break-off point, some 430 miles out: the exosphere, where there is an emptiness.

Unlike cartographers who mapped solid areas of land and sea, those who classified the sky dealt with regions of air that advanced in increasing circles or spheres from the Earth. The troposphere, or turbulent sphere, is the first that extends from the surface and it resembles an oval with a maximum distance of about 60,000 ft at the Equator and a minimum of some 26,000 ft at the poles. The weather is found within its confines and it is characterized by an almost constant decrease in temperature with increase in altitude, the presence of water vapour, and large-scale air turbulence. The upper boundary of the troposphere, which has been designated the tropopause, is the area of high winds and the highest cirrus clouds.

The next sphere to be encountered may sound familiar because the names of several models from the Boeing Aircraft Company have been derived from it: the stratosphere. If the troposphere, which comprises three-quarters of the atmosphere, can be credited with the provision of sufficient oxygen and water necessary for life, then the stratosphere can be credited as the protector of that life as its ozone layer screens out about 99 per cent of the ultraviolet (UV) light which causes the deadly skin cancer, melanoma.

In the main, its features are opposite to those of the troposphere. The oval shape is widest at the poles, where it extends to some 265,000 ft, while at the Equator it is narrow and sometimes nonexistent. The temperature variations are unusual, beginning at lower altitudes with a constant $-56.5\,°C$, progressing to warmer conditions with a maximum of about $35\,°C$ at middle altitudes, and falling to some $-35\,°C$ at the buffer zone that is termed the stratopause (Weisberg 1981). It is distinguished by little turbulence, no moisture, and an ozone belt with concentrations of up to 10 p.p.m.v. (parts per million by volume). Other larger areas follow, the mesosphere, the thermosphere, and the exosphere, but for the purposes of this chapter they are of little consequence.

Of greater use than the classification of the spheres was the discovery of classic laws that govern them, and an understanding of these would later enable man to inhabit the nothingness for brief periods. Besides Newton's law of gravitation, the two which are particularly relevant date back to the seventeenth and eighteenth centuries and are named after Robert Boyle and John Dalton. Boyle's law, whose simplicity is warranted to surprise the uninitiated, demonstrates the upside-down relationship between pressure and volume of a gas. If we ascend the atmosphere, the pressure will decrease while the volume increases, whereas on descent the pressure will increase while the volume decreases. In essence, at constant temperature, the volume of a given mass of gas is inversely proportional to its pressure.

Dalton's law relates to the pressure of a gas mixture. The total pressure of gases in a mixture is the sum of all the partial or individual pressures in that gas mixture. Also each gas enclosed in a fixed volume will exert the same pressure as if it alone occupied the whole volume. An obvious application is that, under low pressures, for an organism to survive, in general it is sufficient to maintain the partial pressure of oxygen (PO_2 or pO_2). This later gave rise to the introduction of supplemental oxygen at altitude.

If there are facts that cannot be repeated often enough here, they are that the nothingness is a hostile place and that mankind did not evolve to survive in it. Whenever we traverse the skies, we are there on borrowed time. In an emergency, when corrective action is necessary, even the best aviators can run out of it. 'Some of the dead pilots needed more time to figure it out', Chuck Yeager, the most experienced of flyers, summed up (Yeager and Janos 1985).

A watchword applicable to our investigation of human factors in civil aviation is 'not too little or too much'. It is the fruits of the research of a man who would later become known as the father of aviation medicine, Paul Bert (1833–86), and is quoted as follows:

> The organisms at present existing in a natural state on the surface of the earth are acclimated to the degree of oxygen tension in which they live: any decrease, any increase seems to be harmful to them when they are in a state of health. Therapeutics can advantageously use these modifications in different pathological conditions.
>
> (Bert 1943: 1037)

He built the world's first pressure chamber to simulate conditions at high altitude and conducted a considerable number of experiments, about 670, to substantiate his theories. Of interest were those with dogs, for he found that when the pressure was decreased, respiration and heart rate increased while intestinal gases expanded and digestion slowed down. Body temperature dropped, the test subject became listless and dull, and in cases of sudden decompression, there was paralysis of the hindquarters, followed by death. In a summary of the experiments, he observed 'that paraplegia is also the most frequent symptom in divers and workmen in caissons' (Bert 1943: 660–83).

He experimented on himself too, and on one occasion spent 45 minutes below 400 mmHg (equal to pressure at an altitude above 16,000 ft) without discomfort when he breathed from a bag full of superoxygenated air. His pulse rate rose from 60 to 86 and, although his stomach remained distended, gas escaped from both his mouth and his bottom from time to time (Bert 1943: 703–8). What he did in microcosm would later be undertaken on a large scale in the following century by the governments of the USA, the UK and France.

Chapter Four

LOW ON HIGH, HIGH ON LOW: HYPOXIA, OR LACK OF OXYGEN

There is a condition which is as prevalent as, if not more so, than the common cold, but few are aware of it because its symptoms are not as obvious as those of a virus infection that causes a sore throat or nasal discharge. The reason is twofold. It can only affect us while we are in an abnormal environment; when we leave, its effect ceases. Also the signs and symptoms are insidious and, as no pain or discomfort results, the condition can be considered to be dangerous. Indeed, the acute phase, Joseph Barcroft (1920) suggested, 'resembles alcoholic intoxication: the symptoms are headache, mental confusion, drowsiness, muscular weakness and incoordination'. Often there is an 'initial state of euphoria, accompanied by a feeling of self-satisfaction and a sense of power. The subject may become hilarious and sing or shout, and manifest other emotional disturbances'.

I refer to hypoxia which is defined in a medical dictionary as 'a decrease below normal levels of oxygen in air, blood or tissue, short of anoxia' (Stedman 1982: 685). We all suffer from bouts of hypoxia, mild or otherwise, whenever we board an aircraft for a flight. The cabin pressurization set at altitudes from 6,000 to 8,000 ft produces an irregular environment in which the condition is found. What this represents is a confined space that contains 20–26 per cent less oxygen (partial pressure) and an equal decrease in pressure to force the air from the lungs into the blood and, as a consequence, cause an oxygen deficiency in the tissues of the body. This level of hypoxia, which is called 'the indifferent stage', causes no unease in healthy passengers although a compensatory mechanism is activated through a slight increase in the heart rate and pulmonary ventilation. A reduction, too, of some 10 per cent in night vision has been detected as well as impairment in mental performance (Ernsting and King 1988).

27

However, the indifferent stage can induce serious problems among passengers with an array of acute and chronic diseases that give rise to oxygen lack at sea-level.

If such a condition appears to be unfamiliar, a comparison with another altitude illness would be appropriate. Picture a beautiful mountain resort that attracts skiers or climbers or trekkers, and you will find mountain sickness, for it afflicts those who are exposed to heights even as modest as 8,000 ft, as was shown in a recent US survey of 3,908 men, women, and children (Houston 1984). Hypoxia is a central feature of it, with cold and exercise as contributory factors. In view of this, the hypoxia encountered in flight could be termed aviation hypoxia or, simply, aerohypoxia. However, there are important differences between the two.

Mountain sickness is a serious illness that in the main can be prevented if sufficient time is taken to reach altitude.[1] Aerohypoxia is not preventable because the nature of air travel makes it uneconomic to maintain an aircraft cabin at sea-level. Therefore, all passengers, irrespective of age or the state of their health, suffer from mild aerohypoxia.

Location also plays a role. In the mountains, you are under open skies with freedom of movement, and have days, if not months, to acclimatize to the rarefied air. Should you feel unwell, the simplest solution is to move to a lower altitude. In the air, you are forced to remain in a restricted space for a fixed period with little room for movement. No allowance is made for your body to acclimatize to the change in pressure. An apt analogy for the experience is to be placed under a giant, cracked bell-jar that permits a limited amount of air to enter at a time.

The stages and symptoms are not dissimilar. With acute mountain sickness (AMS), there are two main forms, the benign and the malignant. In the case of the benign AMS, patients experience headache, vomiting, nausea, sleeplessness, breathing difficulties (dyspnoea), loss of appetite, weakness, 'a feeling of fulness in the chest', or, as Dr John Dickinson of the hospital at Kathmandu points out, 'some combination of these symptoms' (Dickinson 1986). Malignant AMS, which is so named because it can be fatal, is the result of high-altitude pulmonary edema (HAPE) and/or high-altitude cerebral edema (HACE) (Houston 1984: 76). The first, which leads to a build-up of fluid in the lungs, is characterized by dyspnoea, a productive cough with sputum, mental confusion, extreme weakness, sometimes a blueness of the lips (cyanosis), coma, and death. The second is distinguished by a severe headache, drowsiness, abnormal behaviour, unsteadiness on the feet, impaired consciousness, coma, and death. In some cases, 'a patient retires to his or her sleeping bag feeling no more tired than usual, and "wakes-up" unconscious the next morning' (Dickinson 1986).

With aerohypoxia, the effects are less marked, as the subject is resting or inactive without the discomfort of wind and cold, and well documented because they can be studied under the controlled conditions of an altitude or pressure chamber. The methods of classification vary. There is the basis of observer signs and subjective symptoms or the four stages of deterioration in performance. Among the signs noted by an observer are cyanosis, increased rate and depth in breathing, lack of muscle co-ordination, poor judgement, behavioural changes, and unconsciousness. The subjective symptoms include breathlessness, headache, anxiety, dizziness, nausea, fatigue, blurred and tunnel vision, hot and cold flushes, numbness and sometimes euphoria or anger.

Besides the indifferent stage, whose upper limit is 10,000 ft, there are the compensatory (10,000–15,000 ft), the disturbance (15,000–20,000 ft), and the critical (20,000–23,000 ft) stages. See Table 4.1 which shows the stages of aerohypoxia at the respective altitudes and oxygen saturation of the blood. In the compensatory stage, the whole body responds to the decrease in partial pressure of oxygen and the drop in arterial blood saturation. It takes the form of increases in respiratory volume, in cardiac output, in blood pressure, and after a short period the effects on the central nervous system are perceptible. In the disturbance stage, the compensatory measures adopted by the body no longer provide protection against the lack of oxygen. The individual is assailed by a combination of physical and mental impairments and the tragedy is that they are unaware of these disabilities.

Table 4.1 Stages of aerohypoxia

Stage	Altitude in feet	% arterial oxygen saturation
Indifferent	0–10,000	98–87
Compensatory	10,000–15,000	87–80
Disturbance	15,000–20,000	80–65
Critical	20,000–23,000	65–60

Source: DeHart 1985: 98.

This experience could be deemed the prelude to what J.S. Haldane once observed of anoxia which 'not only stops the machine, it wrecks the machinery' (Milledge 1985). By the time the critical stage is reached, consciousness is lost and convulsions may occur. With prolonged anoxia, unconsciousness may result from failure of the heart and circulation, whereas in acute anoxia it may result from injury to the brain. Death follows as anoxia represents a complete absence of oxygen, a state that is incompatible with life in vertebrates.

The worst effects of oxygen lack at high altitude have been demonstrated both inside an aircraft and outside on a mountainous terrain. But there is some way to go before we can grasp the full significance of the subject. As has been made obvious, little of the knowledge that state-of-art pressure cabins cause mild hypoxia has filtered through to the general public. Even less do they realize that medical incidents can be provoked in the unhealthy, both in-flight and post-flight, as a result of hypoxia.

To gain insight into what has been described by its leading exponent as 'the most important single hazard of flight at high altitude' (Ernsting 1984), we have to consult the experts. Some are dead, some alive. There is a story about one of them worthy of a scene out of a black comedy. 'Some years ago,' Dr David Denison recalled,

> [a colleague] asked me to strangle him repeatedly firstly in an air-filled room at ground level and then when he breathed pure oxygen at a pressure of four atmospheres. We set about it by wrapping a sphygmomanometer cuff around his neck and connected the cuff, by a wide-bore tubing and a Douglas tap, to an oil-drum filled with compressed air. (The arrangement provided a satisfyingly abrupt onset to events.) In the air-filled room at ground level his head and neck became ischaemic and the rest of his body asphyxiated, whereas in the compression chamber his head became ischaemic though hyperoxic and the rest of his body hypercapnic (CO_2 excess) but not asphyxiated. The distinctions were not entirely semantic since he regularly lost consciousness after seven or eight seconds in the first situation but was still fully conscious after 20 seconds of strangulation in the pressure chamber. However, at no stage was any part of him anoxic, or even simply hypoxic.
>
> (Denison 1981: 264)[2]

It reminds one of a similar incident that involved a famous admiral and produced the memorable 'Kiss me, Hardy'. Perhaps, in the light of this, it would be appropriate to paraphrase the experiment of the blood-pressure cuff in a terse 'Strangle me, Denison'.

It is a far cry from those days in 1962 when, as a medical officer (research) with the rank of flight lieutenant, David Denison participated in his squadron leader's experiment. Today, Denison is consultant in Respiration Physiology at the three National Heart and Chest Hospitals and Professor of Clinical Physiology (Cardiothoracic Institute) at the University of London. Unlike other clinical physiologists, his experience is unique because of the 14 years he spent at the RAF Institute of Aviation Medicine (IAM), 5 of which were as head of the research team of 15–25 people that studied 'problems of survival in, and escape from, aircraft at high altitudes'. Among the varied information this programme provided was the 'distribution and uses of oxygen in tissues, the effects of mild prolonged hypoxia, a complex-reaction time task for studying rapid changes in consciousness, and the cerebral effects of brief profound hypoxia, hyperventilation and positive-pressure breathing' (Denison 1986).

I talked to him about his lifelong interest not long ago at the Lung Function Unit of the Brompton Hospital, London, where he is based and where for the past 10 years he has directed a group of 15–25 people who provide measurements, both routine and research, of lung function in some 7,000 patients each year. The programme, that covers six topics, includes 'monitoring respiration remotely in the severely ill' and 'determining the role of physical fitness in the detection and management of heart and lung disease'.

The main feature of his modest, narrow office, in which we then sat, was the long working surface that ran the length of one wall. The overall impression that is gained is of a unit where space is at a premium, every nook and cranny is crammed with good equipment. As a result, there is no reception area but an outer office that contains, among other things, a visual display unit connnected with fully automated data acquisition and reporting systems. But the limited accommodation at the Brompton has not curtailed further research, as two laboratories have been established at other hospitals.

Dr Denison leans his elbows on the work-top and describes the relationship between himself and his former superior officer. 'The work we have done is effectively like this,' he says and, with fingers outstretched, bends his hands at the wrist so that they face one another and resemble two trees with branches that interlace but remain separate. 'He taught me practically all I know about aviation hypoxia

31

and I followed him as head of the high-altitude laboratory at Farnborough. I continued the work that he did. But we both know each other's work very well – a lot of it was joint – so in a way it's not material which of us you speak to.'

Earlier, I had enquired whether there had been a division of labour in research at the IAM whereby an individual would assume sole responsibility for a specific field such as mild or severe hypoxia. He had assured me that this was not the case. He chose to begin with the distinction between these two aspects.

'Shall I start by telling you about mild hypoxia then?' he asked rhetorically and rested his head in his hands before closing his eyes, deep in thought. This action signalled a change in his manner for he was no longer the efficient administrator but became the interested teacher who selects his words and paces his delivery to accommodate the most inexperienced note-taker.

'When an aircraft takes off and the cabin pressure inside falls – but not as drastically as that outside, and typically it's not allowed to go above a cabin altitude of 8,000 feet and more commonly it's 5,000 to 6,000 feet – now at that pressure, the lowest value of which is 565 millimetres of mercury, everybody inside who is breathing the air in the cabin is exposed to a very mild degree of oxygen lack. If at some time a hole appears in the aircraft there will be a relatively rapid further decompression and they will then be exposed to severe hypoxia. Immediately, that hole appears, various protective devices will come into operation to minimize the damage. . . . But in principle once the situation is discovered it is put right. So you're exposed to a pulse of brief profound hypoxia as opposed to the sustained exposure in ordinary flight to mild prolonged hypoxia. Therefore, there are two different problems of oxygen lack in aviation, the first created by mild prolonged hypoxia and the second created by brief profound hypoxia.

'Now everybody in medicine believed that in principle they understood what oxygen was needed for in the body and it turns out on the whole that they were slightly wrong, even very wrong. It was very obvious that oxygen was used to release energy from fuel – the sugars, the fats, the protein. That was very clear. And people made the immediate jump to supposing that was the only thing for which oxygen was used. So quite quickly the convention was established that you needed oxygen to provide energy, and if you ran short of oxygen the price you paid for it was that you didn't have access to as much energy to do all sorts of things as before. Energy within a cell to do all sorts of intracellular processes. Now, much later, when people could measure these things, it was possible to show that the energy-releasing attribute of oxygen is an almost inexorable process that will continue even if the oxygen pressure is as low as 1 millimetre of mercury, perhaps even as low as a tenth of a millimetre. So it's the sort of process that you really cannot stop by depriving somebody of oxygen, unless you deprive them of it completely. And this left people with a mystery. Because how was it, then, that people lost consciousness long before oxygen pressures fell to those very low levels? Why were they detectably more stupid at altitudes of about 10,000 to 12,000 feet than they were at ground-level when the oxygen pressure was still really quite high? And the answer to that is that it is now appreciated that oxygen is used by the body in many ways, very many ways. Although only a small percentage of all the oxygen is used in the sophisticated ways, it is that small percentage that is vulnerable to oxygen lack. . . . If you measured how much oxygen people consumed as they lost consciousness due to oxygen lack, you wouldn't see any difference at all. They carry on consuming it at the same rate even though they are unconscious. So it's these subtle processes that make and destroy all of the chemical transmitters in the brain, the hormones in your body, and so on. These account for the effects of oxygen lack much more than the simple respiratory one that people thought of in the past. So that's an important change in attitude that has taken place in the last few years. You can find it summarized in my chapter in that book over there where it is explained in more detail. That is the first thing I would concentrate on because it's very interesting.'

When I later read his chapter, 'The distribution and use of oxygen in tissues' (Cumming *et al.* 1981: 243), I found that the substances he had referred to were enzymes called oxygenases. They were one of three groups of enzymes, the other two being the oxidases and the hydroxylases, that use oxygen in a controlled way and catalyse complex biochemical processes. Although the oxygenases consume a small fraction of the body's total oxygen requirement, some 1 per cent, their function is to produce and to dismember many critical compounds such as amine transmitters of the brain, structural proteins, and steroid hormones.

'In this hospital, for example,' he adds before opening his eyes and straightening himself in the seat, 'when people have got chronic lung disease, they are very much in the same condition as if they were flying all the time. . . . Asthma is like going for a short flight, time and time

again. Chronic bronchitis, you're in the aircraft for a very long time.
[Here] . . . the interest is wider than flying but [aviation] certainly
does explain some of the problems. With mild hypoxia, it appears that
when you go above about 4,000–5,000 feet, you've got detectable
deterioration in night vision. Your body senses that it must breathe
more – it's not that wise if it does, it's actually a disadvantage – but
it obviously knows and is capable of sensing that something's wrong
. . . . There is [also] an interference in your ability to learn and . . .
if you give somebody a not very complicated task that's novel, they
will learn it less quickly at 8,000 or 5,000 feet than they will at
ground-level. . . . If you break it down into the elements of the task,
it will be selective difficulty with the more complicated elements of
the task rather than the simple. . . . Our best bet at the time when
we did the work [a reference to the paper he wrote with F. Ledwith
and E.C. Poulton (Denison *et al.* 1966)] . . . on which our observations
were based, was that in novel and emergency situations where you've
got to take in a lot of information that's unexpected, pilots would be
at a disadvantage if they were breathing in cabin air. That was the
reason why we tried to get the cabin altitude in the Concorde brought
down from 8,000 feet to 5,000 feet.'

What is relevant and not mentioned on this occasion is another
subtle effect of mild hypoxia. It induces an increased sense of fatigue.
He and his colleagues found (in unpublished observations) that subjects
under controlled conditions felt as tired after some 3 hours at 8,000
ft as after 6 hours at ground-level (Edholm and Weiner 1981: 284).
The fact that people at altitude tire more easily and learn more slowly
is a handicap to those passengers like businessmen who work on their
flights. I had often wondered why the cabin altitudes were not nearer
sea-level as this could provide a solution to mild prolonged hypoxia,
but I soon discovered that it was not feasible.

'The trouble with attempting that is that the lower the cabin altitude,
the greater must be the pressure inside the plane and therefore the
stronger its walls must be. Therefore, the heavier the plane will be.
Therefore, it's more difficult to get off the ground, and once it's flying
it's going to consume more fuel. So economically, the attempt to correct
the mild hypoxia of flying is punitive. And there's bound to be
competing views between the engineers who want to design an efficient
plane and the doctors who want to minimize the mild hypoxia. Now
then, the hypoxia is very mild and it's certainly not the sort of thing
that should worry people generally. It's of great theoretical interest and

to some extent it's important to air crew that there can be some errors of judgement . . . which you could perhaps attribute to mild hypoxia. But for most people, it's of no practical importance and it would be very wrong to suggest that flying is in any way unsafe. People accept quite easily that, after a heavy meal, they're sleepy and they don't consider it a serious disadvantage. There's no difference between the sort of mental incapacity at 8,000 feet and the mental incapacity you get after your Christmas dinner!'

'Having said that,' I commented, 'what about people with conditions that affect the brain, the lungs, or the heart and who are in a mild hypoxic atmosphere?'

'Well, there are two situations and it's a question that's asked very commonly. There are two different stresses to flying, other than psychological ones – that people are frightened. From a mechanical point of view, when people fly and the pressure in the cabin drops slowly to the equivalent of 8,000 feet, they are being decompressed and any gas trapped inside them will tend to expand and will tend to burst the walls of its container. There is only one case on record of somebody being damaged in this way and that was quite unexplained. It was a girl of 22 who died on a flight from London to Geneva . . . probably a lung burst. She died, if I remember rightly, about 10 to 20 minutes after leaving Heathrow and the flight continued on to Geneva because it was too late to divert back. But she was certainly dead on arrival and that is unexplained. What is certain is that of the millions of people who have flown, there have been amongst them millions . . . with chronic heart disease who have survived without lung rupture. So it appears that diseased lungs can still empty themselves of air fast enough for the lungs not to burst in ordinary commercial flight. If a window came out of a plane [and explosive decompression occurred] those people would be more likely to die than others. But that's a sort of double emergency. By the time you have catered for getting chronic bronchitics on aircraft, you can't be expected to be responsible for a window coming out as well. We can't cope with that! It is supposed that in a major decompression in an aircraft, you might lose something like one in seven passengers and these would include . . . frailer people with heart and lung conditions. That would be a mixture of the mechanical and the brief profound hypoxia: the mechanics of the explosion, rupturing of the lungs, and being exposed, in addition, to a pulse of severe hypoxia before they got oxygen given to them (see pp. 131–4). But the other problem for people flying,

35

people with heart and lung disease and vessel disease, is that the mild hypoxia in them is added to the hypoxia they've got already and that will make them worse. It can always be treated. It is always easy for an airline to provide sufficient oxygen to bring those people back to the condition at which they are at ground-level. Therefore, experience shows that transporting people with heart and lung disease by air is not a problem provided that it is anticipated. If somebody with severe heart or lung disease doesn't announce it and they walk onto a plane, then it is quite possible that they will become more hypoxic and they may lose consciousness . . . in the aircraft.'

'What about post-flight?' I asked. 'After they've actually landed. Is there not stress or a stressor there?' I had recalled the conversation with Dr Ian Perry, when a patient with a myocardial infarct had died within an hour of arrival (Perry 1983).

'No,' he answered. 'If you make someone profoundly uncomfortable with oxygen lack, the moment you give them oxygen, within about 20 seconds, or certainly a minute, they've recovered consciousness. So it's a very quick phenomenon indeed and there is no important cumulative effect over the duration of an ordinary flight.'

There was a case I wished to take up with him. It concerned a woman who because of her chronic bronchitis had had post-flight problems, both on holiday and back home. I mentioned this.

'Was she given oxygen on the plane?'

'No, she wasn't. But then you see, people don't know.'

'Yes, well they ought to know.'

'I know. It's education.'

'Fine, I accept that. Most doctors are over cautious and that's the problem. If people do go to their doctors the safest course . . . is to say "I think you ought to go by boat" and like that there's no risk at all! That is unnecessary expense and an unnecessary restriction on most people. All airlines are capable of providing oxygen if they're given notice. We see a lot at this hospital because the hospital is devoted to heart and lung disease. One of my jobs is to make sure that as many as possible of those people can go and visit their relatives in Australia and far off places . . . because often with severe heart and lung disease, they are going to die soon and they want to see their families before they die. It's a very important thing . . . to tell them, to reassure them, that now they are going to be perfectly all right. . . .'

'But I've experienced the opposite attitude from doctors. They don't necessarily think immediately, "Ah, the cabin pressure is going to affect your illness'', they say ''Go to a warm climate, it will help your recovery'''.

'Well, that's interesting. But then I think that in one way or another the people in this hospital are different. I mean, they are highly specialized in these things. . . . It's very wrong for people's quality of life to be curtailed, particularly when they're old. They've got lots of things to do before they kick the bucket.'

'But, you see, [what] you are saying . . . is that there can be a risk. Therefore, you've got to have a preventive approach to it. . . .'

'No, not that there can be,' he amended, 'that there is a risk among people. Anybody who is hypoxic at ground-level is going to get more hypoxic when they go into an aircraft. That ought to be corrected and it can easily be corrected if the airlines are given some warning.'

In a chapter on high altitudes and hypoxia in a book entitled *Principles and Practice of Human Physiology*, edited by O.G. Edholm and J.S. Weiner (Denison 1981: 264–5),[3] Dr Denison observes that although the subject of oxygen insufficiency is well understood, the use of some terms associated with it are imprecise. Perhaps, as the terrain has been limited, in the main, to mild and profound hypoxia, it would be opportune to extend it further. Dysoxia, a rather unusual word, describes any 'derangement' of oxygen supply irrespective of whether it is hypo- or hyper- or whether simple or complicated by a variety of factors. Hypoxia, which is oxygen lack under normal conditions at sea-level, cannot (he emphasizes) be merely termed 'inadequate oxygenation since there are some processes that would proceed faster and others that would be affected adversely if more oxygen were made available to healthy people at sea-level'. The paradox is that normal cells are both intoxicated by and deficient in oxygen at the same time.

Anoxia is the most misused term and, on occasion, I have seen it adopted as a synonym for hypoxia. It represents a 'complete absence of oxygen' which is a state incompatible with life in vertebrates and almost impossible to obtain in experiments. Another form of oxygen lack, asphyxia, results from insufficient ventilation that causes blood and tissue carbon dioxide (CO_2) tensions to rise when the supply of oxygen fails. (The effects of hypoxia are modified through the presence of excessive amounts of CO_2 in the blood – hypercapnia.) Ischaemia, which is caused by impaired blood flow, too, is an example of oxygen lack although it involves the restriction and accumulation of other substances. Therefore it is distinct from simple hypoxia and is sometimes known as stagnant hypoxia. Hypobaric hypoxia is due to altitude exposure whereas if oxygen-deficient mixtures of air are breathed at ground-level the condition is known as hypoxic hypoxia. Should the effective haemoglobin content of the blood drop for whatever reason it leads to anaemic hypoxia. Many poisons like cyanide inhibit enzymatic processes and produce histotoxic hypoxia.

When I left the Brompton that day, I came away with a vision of what aviation or aerospace medicine could offer the public in the future. The facilities would be on a par with those for the military and airline pilots. As more and more people take to the air and a greater proportion of these become frequent flyers, a need is created to monitor their health and to set up specialized units. But, we are a long chalk from that. First there is the education of the public and the medical profession on the problems of air travel.

And what of further research on hypoxia? It could well lie in the other pressure zone, the sea. There is no doubt in Dr Denison's mind that the biochemistry of this subject needs additional study and he knows where it should be conducted.

'The impetus and insight for this', he says, 'may well come from investigations on marine animals. These creatures can swim actively throughout a breathold dive of 45 minutes or more. While it is clear that conventional aerobic metabolism of their heart and brain persists due to a remarkable withdrawal of blood flow from the rest of the body, it is not known how the latter, particularly the working muscles, endure what must be very severe tissue asphyxia.'

There is no question about it, hypoxia or oxygen lack is a fascinator. Before I attempt a definition, I should mention an incident that occurred many years ago. On the particular occasion, I had rung the anthropologist, Francis Huxley, to enquire about the word 'fascinator' as I had read somewhere that he was regarded as an authority on such matters. It is unfortunate that the conversation was cut short but he proposed that I pay £100 because that was his fee for an interview. It was an amount I could not afford at the time.

I now know why. One of the origins of the term is the obscure Epode 8 of Horace (1927: 387; 1976: 56; 1960: 213), so obscure in fact because it was omitted in the past from collections of his poems. Today, when it is included, the English translation is less than adequate as reference is made to poker, rod, or hamptons. 'Fascinator' is derived from the Latin verb, *fascinare*, to bewitch or enchant, and I suspect earlier from the Greek *baskainein* (Licht 1933: 369). The word appears to have had another meaning as a charm or sacred object and as such was symbolized by the male generative organ. As a result, it could be used to break a spell like the evil-eye or to provoke awe in the beholder to the extent that they would be blind to outside influences. (An attraction that could prove to be fatal.)

In this context, it would be appropriate to speak of it in terms of a sacred object or god who provokes awe to the extent that the beholder is blinded to all outside influences. What is implied in the meaning is that attraction can prove to be fatal. Take the example of the beautiful woman or Lorelei who can lure men to their doom. Or the stoat that bewitches the rabbit to the degree that the rabbit's only response is a high-pitched sound until it is attacked and killed. The phallic preoccupation of some primitive tribes may seem to outsiders as pleasurable, but for the tribesmen it is not without pain as a complex system of taboos may be in operation.

Down the ages, there has been a fascination for hypoxia, and its existence appears first to be noted by Aristotle (Boyle 1660: 357). He recorded that people became light-headed and ill on Mt Olympus where the altitude was some 10,000 ft and they had to breathe through wet sponges to be comfortable. The Chinese, too, made reference to it as early as 30 BC in the *Tseen Han Shoo*, when it was proposed to send an escort for an envoy from the mountainous region of Western China to the Hindu Kush in Afghanistan. Mention was made of the journey past the Great Headache Mountain, the Little Headache Mountain, and the Fever Slope, areas where 'men's bodies become feverish, they lose colour, and are attacked with headache and vomiting' (West 1981: 3). These are symptoms of oxygen deficiency and because of our differentiation of its origin today it is called mountain sickness.

Another chronicler of this condition was a Spanish priest, Joseph de Acosta, whose experiences among the inhabitants of high-altitude areas in Peru were published in Spanish in 1590. He gave a fuller account of the problems and also included symptoms of nausea, shortness of breath, and impaired ability in concentration and in the performance of difficult tasks (Fulton 1948: 13).

Now we enter the realm of the experimenters. First they used objects and animals, and then the ultimate, themselves. For who could resist the fatal attraction of the fascinator? Foremost among the experimenters was Robert Boyle who observed that when a viper was deprived of air in his exhaustion chamber, a bubble formed in its eye. In 1674, John Mayow put a mouse under a bell-jar which in part was immersed in water. Stephen Hales went further with the bell-jar in 1727 for he calculated that a rat breathed a thirteenth part of the total volume, or 45 cu. in., of air before its death 10 hours later, while a candle was extinguished in a minute, after it had consumed 54 cu. in. – an eleventh part. When he attempted something similar on himself and breathed from a bag, he discovered that, as the volume decreased, he became giddy (Fulton 1948: 49, 8, 22–4, 165). Paul Bert was so spellbound that his exuberant tribute to it, *La Pression Bárometrique*, ran to some 1,200 pages and earned him an accolade from future aviation or aerospace doctors (Bert 1943: VIII). Last in this line of pioneers was Joseph Barcroft who lived for 6 days in a glass box where there was a gradual depletion of oxygen until on the last day it was down to 10 per cent – the equivalent to an altitude of over 19,000 feet. It was termed 'a heroic experiment' and 'he felt quite ill' at the end (Milledge 1985: 1410).

As soon as aircraft transport became viable it was the turn of the aviators to stand in awe of the sacred condition, and the First World War provided the ideal opportunity. Armed with goggles and a white scarf, they would ascend to 20,000 ft and return to boast of 'never having felt better'. That was proof of their virility. Little wonder that it was difficult for medical officers to introduce the use of oxygen at high altitudes in spite of the harmful consequences of not doing so. But the allure of hypoxia never palled, it only grew. Look at an extract from the report filed by Captain R.W. Schroeder when he set the altitude record of 29,000 ft in 1918.

At 20,000 ft. while still climbing in large circles, my goggles became frosted, making it difficult for me to watch my instruments. When I reached 25,000 ft. I noticed the sun growing very dim. I could hardly hear my motor run, and I felt very hungry. The trend of my thoughts was that it must be getting late . . . I went on talking to myself and this I felt was a good sign to begin taking oxygen, so I did. I was then over 25,000 ft., and as soon as I started to inhale oxygen the sun grew bright again, my motor began to exhaust so loud that it seemed something must be wrong with it. I was no longer hungry and the day seemed to be a most beautiful one. . . .

(DeHart 1985: 96)

It was not sufficient that the pilots experienced oxygen lack, they forced the few passengers that flew with them to share it too. Tommy Tomlinson recalled those days in the 1920s when he would hit altitude rather than slam into those mountains east of Los Angeles. 'I would get a Ford or Fokker up to eighteen thousand feet, even twenty-one or twenty-two thousand feet, and fly reasonably well. Not for long, though. The passengers passed out' (Solberg 1979: 114).

The military were in the forefront of the field. There were General Harry G. Armstrong in the USA and Sir Bryan Matthews in the UK to name just two. As one of the early flying doctors with inadequate staff – one enlisted man – and a limited budget, Harry Armstrong was obliged to use himself as a test subject and whatever animals he could find for experiments in the simulated altitude of a pressure chamber (Engle and Lott 1979: 62–3). He too had been interested in Boyle's bubble, the nitrogen bubble that enlarged whenever there was a shortage of air. Once he had noticed a series of bubbles in the tendons of his fingers which he was able to move back and forth. To further his quest he took to riding up and down the pressure chamber with a rabbit. On the ascent it was alive; at 35,000 ft it was dead, and on descent it was dissected in an effort to find bubbles in the blood. Armstrong too became a casualty. Once, in spite of his protests that he had not completed his task, the operator brought him down to sea-level. What had happened was that he had fallen off the stool, unconscious, onto the floor at maximum altitude, revived at 20,000 ft and resumed the dissection, only to discover that the altimeter was losing height. If it had not been for the large bump on his head, he would never have believed that the incident had occurred (Engle and Lott 1979: 331). Today he is remembered for the Armstrong Line – the zone encountered at 63,000 ft where man's body fluids and blood will boil in an unprotected environment – and as he is a founder of aviation medicine in the USA he is honoured by an annual lecture given to members of the Aerospace Medical Association in his name.

On the other side of the Atlantic, Sir Bryan Matthews conducted similar experiments. Day in and day out, Sir Bryan and two colleagues, Alan Hodgkin and T.C. Macdonald, simulated high-altitude 'runs' in a corrugated iron lean-to on a site that would later become the renowned Institute of Aviation Medicine at Farnborough. These 'runs' were undertaken against the advice of the resident neurologist who was appalled at the risks involved. Apart from the severe pains in their joints caused by the presence of nitrogen bubbles, a condition which was later called 'the bends', they suffered from partial paralysis and from blindness. There was also 'individual variation, Macdonald being worst affected, Matthews often suffering from disturbing visual symptoms and Hodgkin being least affected' (Gibson and

41

Harrison 1984). Sir Bryan categorized the symptoms and in 1939 coined the term 'decompression sickness'. But there was the inevitable price – permanent damage to his vision.

Between the earthbound experimenters and the aviators were the fanatical mountaineers who climbed without oxygen. One such example, Rudolf Messmer, ascended Mt Everest that way. He related in his book *Everest: Expedition to the Ultimate* (1979) how he collapsed every ten or fifteen steps to crawl on again, and how breathing became virtually impossible. But he continued for the fascinator had him in complete thrall and acted as an intoxicant. 'My mind is disconnected, dead,' he wrote.

> But my soul is alive and receptive, grown huge and palpable. It wants to reach the very top so that it can swing back into equilibrium. The last few metres to the summit no longer seem so hard. On reaching the top, I sit down and let my legs dangle into space. . . . In my state of spiritual abstraction, I no longer belong to myself and to my eyesight. I am nothing more than a single, gasping lung, floating over the mists and the summits.
>
> (Messmer 1979: 180)

There is the temptation to catch others in the awesome act and, if it teaches us anything, it is how close the tragic is to the comic. United Airlines (Rule 1986) has an excellent film on hypoxia that is always doing the rounds in the industry to train cabin staff. It stars a captain with a Russian-sounding name and a crew-cut that gives him an indeterminate age, and a flight attendant called Marsha. The action occurs in a pressure chamber among other flight crew and a taskmaster who is the sole person to wear an oxygen mask throughout the show. They undergo a rapid ascent to the average cruising altitude of a jetliner where the time of useful consciousness is about one minute. The fun and games begin when the participants are asked to perform simple tasks. They have to point to numerals displayed on a board, tell the time, and play pat-a-cake. As they repeat each task, their reaction times become slower and their muscles less co-ordinated. In all, their performances deteriorate and yet they appear to enjoy themselves in the manner of those inebriated. These antics are sure to produce laughter from the audience. Marsha's moment arrives when she is asked to put on some makeup. The lipstick is smeared on her nose and the eyeliner lands on parts other than the outline of her eyes. But her hypoxic self is delighted with the effects – as indeed are the new batch of trainees who never expected to see such a hilarious film – and once back at ground level, she is near a nervous collapse when a mirror confronts her with the reality.

The captain in true aviator tradition plays the role of the tough guy as he is the last to don the oxygen mask. The dramatic scene comes when he tugs at the mask tubing in an effort to pull it towards him and instead falls backwards in his seat. Twice the taskmaster shouts at him to convey the urgency of the situation before he connects and some of those watching the film have to curb the impulse to cheer him on like a popular rugby player who almost fumbles a catch. At the end of the film, when all the participants line up for the review, he is the only one who appears not to be himself. One later learns through the airline grapevine that our brave pilot may have suffered from brain damage since.

Although today the physiognomy of the fascinator is well charted, as is its inclination to have a different effect on each victim, its embrace can still be lethal and its symptoms insidious. Beware.

Air Commodore John Ernsting is perhaps the world's foremost authority on oxygen lack – the uncrowned king of hypoxia, so to speak – and is one of a handful of physiologists who in the past have been prepared to use, or indeed use up, their bodies for the purposes of research. (A sacrifice which, I was later informed, is no longer permitted by the scientific establishment.) His rise may seem unspectacular for he joined the Royal Air Force in 1954 on a 3-year short service commission, and stayed put. At the time he was a doctor with an honours degree in physiology and a penchant for investigation.

But what, we may ask, distinguishes the brilliant from the mediocre career? Is it the inexorable pursuit, the enthusiasm, the altruism, luck, or an empathic disposition? Even a combination of these things? There must be many occasions when the experimenter projects himself into the cockpit of a high-performance jet and plays the game of 'what if?' this or that physiological disaster occurs. It is said that a good doctor empathizes with his patients. Therefore, Ernsting would assume the role of the fighter pilot which, as an official history of the RAF observes, is not an easy task. 'Since he is operating in an environment that is hostile in both a military and physiological sense, his ability to survive to do his job depends on the degree of protection with which he is provided' (Gibson and Harrison 1984).

One day he pictures an emergency out there in the blue. It is an incident of acute hypoxia at 60,000 ft and the question is, how much time does the pilot have before a vacuum is achieved? He knows he has 8 seconds because that is the period the blood takes to travel from the lungs to the brain. But how could the time of useful consciousness (TUC) be prolonged?[4] Any extra seconds might save the pilot's life. What if there was a store of oxygen in the brain? Assumptions had been made but never proved.

He set up a series of tests to prove or disprove the hypothesis. In the annals of natural science, the experiment must rank as one of the most gruesome undertaken. For the cause, some scientists have been fired into the air at 290 m.p.h. on rocket-assisted ejection seats (e.g. Peter Howard), others had tubes stuck into their veins to be pushed up towards the heart (e.g. David Glaister) or been given injections of toxic substances (e.g. David Denison), but none of them had been throttled.

The suggestion was grotesque. It was similar to an invitation to test the iron collar of a garrotte or the running knot of a hangman's noose. One slip and it would be fatal. But there could be a fighter pilot somewhere in the sky, where the countdown had begun. . . . Perhaps the feeling of repulsion for the ordeal was mitigated by some such thought?

A blood-pressure cuff was wrapped round his neck blown up very high and he was strangled into unconsciousness again and again. (Whether the skin was bruised afterwards was not mentioned.) It took him between 5 and 7 seconds to black out and the conclusive proof was obtained when the experiment was repeated in a hyperbaric chamber where he breathed 100 per cent oxygen at a pressure of 4 atmospheres. As a result, it was confirmed that another 5 to 7 seconds could be gained because 'the brain itself has oxygen solution in store'. In all, therefore, the pilot has a maximum of 15 seconds before TUC. The studies are unpublished.

This story should be contrasted with the rare find of another store in the body which, if anything, shows the indomitable physiologist at work. In 1921, *en route* to the Andes in Peru where he was to make observations on altitude physiology, Joseph Barcroft noticed that his blood had become both thicker and darker when the ship on which he was travelling reached the tropics at the Panama Canal. He realized that the red (blood) cells, those carriers of oxygen, must have been released from a reservoir because their manufacture does not occur quickly. There were several possible sites for blood-stores but he had a hunch that it was the spleen and used an ingenious method to check it.

He placed rats in an environment where they would inhale carbon monoxide (CO). The gas acts as a poison to the red cells – it suffocates them – for they are unable to obtain oxygen and perform their functions. (This fact is relevant to a later discussion when the closed space of the aircraft cabin is considered, as cigarette smoking also produces carbon monoxide.)

Rats were killed at intervals and he found that it took longer for the poison to reach the spleen, 'a lag of about half an hour', than any other organ. This organ would appear to be the last bastion of unpoisoned red cells and a rat without a spleen would have less of a chance of survival as it had no store from which it could draw healthy red cells. Therefore Barcroft had obtained his proof (Eckstein 1970: 163–4).

Another feature that interested him was the effect of exercise. Since more air is expended during it, more red cells are needed. On this occasion rats were stalked, forced to swim, and hit on the head. Compared to the rats in the control who had been only stalked during sleep, it was discovered that the exercised rats had smaller spleens. This is also the case in a haemorrhage and when an animal shows emotion. Barcroft cites the example of a dog whose spleen will undergo a degree of contraction if subjected to the scent, the sound, and the presence of a cat. The contraction begins when the feline pheromones are first sniffed. But should the cat appear and miaow the spleen reduces to half its size and to a quarter if a chase ensues.

I had arranged to meet John Ernsting who is the head of research at the RAF Institute of Aviation Medicine where some 200 people work – a third are specialist officers and NCOs while two-thirds are civilian scientists. The motto of the institute is apposite – *Ut secure volent*, 'That they may fly safely' – and has over the years inspired those within its precincts to heights of dedication and courage.

To reach Farnborough where the IAM is located, you have to drive through Aldershot where a large signpost welcomes the visitor and announces that it is 'The Home Of The British Army'. This is an apt reminder for the institute, too, is part of a military complex. Under the control of the Ministry of Defence through the Director General of Medical Services Royal Air Force, its chief function is the provision of specialized advice to the Air Staffs on the human factors concerned with aviation. Since 1985 IAM has been a unit of RAF Strike Command. In addition, as the glossy official brochure states, it is a large research and teaching organization studying all non-clinical aspects of environmental medicine of flight, with particular reference to physiology, psychology and the related sciences, the aim being to gain a better understanding of those human factors which affect the safety and efficiency of aircrew. To this end the Institute has always had its complement of aircraft – usually flown by medical officer pilots – for it is considered essential that laboratory scientists should be prepared to validate their experiments in flight.

(RAF AIM 1983: 2–3)

At present they are down to one aircraft, a Hunter T7, which nevertheless places them in an enviable position *vis-à-vis* other western institutes.

I also learn from the brochure that Farnborough is known as 'The cradle of British Aviation' for it was here in 1908 that the first powered and manned flight occurred when Samuel Franklin Cody piloted the British Army Aeroplane No. 1 over 1,390 ft in distance (Taylor and Mondey 1983). (The RAF mess there is known as No. 1 Officers' Mess.) Earlier, together with Aldershot and nearby Laffan's Plain, it was the site of miltary ballooning. The activities now carried out are impressive for they include research into altitude, behavioural sciences, biodynamics, environmental sciences, and neuro-sciences; there is a Control and Data Division and a teaching section.

On the particular day, I skirted the Queen's Roundabout, which is the usual point of reference given to visitors because of a hotel with the same name that is sited there, and drove towards the guardhouse nearby. As I parked, well before the time set for the appointment, I knew that there was no certainty that I would emerge with the requisite MOD form A98 which would permit entry to the institute. In the early stages of researching for this book, I had once been debarred from these very gates, and the only method to circumvent the directive was to be provided with an armed escort. I must confess that at the time I was prepared to brook such incongruity in the library – for that was my destination – as I was eager to browse in their specialist collection. But it was not to be. I had been misinformed.[5]

The grey and square, two-storey, modern block, which is at odds with the long, low buildings that predominate and no doubt have been influenced by the quintessential aeronautical form, the hangar, has prompted one wit to dub it 'the home of the *cognoscenti*' and it is where the Air Commodore's office is situated. An airman accompanied me to the entrance. In a way, John Ernsting could be described as 'hypoxia personified' for to date his body of work on the subject is unrivalled. It could be argued that on the whole the application is confined to a narrow field as most military aircraft have a low differential cabin pressurization and the test subjects reflect the average aircrew, who are young, fit, and healthy. There is his book, for example, that is devoted to the specialized area of high-pressure breathing at high altitudes, of which the blurb-writer writes, 'will be all-absorbing to those engaged in the design and practicability of manned space vehicles' and predicts that in the current 'climate of explosive expansion of space and aviation medicine . . . will become a classic . . .' (Ernsting 1978). Published by NATO in 1966, it was called *Some Effects of Raised Intrapulmonary Pressure in Man*, and when it was first presented as a thesis for a Ph.D. to the examiners at the Faculty of Medicine of the University of London, they were 'disturbed' by its length and depth. (I was later told by an expert that it is a classic and a monumental piece of work!)

However, the cornerstone of his research does have relevance in civil aviation. In the tenth Harry G. Armstrong lecture (1975) which was titled 'Prevention of hypoxia – acceptable compromises', and which is considered an excellent review of aviation hypoxia in line with those of Professor Ross McFarland and General H.G. Armstrong in the past, he gives an account of the work.

Interest in the impairment of performance induced by mild hypoxia was stimulated at the RAF Institute of Aviation Medicine in 1960 . . . by the chance observation that the ability of subjects to reproduce a recently learnt sequence of eight digital operations was impaired when they learnt the task whilst breathing air at 8,000 ft compared with their performance when the task has been learnt whilst breathing 100% oxygen at 8,000 ft. This discovery was followed up in a series of experiments designed specifically to investigate the effects of hypoxia upon the process of learning a novel task. Denison, Ledwith, and Poulton compared the performance of matched groups of subjects learning a complex orientation task whilst exposed to inspired PO_2s equivalent to breathing air at one of three altitudes; namely, ground level, 5,000 and 8,000 ft. Throughout each experimental period, the subject pedalled on a bicycle at a load which produced an oxygen consumption of 0.6L.(NTP)/min. He was required as a secondary task to maintain a constant preset rate of pedalling. . . . The results suggested that performance at the complex orientation task used in the study was impaired by the mild hypoxia induced by breathing air at either 5,000 or 8,000 ft whilst the test was being learnt but not after the subjects had practised it. Impairment during the learning phase was only just detectable at 5,000 ft but considerable at 8,000 ft.

Since the original experiments,[6] which were conducted between 1960 and 1965, there have been several independent studies, which have confirmed that very mild hypoxia impairs performance at complex tasks during the learning phase. . . . The pattern which emerges from the various studies of the effects of mild hypoxia upon psychomotor and mental performance which have been performed in the last decade is that the most clear-cut effect induced by breathing air at altitudes of up to 10,000 ft is a prolongation of the time taken to learn a new task. The intensity of this effect increases with the complexity of the task, but even choice reaction times are prolonged by breathing air at 5,000 to 7,000 ft. . . . Synthesis of these results of laboratory studies (which have shown that hypoxia increases fatigue) suggest that, when air is breathed, the maximum cabin altitude during routine flight should not exceed 6,000 ft. Practical experience in transport operations also gives support of this conclusion since reduction of the cabin altitude from 8,000 ft to 6,000 ft is associated with a lower incidence of otitic barotrauma and disturbances in passengers with cardiorespiratory disease.

(Ernsting 1978: 498–9)

We sat on a modern corner-sofa, which I suspect is a standard fitting for senior officers, in the spacious office of John Ernsting's suite which includes a reception area and a boardroom. Here it was back to basics for we began at the very beginning of respiratory physiology, i.e. with breathing. The supply of oxygen, or for that matter carbon dioxide from the environment, to the tissues is achieved through gas tension gradients. It is usual to depict this as a down slope from dry air, wet tracheal air, alveolar gas in the lungs, arterial blood, venous blood, to the lowest pressure or tension in the tissues.

'The important thing is to determine', he says, 'the partial pressure of oxygen . . . at the reacting face . . . because it's the pressure head of oxygen which drives the whole mechanism in the body. And why you need oxygen is that your final process in release . . . whether it be in the brain or muscular activity or heart activity or digestion in most tissues, is an oxidation process.

'I'm going right down to the tissues,' he explains in his interpretation of the oxygen tension cascade, 'and there you need to maintain . . . a partial pressure of oxygen for most tissues to operate normally of between 2 to 5 millimetres of mercury. Now that compares with us breathing air in this room at a partial pressure of oxygen at 150 mmHg and the transport mechanisms in the body, in fact, usually maintain, in a normal working tissue, the partial pressure of oxygen considerably above that of 2 to 5 mmHg, usually about 20 to 30 mmHg. So if you're thinking about typical tissue in the body compared with the outside environment, breathing air at sea-level with a partial pressure of 150 . . . down at tissue level it's about 30.'

'If you want to talk about how the gradient changes down the system . . . you've got oxygen disappearing from the gas you breathe in, going into the blood and you've got carbon dioxide coming out . . . [as a result] the lung gas contains normally about 5 to 5.5 per cent carbon dioxide which exerts a partial pressure of 40 mmHg. So if you've got 40 mmHg for carbon dioxide . . . you must have less room for oxygen in the lungs. You've got a partial pressure of 100 mmHg for oxygen as it drops from 150 mmHg in the atmosphere to roughly 100 mmHg in the lungs. The gas exchange mechanism is very effective for it has a very large surface area of thin membranes, separating the gas from the blood. When the blood leaves the lungs it's almost full of oxygen, up there at 100 mmHg, and as it flows through the heart, it goes into the arteries where the partial pressure of oxygen is about 8 mmHg lower than the lung gas, at about 90 to 95 mmHg. [Later] as it flows through the tissues, the oxygen diffuses out because the partial pressure is higher in the blood than in the tissues and when it gets to the venous end, at the far end of the tissues, the partial pressure of oxygen will be about 40 mmHg. That's the partial pressure of oxygen in the blood that comes back to the lungs. And in the lungs, then, you've got blood coming into it at a partial pressure of oxygen of 40 mmHg while the lung gases have got a partial pressure of 100. So that's the driving force of 60 mmHg to push the oxygen into the blood.

'And as you go to altitude, you get compensation, in that above 10,000 or 12,000 ft the falling partial pressure of oxygen that occurs in the blood stimulates respiration through some receptors in the neck, in the carotid artery. . . . They continually sense the partial pressure of oxygen in the blood and if it falls below a certain level then they stimulate respiration. You see, respiration starts increasing when you go above altitudes of about 10,000 to 12,000 feet to about the time you get to half an atmosphere, 18,000 feet, the partial pressure may be nearly down to half of what it was at sea-level.'

'But then don't you start hyperventilating?' I ask.

'Yes, that is termed hyperventilation – the washing out of carbon dioxide. The advantage of that is it gives more room for oxygen, of course. The disadvantage is that [the reduction in the partial pressure of carbon dioxide] in the blood leads to constriction, contraction of the blood vessels of the brain. Therefore, the blood flows more slowly through the brain and each unit volume of blood going through the brain . . . has to give up more oxygen. So the partial pressure of oxygen in the blood falls to a lower level, thus making the brain tissue more hypoxic. Although you gain by hyperventilating when you're hypoxic at altitudes . . . in fact at the brain level you lose out.'

One aspect that is not mentioned here is the carriage of oxygen by the blood. It is done through simple physical solution and in reversible chemical combination with the haemoglobin of the red cells in the form of oxyhaemoglobin. Also, it is governed by Fick's law whereby 'the concentration of dissolved oxygen varies directly with the tension of the gas'. The definition is extracted from Dhenin's textbook on *Aviation Medicine* published by Tri-Med Books of which he was the editor (Dhenin 1978). As hyperventilation can in rare cases cause unconsciousness, I enquired about this condition, which is otherwise known as syncope or fainting, and is quite common among air passengers. I took the example of the old lady who faints on board.

'Well, it may be due to many things . . . the common cause of a faint in a person who's upright is emotional disturbance, fear, and anxiety. . . . Take a group of healthy subjects and make them hypoxic until they're unconscious. Roughly a fifth of them will lose consciousness due to a faint – they will have what is known as a full-blown faint – the other 80 per cent will not faint, they'll lose consciousness with a well-maintained blood pressure. When a person faints . . . the mechanism – why you lose consciousness when you faint – is that the arterial blood pressure falls because the resistance vessels in the muscles of the body have all opened up suddenly. That can be due to loss of circulating blood volume like in a haemorrhage; it can be due to standing upright for long periods like soldiers on parade . . . emotion can do it and as I said hypoxia. It's a very specific thing, a faint, and it is not a general mechanism of loss of consciousness. You lose consciousness because blood flow to the brain ceases as there is no blood pressure. That is a protective mechanism because normally, of course, you'd fall flat. It's very difficult to make somebody faint when they are lying flat. . . . When you're seated you can faint quite easily.'

'To return to the protective mechanism,' I suggested, 'how does the brain protect itself in the case of oxygen lack?'

'First of all . . . [through] increased ventilation. The second mechanism, unless you do faint, is a well-maintained blood pressure which may well increase slightly in hypoxia. And the third, which occurs in severe hypoxia, is the dilation of the cerebral arterioles which leads to an increase in blood flow to the brain, thus reducing the fall of PO [partial pressure of oxygen] in the brain tissue. But eventually that still may not be adequate, for at about 20,000 feet to 25,000 feet most people if you leave them long enough will lose consciousness. Certainly above 25,000 feet. And that's because those protective mechanisms will no longer maintain the partial pressure of oxygen in their tissues.'

Halfway through the talk we exchanged anecdotes on hypoxic incidents. Ernsting's favourite was about a pilot who attempted to land on a cloud. It occurred during the Second World War when an RAF bomber pilot had been at 20,000 ft for 2 hours with a defective oxygen system. The navigator of the particular Halifax aircraft gave an account of the event that later appeared in the Gillies textbook of *Aviation Medicine* to which Ernsting was a contributor.

> When we realised that the aircraft was out of control the engineer trimmed the aircraft. The pilot resented this and assaulted the engineer. He then gave the order to bale out which we cancelled. He opened the window to look out, and was only prevented from falling out by the engineer who hauled him in. He said that he felt very happy, and had no feeling of fear even when he tried to force land on a cloud, thinking he was near the ground. On one occasion he informed us that we were below ground. After being forced to take oxygen from the spare helmet and mask he gradually recovered his senses and was able to fly the required course to base, although he suffered from headache which persisted after landing.
>
> (Gillies 1965: 212)

There appears to be little in the open literature on the long-term effects of hypoxia and I broached the subject with Ernsting. It is accepted in general that the administration of oxygen or an increase in environmental pressure is sufficient to ensure a rapid recovery. The only symptom that tends to persist is a headache if the exposure was prolonged. However, there are exceptions, for the immediate restoration of alveolar oxygen tension in some subjects may result in 'a transient increase in the severity of the symptoms for 15–60 seconds', as is noted in the Dhenin textbook.

> The *oxygen paradox*, as it is termed, is usually mild, but sometimes the administration of oxygen may induce clonic spasms and loss of consciousness. A large proportion of subjects show a transient worsening of performance at complex tasks in the 15–60 seconds after restoration of oxygen supply. The mechanism responsible for this condition is uncertain.
>
> (Gillies 1965: 212)

It all serves to confirm that the area has remained unexplored and open to speculation. I recalled how Sir Bryan Matthews suffered a loss of peripheral vision through the effects of decompression sickness which, though not associated with hypoxia and trapped-gas expansion, also occurs at lower barometric pressure.

'That's still true,' Ernsting commented when I asked him about the use of oxygen as a resuscitative technique. 'Unless', he continued, 'you produce permanent brain damage.'

'Under what conditions could one do that?' I asked.

He explained that during the last war there were many deaths due to hypoxia. (The extent of this was covered by Ross McFarland in *Human Factors in Air Transport Design* who reported that fatalities among American bomber crew on high-altitude flights were at one stage as high as 21.6 deaths per 100,000 man–missions (McFarland 1946: 597).) There were also a larger number who recovered from hypoxic incidents as well as a few who suffered from permanent brain damage. He contrasted this with the situation of a cardiac arrest where 'you know very well that if you don't get the circulation going again effectively to the brain within 4 minutes or so, you're certainly going to have some permanent brain damage. Even maybe a little earlier than that.

'In fact, it was Group Captain Nicholson in our joint experiments in relation to Concorde who really brought out that acute hypoxia can, in animals, in primates – monkeys – produce permanent brain damage. We were interested in looking at the original plans for the design of the pressure cabin which related very much to the size of windows, the duplication or quadruplication of control systems . . . and we examined various cabin altitudes – time profiles simulating descent from 60,000 feet following the initiation of a decompression. We did that work here at the IAM and put monkeys (*Macaca mulatta*) through these profiles and then followed them for the next 5 or 6 days afterwards; we found some of them had permanent brain damage or, if they survived, paralysis. Yes, that's all in the *Aerospace Journal*, published by Nicholson and myself. But there are a whole series of papers on that. And when we went on to look at the level of hypoxia which would produce permanent brain damage among monkeys, I think we ended up at 37,000 feet breathing air for something like 15 minutes. . . .

'It was partly the results of those experiments which drove the Concorde windows to be as small as they are now and the triplication or quadruplication of the control system. We had done the work to show that failure of windows as large as those in subsonic jets would get you into very, very serious problems. So there was a feed into Concorde and SST requirements very much related to the sort of picture that you have of the aircraft flying at 60,000 feet. It loses cabin pressure and has a relatively restricted rate of descent compared with a fighter because of problems of exceeding the critical Mach number and loss of control. If you look then, at what happens to the cabin altitude against time, cabin altitude, that's very much a function of, first of all, the rate at which obviously the aircraft can descend, but secondly, the size of the hole in the cabin.'

Later, when I read the series of studies on the neurological effects of profound hypoxia, I found how accurate the results were. In one paper by A.E. Blagbrough and A.N. Nicholson (1975), they mentioned the tragic accident of a balloonist who, during an attempt on the world's altitude-jumping record, was decompressed at 57,000 ft. Although automatic descent procedures became operative within a few seconds, he was exposed for 3 minutes to altitudes of over 40,000 ft and it took him some 25 minutes to reach ground-level. Severe neurological disturbances were demonstrated and he died after 4 months without regaining consciousness. 'Post-mortem examination of the brain revealed severe damage to the cerebral cortex similar to that which had been found in the baboons' (Blagbrough and Nicholson 1975: 199).

It was towards the end of the hour talk that he showed he still is the researcher *par excellence*, in spite of an observation earlier that he had finished his experimental career. He came up with something that revealed a gap in an otherwise fail-safe system of the SST. For the relentless prober with an inherent concern for human life, it is a consequence of innumerable 'what if' speculations. But this time, the general public are involved, not the single fighter pilot. It can be summed up as a disaster scenario for the Concorde.

I had switched back to a point he had made before about the quadruplication of pressure control systems and their operation.

'Instead of just having a simple valve controlling the outlet,' he replied, 'you put another one in series with it, so you can shut it. If that one fails, there's the next one.' He assured me that the engineering reliability was high and, as he admitted to being rusty on the design specifications, consulted Dhenin's textbook (1978). ' "The cabin altitude should not exceed 15,000 ft" ', he read, ' "after a probable failure of pressure cabin, and that's 1 in 10^3 to 1 in 10^5 flying hours. It should not exceed 25,000 ft after a remote failure, which is 1 in 10^5 to 1 in 10^7 flying hours and will not exceed 25,000 ft – extremely remote – and that's less than 1 in 10^7 flying hours which is a major structural failure on reliability level. . . . So in that aeroplane, the chances of loss of pressure being very severe is very, very remote. No, the bigger problem with both Concorde and subsonic jets operating over . . . the Atlantic is what you do after loss of pressure when you come down. Because of having to continue the flight unpressurized, that's more (dangerous)." '

'Could you rephrase that?'

'The philosophy there depends on getting the passengers down to an altitude where you can breathe air safely. Because of the many studies done, quite a lot by Charles Billings at Ohio State, where you take normal groups of people, give them a full airline briefing and put them in a decompression chamber and suddenly the altitude is at 35,000 ft, (we know that) many of them will not even use drop-down masks. If you look around the back-end of a standard civil transport aircraft, you know people are asleep or eating . . . only a small proportion of the population would probably make use of the drop-down systems in the event of a severe decompression. The whole philosophy of saving their lives in that situation is to ensure that the crew won't become hypoxic, then they can rapidly reduce the altitude. However, if you're in the mid-Atlantic, for instance, because your fuel consumption goes up so rapidly with decreasing altitude, many aircraft are forced to return to altitudes of between 15,000 and 20,000 feet. Then you have a major problem because government regulations only require you to carry enough oxygen for 15 per cent of the passengers.

'Enough for 15 per cent.'

'That's it. How do you decide which 15 per cent need it?'

'Are you saying that if there is a loss of pressure only 15 per cent of the masks will come down?'

'No. What I'm saying is, on a rapid decompression, they all come down and regulations require you to carry sufficient oxygen for all the passengers until the aircraft has descended back down to 10,000 feet or so. Then, you've got to re-ascend – if that accident happens in the middle of the Atlantic – to 15,000, 16,000 feet because of fuel consideration to get back to land. The international regulations . . . [require] you only to carry enough oxygen for 15 per cent of your passengers for that 2 hours.'

'Who decides what?'

'The cabin staff.'

'So it depends who is in what condition?'

'Yes. Even a trained doctor would have difficulty in deciding [who gets the oxygen]. The regulations, like many set regulations, come about from negotiation. . . . You have to rate the chances of that happening against the routine penalties of carrying a lot more oxygen in the aeroplane. So those sorts of decisions are arbitrary but are usually done on an international basis so that everybody is using the same regulations.'

The predicament itself would cause considerable chaos. Not all the passengers would don their oxygen masks when these appeared in the initial phase. Charles E. Billings and his colleagues noted in their observations on the behaviour of naïve subjects during rapid decompression that some 40 per cent might be at risk through either this failure or prolonged donning times (Chisolm *et al.* 1974). There is the additional complication that the 85 per cent without masks, besides suffering impairment of their own health, would constitute a flight hazard because they would all be in the disturbance stage of hypoxia which is characterized by personality changes in individuals. They exhibit euphoria, elation, pugnacity, moroseness, and over-confidence, and become physically violent. But whatever the consequences to the passengers, the Civil Aviation Authority regulation is incorporated in Air Navigation Order Schedule 5: Scale K. (It is of interest to note that in the USA, the Federal Aviation regulation of Part 121.329 which deals with a similar situation requires double the percentage of passengers, i.e. 30 per cent, to be provided with oxygen between 14,000 and 15,000 ft cabin altitude, while above

15,000 ft oxygen should be provided for all passengers because of the occurrence of serious impairment.)

I was also made aware, on another occasion, of the interchange Dr Ernsting has initiated through his academic appointments between his field, diving medicine, and modern areas of clinical medicine. It has been known for some time that a large number of diseases produce their effects through hypoxia. In certain types of cancer, for example, it was found that cells at the centre of the tumour were resistant to radiotherapy because of their very low oxygen partial pressure – two and a half times less than that of normal tissues. Therefore, in some medical institutions, such as St Thomas's Hospital, London, where he is the Visiting Professor in Physiology, the patients undergo hyperbaric oxygenation. 'You give oxygen at very high pressure', he told me, 'and then expose the patient's body to X-rays. On that basis you bring all the cells up, not only the body cells but the cancer cells, and make them more sensitive [to radiation]' (Ernsting 1986).

Before I left that day, I saw yet another side of John Ernsting's personality. A side that enables him to transcend the high fences, the barbed wire, the preoccupation with rank, and a thousand other minutiae necessary to a military establishment. It was a simple act of kindness that endeared him to me. He had been informed of my attempt to visit the library and had enquired why it had been abortive. How can one answer such a question? Perhaps I should have said, 'In the interests of knowledge', or invoked the name of that institution's champion Dr Vartan Gregorian of the New York Public Library? However, as the time was inappropriate, I settled for a perfunctory remark. He then offered to lend me journals and books from his own collection. One was a rare first edition, the English version of Paul Bert's famous book that had to wait 65 years before it was translated. From the signatures inside, it was obvious that it had belonged to both the first head of the RAF IAM, Air Vice-Marshal W.K. Stewart, and his successor, Air Vice-Marshal H.L. Roxburgh. When I offered to return the journals personally within a fortnight, he smiled. 'If you do,' he said, 'warn my secretary. Otherwise they might think your parcel could contain a bomb.'

Chapter Five

THE GREAT MIMIC: HYPERVENTILATION, OR OVER-BREATHING

It happens on the ground and it occurs in the air, where, according to the American Medical Association, it is the most common medical complication encountered in commercial flights (AMACEMS 1982: 1010). Hyperventilation or 'over-breathing' is a condition that lowers the carbon dioxide tensions in the body and appears to be caused by fear, excitement, or anxiety. The symptoms resemble those of hypoxia. In the main, the breathlessness is followed by numbness, tingling of the face and limbs, and, if it is not controlled, it can lead to muscle spasms, blurred vision, and unconsciousness.

Yet it would be easy to delude oneself over hyperventilation because of the simple mechanism involved and the cure. In our age of modern drugs, who could afford to be serious about an antidote such as a paper bag? Part of the dismissive attitude derives from the fact that the condition is often misdiagnosed as respiratory distress or coronary heart disease, and on occasion its symptoms have been attributed to thyroid, gastrointestinal or central nervous diseases. Such a situation would lead to the compilation of a useless dosier on a patient and has prompted a consultant chest physician, Dr L.C. Lum, to dub it as the worthy successor to syphilis as the great mimic. (Lum 1981: 1). If an archetypal syndrome could be found for it, it would be Da Costa's as the physiological dysfunction – the palpitations and shortness of breath – could be mistaken for a disorder of the heart.

Since we are concerned with the occurrence of hyperventilation in-flight where the facilities for observation are nonexistent, it is important to review some of the clinical studies carried out on the ground. There is little doubt that the patients are regarded as neurotic and if there is a question to pose it is whether the anxiety causes the symptoms or the symptoms cause the anxiety.

In addition to the symptoms already mentioned, there are quite a few others. Of particular interest is the gastrointestinal type that includes difficulty in swallowing (dysphagia), heartburn, burping, choking sensation (globus), and oesophageal reflux because a major airline reported a 50 per cent increase in such incidents on international flights during the period 1984 to 1985 (Harrex 1985). Perhaps the great mimic hyperventilation was responsible and not the reason offered at the time, that it was 'no doubt due to greater awareness of both passengers and cabin crew following the outbreak of food poisoning in early 1984' (Harrex 1985: 29). Fatigue, an irritable, unproductive cough, muscular cramps, tetany (uncommon), fibrositis of different parts of the torso, sleep disturbance, nightmares, and 'emotional sweating' (palms and armpits) are listed as well but the most unusual are psychic experiences that vary from hallucinations, depersonalization, 'unreal' feelings, free-floating anxiety, to simple tension (Lum 1981: 1). Among the most predictable that Dr Lum discovered in his extensive survey of 1,735 patients over a period of some 20 years at the Papworth Hospital, Cambridge, were 'general exhaustion, lack of concentration and diminished performance' (Lum 1981: 1, 4). It is uncanny how the last two are similar to the signs of hypoxia; this demonstrates the difficulty of the professional, and more so of the non-professional, in making a positive diagnosis on board an aircraft.

What then are the causes of hyperventilation? From the diverse symptoms recorded, there may be the temptation to ascribe them all to the psychological factor and use the convenient term, neurosis. But this would be inaccurate, as Squadron Leader T.M. Gibson of the RAF has shown in his research with military pilots who appear to be prone to it while they undergo training, particularly in high-performance aircraft (Gibson 1984: 411–12). (It is claimed some 20–40 per cent are affected.) Experienced aircrew too can be affected when under severe mental stress in an in-flight emergency. Environmental, pharmacological, and pathological factors also play a part. The flight environment itself can provide stimuli which include hypoxia, whole-body vibration (at 4–8 Hz), heat stress, motion sickness and when there is increased resistance to breathing with oxygen equipment. Certain drug groups such as female sex hormones, stimulants of the central nervous system, salicylates, and catecholamines can provoke the condition while the same can be said for fevers, anaemia, pulmonary disorders, degenerative heart disease, metabolic acidosis that arises in diabetes or in uraemia, and peripheral chemoreceptor stimulation which originates from histotoxic poisoning. Besides the anxiety state, anger, pain, and extreme emotion are cited as effective causes in healthy subjects.

The extent of this problem can only be appreciated once the physiological consequences are known. When hyperventilation happens, excessive amounts of carbon dioxide are lost, blown off, and the low level of it in the blood is called hypocarbia or hypocapnia. At the same time the acid–alkali balance, expressed as pH of about 7.4, alters and the blood becomes more alkaline, a condition known as alkalosis or respiratory alkalosis. In the main it inhibits the catalytic activity of enzymes. This in turn affects the cardiovascular and central nervous systems and in the case of the latter can produce bizarre situations. Neurophysiological research over the past 30 years has shown that changes in the carbon dioxide level exercise a strong influence over the function of the nervous system. In an excellent review on the subject which was published in the *Journal of the Royal Society of Medicine* (Lum 1981), Dr Lum describes an aspect of this.

> At neuronal level, carbon dioxide acts directly on the nerve cell. Its molecular size allows it to diffuse in and out of the cell even faster than water: it is one of the fastest diffusing molecules. A fall in arterial and cerebrospinal PCO_2 is immediately followed by migration of CO_2 from the neurone. The intracellular pH rises, and with it there is a demonstrable increase in neuronal activity and electrical discharge in associated nerve fibres.
>
> (ibid: 2)

Such a stimulatory effect will occur even under minor degrees of hypocarbia when there is a decrease, for example, from the norm of 40 to 35 mmHg. In the case of profound falls, a change in the neuronal metabolism results. 'Then', as Dr Lum notes,

> anaerobic glycolysis begins to produce lactic acid which lowers the pH again, with consequent diminution of neuronal activity so that in extreme degrees of hypocarbia, the neurone may eventually become inert. Thus the response is biphasic: initially excitation; later, with more profound hypocarbia, a progressive depression. Clinically this manifests itself as excitability in the early and mild stages: later, if hyperventilation continues and increases, progressing to exhaustion. In extreme cases, stupor or coma supervene.
>
> (ibid: 2)

To show how this becomes evident in an individual, a specific instance is given. Under a moderate degree of hyperventilation, there is the classic fight or flight syndrome in which sensory perception is heightened – sounds are louder, lights are brighter – reflexes are quickened and the musculature is tense and alert. If this state deteriorates to severe hypocarbia, many of these responses cease and the victim is rooted to the spot – the phenomenon of paralysis through fright. The nerve fibres react in a definite order of impairment whereby touch is the first, followed by position, pressure, and vibration, next is the motor function which is succeeded by cold, heat, and, in the end, pain fibres.

The cardiovascular effects include a rapid pulse rate (tachycardia), a redistributed cardiac output, a decline in blood pressure and vascular resistance, while the vasoconstriction of the small cerebral arteries decreases the blood flow to the brain.

However, once the CO_2 stores in the body are depleted, it requires time for them to be restored. In the case where a person has hyperventilated for a few minutes, it can take hours for the levels to become normal. With chronic cases, in particular in women, Dr Gibson observes that they will have a low PCO_2 for months after the symptoms have ceased (Gibson 1984: 413).

For a disorder that confounds the diagnostician and undermines the body, one would not expect to be able to put it to good use. But this is possible both in the conventional and unconventional sense. In hypnotism, it is an important aid to induce hypnosis and as such has become a standard procedure. Perhaps the neurological effects of hypocarbia account in part for this state of mind. It also has a place in societies in which rites are still practised. But here it is the unusual feature, the insensitivity to pain that it creates, which is utilized. Where mutilation is an integral part of tribal or voodoo ceremonies, initiates are stimulated to hyperventilate by the singing, dancing, drumbeats, and general excitement that accompany these occasions, and will exhibit greater endurance during painful procedures than otherwise.

As to the question whether anxiety arises from hyperventilation or vice versa, the current medical opinion (based on R.L. Rice's work in 1950), which is a reversal of the one held in the past, is 'that the anxiety was produced by the symptoms and, furthermore, that patients could be cured by eliminating faulty breathing habits. Lewis (1964) identified the role of anxiety as a trigger, rather than the prime cause' (Lum 1981: 4). It is not infrequently that a vicious cycle develops through an assortment of triggers both psychological and physiological.

Dr Denison points out that hypocarbia is much more obvious on long-haul flights when passengers are nervous and the cabin is hot and stuffy (Denison 1989). Additional factors, identified by Dr Gibson, that contribute to or exacerbate the effects of the condition in flight are positive acceleration and hypoglycaemia (Gibson 1984: 412). However, a cure rate of 70–75 per cent has been obtained for chronic hyperventilators, the majority of whom are profiled as either perfectionist or slightly obsessional and, in the case of men, type A personalities. As hypocarbia is known to potentiate the effects of alcohol these chronic sufferers should abstain from drinking when they fly or drive.

And now for the denouement. In aviation medical studies on this complex subject, it would appear that the outer form, the rapid, shallow breathing, has taken precedence over other aspects. This has led us to understate or even overlook the fact that the pressure cabin itself causes hypocarbia. By virtue of Boyle's law there will be a decrease in the pressure of CO_2 in this environment. In Table 5.1 it will be seen that at a cabin altitude of between 6,000 and 8,000 ft, the partial pressure of CO_2 will vary between 37 and 36 mmHg. Therefore every passenger will suffer from mild hypocarbia.

Table 5.1 Partial pressure of carbon dioxide at altitude

Altitude ft	Pressure Air (mmHg)	$PACO_2$* (mmHg)
0	759.97	40.0
1,000	733.04	39.4
2,000	706.63	39.0
3,000	681.23	38.4
4,000	656.34	38.0
5,000	632.46	37.4
6,000	609.09	37.0
7,000	586.49	36.4
8,000	564.64	36.0

Source: DeHart 1985
Note: *$PACO_2$ – partial pressure of carbon dioxide.

Chapter Six

THE BODY AS A BALLOON: GAS EXPANSION

At a time when the scheduled airliner had just become a reality and it was important to show the public whenever possible how safe and comfortable air travel was, the first small child flew across the American continent, from New York to Los Angeles, in a journey that took 48 hours and was combined with fast train connections because there were no flights at night. It was a feat that would earn 4-year-old Gore Vidal a footnote in the history of aviation, much to his satisfaction, and he, the ever-observant, still has memories of that event: 'the lurid flames from the exhaust through the window' and 'a sudden loss of altitude over Los Angeles, during which my eardrums burst' (Vidal 1985). But the blooding of the author, for he later appeared in newspaper photographs of 1929 with a trickle of blood down each earlobe, has a significance that he has missed and would enable him to gain yet another footnote, on this occasion in the field of aviation medicine. His would be the first recorded case of otitic barotrauma or aerotitis media in an infant. This condition, described by H.G. Armstrong and J.W. Heim in 1937 as a new clinical entity, is caused by inadequate ventilation of the middle ear during descent and may arise in conjunction with infections of the upper respiratory tract or as a result of a too rapid descent and a failure to vent the ears (Armstrong 1961: 164).

The incident is also a sure sign that the body inflates and deflates like a balloon as a consequence of flight. To be specific, gas contained or trapped in the closed or semi-closed cavities of the body will expand or contract with the respective increase or decrease of altitude in accordance with Boyle's law. As an illustration of expansion, the volume of trapped gas will expand 20 per cent at 5000 ft, 25 per cent at 6,000 ft, 35 per cent at 8,000 ft, and will double at 18,000 ft. (Table 6.1 details these percentages further at various altitudes.) Although

Table 6.1 Gas expansion at altitude

Altitude (ft)	Atmospheric pressure (p.s.i.)	Volume increase (%)
0	14.7	0
1,000	14.2	3
5,000	12.2	20
6,000	11.8	25
7,000	11.3	30
8,000	10.9	35
10,000	10.1	46
18,000	7.3	100

Source: Adapted from DeHart (1985) by F.S. Kahn

this represents on average a 30 per cent increase in volume on board a commercial aircraft, the figure is modified through the presence of water vapour because the walls of the cavities are always moist. At face value, these changes do not appear to have much impact on our bodies, as indeed most passengers would attest. In the case of the alimentary tract, if any discomfort is felt, the gas can be discharged without any problems. Yet Dhenin's textbook notes that 'certain individuals, usually inexperienced aviators, have difficulty in venting gas from the mouth and anus even with low rates of ascent' (Dhenin 1978: 24) The lungs, on the other hand, have a limited flexibility and in principle could burst at a pressure of 2 p.s.i. However, in practice this is a rare occurrence.

But there are instances where gas contained in the semi-closed cavities of the ear, the sinuses, and the lungs, and the closed cavities of the alimentary canal and the teeth, can cause serious complications. These can occur either when there is a pre-existing condition or after recent surgery or during rapid decompression. Of the semi-closed cavities, the ear is the most likely to cause problems by virtue of its anatomical structure. Two out of the three chambers of which it is composed, and the eustachian tube to which it is connected with the upper part of the throat or the nasopharynx, reflect the changes in pressure. The external ear is separated from the middle ear by the tympanic membrane (ear-drum) and it is essential that the pressure on either side is always equal. This is achieved by the location of the eustachian tube in the middle ear that provides an outlet in the form of a one-way valve.

On ascent, gas expands in the middle ear and escapes through the valve into the nasopharynx at a rate of once every 500 to 1,000 ft. When this occurs, the passenger experiences a 'popping' in the ears – a sensation caused by the ear-drum as it rebounds. On descent, gas that had earlier been vented now finds an obstruction and cannot enter the folds that form the mucous membrane lining of the eustachian tube. But it is necessary to equalize the pressure in the external ear, and until that is attained the ear-drum is forced inwards. The distortion of the membrane results in a feeling of fullness in the ears, a slight deafness, and, later, severe pain prior to rupture. It can also affect, in unusual circumstances, the organs of balance in the inner ear with the resultant disorientation. However, the remedies are simple. All that is required in most cases to actuate the eustachian tube is to swallow, to yawn, or to move the lower jaw from side to side. If this does not clear the ears, the Valsalva manoeuvre has to be used. Here the individual inhales, closes the nose with thumb and forefinger, and exhales with the mouth closed. It is obvious that where one is asleep or under heavy sedation the preventive measures cannot be taken.

Diseases of the ear and minor infections can predispose passengers to 'ear block' and of these the most common determinant is when the eustachian tube is swollen due to a cold, sinusitis, or an allergy. Contributory factors can include enlarged adenoids, chronic tonsilitis, or old facial and nasal fractures. One or both ears may be affected by the pain which could be so intense as to produce a faint and in rare incidents, about 5 per cent, a perforation of the ear-drum. If this does not heal, it can cause permanent deafness. Tinnitus (that buzz in the ear) and vertigo may accompany the condition. By now it should be clear that Gore Vidal's memory of the historic trip had failed him in one respect. He had blotted out the sensation of pain that had excruciated his tiny body. If there is a lesson to be learnt, it is that parents should ensure that children who have upper respiratory tract infections do not travel by air.

Although the incidence of aerosinusitis or sinus barotrauma is far less than that of aerotitis media, its predominant symptom also is pain. Both the frontal and the other sinuses are connected to the nose and on ascent or descent the gas contained within them is free to expand or contract. Should these cavities be restricted or narrowed, the condition will develop. The pain that can cause incapacitation occurs in the cheeks, the forehead, or deep in the head and may be accompanied by tears and a nosebleed. Nasal decongestants could offer relief and aerate the particular sinus. However, it should be noted that, because of their rigid walls, sinuses can on occasion pose serious problems. A build-up of positive pressure of up to 200 mmHg is possible on ascent and this can 'obstruct the blood flow to the mucosa and may rupture the sinus' (Denison and Preston 1983: 6.70). There can be a further complication, as Dr D.M. Denison and Dr. F.S. Preston observed in their chapter on Aviation Medicine in the *Oxford Textbook of Medicine* (1983), should infected material be forced through the thin roof of the ethmoid sinuses into the skull,

> leading to cerebral abscess. If a sinus that was patent on ascent obstructed during descent, its cavity would contain a relative vacuum that could reach – 200 mmHg. This is sufficient to cause gross mural oedema and to rupture some vessels, filling the cavity with blood.
>
> (Denison and Preston 1983)

The lungs do not usually present a problem but have been included here because of the exceptional case of pneumothorax. With this condition, gas which has escaped from the surface of a lung is trapped in the pleural cavity that surrounds it. As there is a risk that the gas may expand by 35 per cent and induce complications, the disorder is contraindicative to flight. The same stricture applies to very severe asthma and tense cysts (see Chapter 12).

The closed cavity constitutes less of a problem than its semi-closed counterpart. The volume of air contained in the alimentary tract varies between 0 and 400 ml, and is a result of swallowed air, of the action of bacteria present, and of the exchange of gases from the tissues and blood. It is vented without difficulty unless an infection is present or a considerable amount of gas-forming food or drink is consumed. This can include champagne or other carbonated beverages, roughage, beans, peas, cabbage, and cauliflower. There are instances where the expansion of a pocket of gas in the small intestine may lead to discomfort, nausea, vomiting, severe pain or even fainting (a vasovagal syncope). In theory, the expansion would be sufficient to rupture a diseased part of the intestine, in particular in the presence of colitis, septic or duodenal ulcers, diverticulitis, and recent abdominal surgery.

Aerodontalgia: yes, teeth too can be affected on ascent. Defective fillings, abscesses (apical), and carious deposits may result in toothache because of the existence of cavities.

The penultimate instance in this barrel of oddities concerns the scuba or aqualung diver. While underwater, there is a rapid increase of pressure, 1 atmosphere for every 33 ft (10 m) of depth, and in accordance with Henry's law the amount of gas held in solution also increases. To be specific, more nitrogen dissolves in the body fluids and tissues. If the rules of diving tables are followed, no difficulties will be encountered when the diver surfaces. But if air travel is under-taken soon after, the diver can suffer from decompression sickness, which is also known as 'bends', aeroembolism, and dysbarism. What this shows is that there has been a rapid release of nitrogen, in the main from fatty tissues, due to the lower pressure of the cabin environ-ment. The siutation is analogous to the bubbles that appear in a bottle of lemonade when it is opened. This formation of bubbles, which can obstruct the flow in small blood vessels, produces the various manifesta-tions of the condition. The most common symptom is 'bends', pain in joints or a limb. Others are disturbances of the skin ('the creeps'), the respiration ('the chokes'), the nervous system ('the staggers'), vision, and can result in a state of collapse. Therefore, the recommen-dation is to allow several hours between the last dive and the depar-ture of the flight. The American Medical Association suggests 12 hours, and if a depth of 30 ft is exceeded, at least 24 hours.

However innocent and isolated these incidents appear to be, there is a chance that they may develop into an emergency, of whom, who knows, the reader may become the subject. Take a look at this news item from the *British Medical Journal*:

> Even modern aircraft still expose their passengers to some risks from lowered atmospheric pressure. A gruesome account in the *Canadian Medical Association Journal* (Parsons and Bobechko 1982: 237–43) describes a 12-year-old boy whose legs, enclosed in plaster casts, became gangrenous on a seven-hour flight to South America. The cause was thought to be some degree of hypoxia plus vascular compression from expanding gases in the virtually air-tight casts.
>
> ('Minerva' 1982)

Chapter Seven

THE JET SYNDROME

I stand before the next topic, jet syndrome, much as an archaeologist faces a mound of earth that represents the various strata of an ancient and forgotten city, because such is the interest generated by the disruption of circadian rhythms that the papers from diverse disciplines pile up thick and fast. Perhaps the colloquial equivalent term, 'jet lag', is responsible for this interdisciplinary activity as by connotation it confers an international status on the sufferer; or, if you prefer, the term has become an international status symbol. Whatever the reason, I see no sign of abatement in these contributions. They began in the late 1950s when jet-powered air transports were introduced, and, indeed, I must confess here that I too have been tempted to add my halfpennyworth, as you will see later.

The latest to come my way is titled 'Bright light resets the human circadian pacemaker independent of the timing of the sleep–wake cycle' and is a team effort from Harvard that combines the divisions of Endocrinology (Neuroendocrinology Laboratory) and Applied Sciences (Czeisler *et al.* 1986: 667–71). Among the other disciplines, besides aerospace medicine, involved in the alleviation or cure of jet syndrome are Biochemistry, Physiology, Psychology, Ergonomics, Chronobiology, Psychophysiology, Biological Psychology and Psychiatry, Occupational Medicine, Theoretical Biology, Chrono-pharmacology, and even a form of alternative medicine, Aromatherapy.

Confronted by such a spate of literature, which at the last count, by Ross McFarland in 1974 (McFarland 1974: 649) had amounted to 200 scientific papers and 10 monographs, I have little choice but to resort again to the analogy of archaeology and on this occasion to methods of excavation. In the instance of Flinders-Petrie, it would entail a painstaking process whereby each artefact is numbered, recorded, and described with the result that the removal of detritus is slow. However, as space in the book is limited for the subject, I shall instead adopt the technique of that famous amateur, Heinrich Schliemann, who spared no effort to get to the fundamental layer fast.

We have a classic case, the 8-day global flight of Wiley Post in 1931. This man, a former barnstormer with an admiration for Christopher Columbus, succumbed to an urge to go 'round the world', which even today is a common aspiration, and he became the first person to both anticipate and experience the disruption of his 'circadian rhythm', as our 24-hour physiological cycle has been named by Franz Halberg. Although he would deny that his exploits or those of other pilots in those early years had transformed them into heroes or given them 'superhuman qualities' and rather would offer the reason that they 'were just doing what they set out to do', he nevertheless must be singled out as a remarkable figure. For not only did he accomplish the feat (that he was later to better through a solo performance in 7 days), but with no formal training, except several years of flying experience which he admits was 'of the hardest sort', he made an unusual contribution to aerospace medicine. He recognized that time displacements would have adverse effects on his eating and sleeping cycles, which in turn would impair his proficiency as a pilot. Therefore, he set out to counter these effects and was successful. The results, though not embodied in a scientific paper, have been given credit in a comprehensive survey (Siegel *et al.* 1969) for the American Association for the Advancement of Science.

> He also experimented with an irregular schedule of meals and worked out a conditioning program designed to break his habitual sleeping and eating patterns. . . . Post felt that the time-zone effects were significant and that the steps he took to adjust to them were beneficial.
>
> (ibid: 1251)

It should be mentioned that if his work is of an anecdotal nature, it still has relevance today because he exposed the bare bones of the problem and proposed a feasible solution that, as will be demonstrated, forms the basis of some current studies.

However, it is important to return to the original source and allow Wiley Post to speak up for himself – which, I may add, he does well in spite of a preference to fly rather than to write about flight. In the book *Around the World in Eight Days*, subtitled *The Flight of the Winnie*

Mae, that he wrote with his navigator, Harold Gatty, he is candid about the preparations he undertook some 8 months before take-off. 'Part of it', he said, 'was training my mind and body for the long grind ahead. I didn't want to take any chances of causing delays on the flight because of physical incapacity or mental fatigue' (Post and Gatty 1931: 26).

His task was twofold for he had to deal with the aircraft as well as the time-zone shifts:

> As I flew about the country in the regular routine of my job, I tried my best to keep my mind a total blank. That may sound easy, but it is one of the hardest things I ever had to do. According to my theory, it was of primary importance in overcoming one of the greatest dangers on the flight – slowed-up reactions at the end of a long hop. These might easily result in ground-looping or some other form of minor accident in landing.

> By keeping my mind a blank, I do not mean that I paid no attention to the business of handling the ship. I mean that I did it automatically, without mental effort, letting my actions be wholly controlled by my subconscious mind. I am not a psychologist by any stretch of the imagination, but I have analysed some of the events leading up to bad landings after long flights. I have seen pilots who are numbered among the best 'stick technicians' in the country, plop their planes down, when they were tired so that only the good turf on the airport saved them from breaking something. Those landings were perfectly safe, of course, but as Gatty and I were not going to carry any spares on the trip, one broken shock absorber or blown tyre in the far reaches of Siberia might mean a month's delay and the failure of our plan to break the record.

> Another thing I had to learn was to control my sleep. I knew that the variance in time as we progressed would bring an acute fatigue if I were used to regular hours. So, for the greater part of the winter before the flight, I never slept during the same hours on any two days in the same week. Breaking oneself of such common habits as regular sleeping hours is far more difficult than flying an aeroplane!

> Other habits also had to be regulated in accordance with my special home-made course in physical and mental training. I found one interesting thing. By limiting my diet, I could get along without much sleep. Several times Mrs. Post accused me of trying to reduce. She said, 'If your margin is so small that the few pounds

you take off by dieting mean so much, I don't think much of your chances of getting through.

(Post and Gatty 1931: 27)

But he did. Together with his navigator, he encircled the upper part of the Earth, over a distance of 15,477 miles, from New York through Harbour Grace (Newfoundland), Chester, Berlin, Moscow, Siberia (where there were three stops), Fairbanks (Alaska), Edmonton, and back again to a ticker-tape reception. Once the fanfare had subsided, what did he find he had achieved in real terms? There is no doubt that the method (although undocumented) to counteract the time-zone effects had succeeded. He had demonstrated the feasibility of long-distance travel and in that role he could be des cribed as the archetype of the frequent flyer or business traveller who now chalks up between 100,000 and 200,000 miles a year in the air.

However, there is another factor that is not so easy to assimilate. Our concept of time was changed. Prior to the flight on 6 June 1931, we could still entertain the rigid, the objective, or the fanciful notion, much in the same way as a character does in the short story 'Disguised' by Isaac Bashevis Singer. 'America, where, she was told, it was night time when it was daytime in Poland, and where people walked upside down. . . .' (Singer 1986: 35). By 1 July 1931, after the trip, the notion had become obsolescent. For this pioneer had come up against time in all three of its guises at once within the confines of the cockpit: local time set on the dash clock, the Greenwich time of the chronometer, and the time back home on his wrist watch, and he had returned in one piece. He even bore witness to one of its tricks when he covered 2,441 miles in 3¼ hours in an aircraft capable of an average speed of 150 m.p.h. In his account of that memorable event he mentions that 'we passed from about 11 a.m. Tuesday, June 30, into 11 a.m. Monday, June 29 by crossing the International Date Line on the 180th meridian'. To him, it was 'more amazing than the yarn about Columbus standing the egg on its point' (Post and Gatty 1931: 212). So somewhere off Cape Navarin where icebergs give way to clear water, man the slave to time became the conjuror of time. There, a day can be turned into two or can disappear altogether. From then on whenever man flew from west to east or from east to west, he could shorten the period or lengthen it. Indeed, such is the phenomenon that a poet can convert a dream into reality:

Time present and time past
Are both perhaps present in time future

(Eliot 1949)

Wiley Post's circumnavigation had another impact on the life of humans. For millions of years they had been stuck to the surface, not dissimilar to flies on flypaper, and now they were free to race the sun around the Earth. (Indeed, Howard Hughes saw the sun set and rise five times in four days on his record trip in 1938.) This scramble or mass migration, every year now equivalent to the movement of the combined populations of North America and Europe (excluding the USSR), is so thorough that it can cause an inversion of our circadian rhythms. A fact that was noted by Dr Hubertus Strughold in 1952 when he presented a paper titled 'Physiological day–night cycle in global flights' (in the main as prognostic as the space medicine department of which he was the head) to airline medical directors; he termed it the 'Physiological Time Inversion Point' (Strughold 1952: 470). What interested him at the time was the strong influence exerted on sleep and wakefulness or the alternate phases of rest and activity by the Earth's rotation on its axis once every 24 hours. These phases as a result had become established to such a degree that he was inclined to describe them as 'a kind of conditioned reflex' (Strughold 1952: 464) in man and in some higher animals, and this could be demonstrated by three facts. First, there was 'the impossibility of breaking this cycle over a longer period of time' (Strughold 1952: 465) and examples were given of sleep deprivation that caused the death of a dog after 14 days through 'severe degeneration of the ganglion cells', and such neurotic behaviour in a young human subject after 10 days that the experiment had to be abandoned. Second, 'the diurnal cycle can be lengthened or shortened to a limited degree only'; and third, 'a shift in the phases in the day–night cycle cannot be achieved instantly, but rather demands a certain amount of time for adjustment'. If this last fact was well known through studies of shift-work, what was new was that the shift or disruption could be imposed by air travel.

Over the next three decades or so, there has been a continual series, not unlike a television soap opera, on the effects of and therapies for jet syndrome, jet lag, desynchronosis of biological rhythms, dysrhythmia, dyschrony, or call it what you will. Wiley Post, who was the first to recognize its symptoms and find a remedy, did not have to live with it as hundreds of millions of flyers do nowadays. Some

71

of them, military or airline pilots, are privileged as they are provided with medical care in this as in other aspects of their health by top aerospace or aviation specialists. The majority of air travellers, however, are still ignorant of the stress it imposes on their bodies and how it impairs their performance. There exists at least one case of adverse testimony from this quarter. It was given by a US Secretary of State, John Foster Dulles, on his deathbed, and it should be treated with the seriousness such an attempt deserves. In an interview with a columnist, he admitted to a mistake that led to the Suez crisis with the subsequent nationalization of the Suez Canal and war with Egypt. The action that triggered it was severe jet lag for he had made a decision to cancel the loan on the Aswan dam soon after his return to Washington from a Middle East diplomatic shuttle when he had learnt of President Nasser's agreement to purchase arms from the USSR. With hindsight, he blamed the time-zone effects for this ill-considered judgement (Kowet 1984: 9-10). Perhaps there is a lesson here for air passengers, which is not to act in haste unless they want to indulge in confessions for posterity later.

Before an attempt is made to comprehend the subject, we must cast aside for a moment the illusion of air travel that is created within the cabin by an absence of stimuli from the reality outside, and an emphasis on entertainment whether it be in the form of refreshments, movies, music, or attractive flight attendants. Two main aspects are obscured from our view. The first is the conveyance itself – a fragile pressure-vessel propelled by two or more paraffin rockets which contain hot metal rotating at high speed and sited near fuel tanks and pipelines under pressure. The thought is enough to unsettle anyone's psyche. The second is the surface of the Earth which we overfly at subsonic or sometimes supersonic speeds, and is as solid and conspicuous as the network of Standard Time is arbitrary and inconspicuous. The almost spherical shape has been divided into zones of longitude by 360 imaginary lines that have been drawn from pole to pole and designated meridians. The prime or zero meridian is the longitudinal line at Greenwich in the UK. As the Earth rotates, daylight moves from one meridian to another in a matter of 4 minutes and covers fifteen meridians in an hour. This geographical time difference represents one time-zone, of which there are a total of twenty-four round the world. The two oddest of these are those on either side of the International Date Line that marks the start of the calendar day, as a whole 24 hours separates them and not the usual 1 hour.

Juxtaposed with Standard Time is our own body's system of time, or, as it is called, physiological time, and it is this element which, if at variance with local time, leads to problems and the attendant penalty. As a general rule, for every time-zone we cross, it takes 1 day to recover. Therefore, in the case of a transatlantic flight, 5–6 days are necessary if the body is to readjust. However, in my effort to be lucid I have overshot the mark.

But if a reasonable question is to be asked, what is the mark? In such a voluminous field that causes the researcher to suffer something akin to disorientation from his forays across various disciplines and where the subject itself had to be redefined because it would appear to have become convoluted too, that is a good question. To provide an adequate answer, we have to turn to a paper written by four scientists, one of whom won an award for original research, and which was selected for publication by the Science and Technological Committee that is composed of thirty-three members of the Aerospace Medical Association. I refer to 'A review of human physiology and performance changes associated with desynchronosis of biological rhythms' by Charles M. Winget (Arnold D. Tuttle Award, 1982), Charles W. Deroshia, Carol L. Markley, and Daniel C. Holley, that appeared in *Aviation, Space and Environmental Medicine*, (Winget *et al.* 1984). The authors, in an attempt not to be procrustean, for that could be an expedient solution in such a situation, cite some 119 references from interdisciplinary sources and draw attention to the fact that should desynchronosis be controlled there would be practical applications in medicine, civil and military aviation, pharmacology, and shift-work schedules. Although further research is advocated, no mention is made of the possible long-term effects on professional air travellers; it could be argued, if our physiological clock is in a constant state of resynchronization, might not a part of that complex mechanism become impaired or even break down after a period? It might constitute a significant study. But that lack can be explained in the context of the prime aim of aerospace medicine, which is to enable aviators to survive the hazardous environment as well as possible or, if you wish, to keep them flying for as long as possible. However, as I have already shown, there are more important elements of health, some life-threatening, to consider if that is to be achieved. This would also account for the brief entries about the subject in specialist textbooks.

What are we up against, then? I address diplomats, athletes, corporate executives, soldiers, musicians, actors, politicians, and others who, after encountering multiple time-zone changes, have to demonstrate efficiency at their destination – unlike their counterparts, the airline pilots, who go off-duty on arrival. As well as the 'adverse effects on performance and well-being', the review notes that

> the desynchronised individual may experience states of irritability, disorientation or confusion, distortion of time and distance, aches of various types, digestive upsets which include constipation, decrements of physical and mental efficiency, and disturbances in sleep habits. . . . The potential safety hazards of sleepiness and fatigue induced by circadian desynchrony may be of serious consequence among airline pilots, astronauts, cosmonauts, and their supporting crews.
>
> (Winget *et al.* 1984: 1085)

To the latter, of course, may be added any troubleshooters from engineers to surgeons who fly halfway across the world to contend with emergencies.

A factor that is noticeable to air travellers is that dysrhythmia causes a shift in the major bodily functions with the result that sleep, hunger, and defecation tend to occur at inapposite moments for variable periods. What is not so obvious is that over 100 biological functions and activities are affected (McFarland 1974: 650). These, which are well-documented by J. Aschoff, oscillate between maximum and minimum values diurnally and include sleep and wakefulness periods that are relative to day–night cycles, mental alertness, visceral and glandular activities as well as variations in pulse and temperature. There are two forms of biological rhythms. The exogenous where oscillations are dependent on impulses from the environment and the endogenous in which the oscillations are self-sustained, such as the classic case of the daily rise and fall of body temperature. 'The spectrum of biological periodicity includes ultradian rhythms with periods less than 20h, circadian rhythms with periods of about 24h and infradian rhythms with a period greater than 24h' (Winget *et al.* 1984: 1086). Before I proceed any further, I have to emphasize that these rhythms have little to do with the popular biorhythm theory which, as the authors of the review point out, 'are too simplistic to account for the complexities of everyday life' (ibid: 1086).

It has been demonstrated through experimental evidence that circadian rhythms are not only endogenous and autonomous but are synchronized by environmental cues. These synchronizers, or zeitgebers, as they are also called, facilitate the entrainment of the rhythms. However, other factors, e.g. social interactions, could override both the primary zeitgeber of day–night, and a secondary one like temperature. To establish the actual periodicity of the endogenous circadian system – in other words, how long our body clock will run before it initiates a new cycle – an unusual study was undertaken by Franz Halberg (Engle and Lott 1979: 311). Seven women were settled in a cave for 2 weeks and he noted that their cycle was 24 hours 42 minutes. Such a fact prompted Hubertus Strughold to speculate that mankind may have originated from Mars as that time coincides with that planet's rotational period (Engle and Lott 1979: 310). From other studies, it was determined that

> humans have separate, individually synchronised, free-running circadian rhythms of body temperature, activity, urinary variables, and performance on various tasks. Even though the different rhythms are not always in phase, their periods are all approximately 25h.
>
> (Winget *et al* 1984: 1086)

Under the conditions of transmeridian flight, a phase shift will occur between the circadian rhythms that are sychronized to the departure time and the zeitgebers at the destination. As should now be apparent, it will 'involve a differential restructuring of the many oscillating body systems, resulting in internal circadian desynchronization and associated symptoms' (Winget *et al.* 1984: 1087). One unfamiliar feature of interest to female passengers is the effects this has on menstruation. Stewardesses have a 'significantly higher incidence of irregular menstrual cycles and exacerbated dysmenorrhea' (Winget *et al.* 1984: 1087). Among the anticipated problems were sleep and gastrointestinal disturbances. In the case of sleep this arose in 59–78 per cent of the flight crews on the first night after travel across timezones and fell to 25–30 per cent on the third night post-flight (Winget *et al.* 1984: 1087). These figures should be compared with a later study by R.T.W.L. Conroy (Conroy 1971: 69–72) that involved 315 American and British senior executives where a high number, 87 per cent, reported sleep disruption. 'Up to 41 per cent of the crew members experienced gastrointestinal problems' (Winget *et al.* 1984: 1087). Other physiological rhythms upset by external desynchronosis were respiration, arterial pressure, and frequent urination (diuresis).

The onset of hunger at odd times appears to be a common complaint of long-haul passengers.

While an upset eating schedule may be reflected in disturbances of the cycles of waste elimination, blood amino acid levels, and other visceral activities, the timing of meals does not appear to act as a strong Zeitgeber in humans. Circadian rhythms persist in humans virtually without alteration, both in subjects who are fasted and those who receive constant amounts of food at short intervals. However, real timing does affect some rhythmic variables. For example, the internal timing of blood hormones (insulin, glucagon, somatotropin, and cortisol), as well as rhythms in blood pressure and pulse, can differ on a regimen of breakfast only or dinner only. However, changes in meal timing alone do not shift the rhythms for simple task performance, such as eye–hand co-ordination, adding speed, or grip strength.

(Winget *et al.* 1984: 1088)

If there is a significant result that emerges from the physiological data accumulated since the 1950s and which encompasses studies that vary from hormonal changes through to profiles of rhythm chronotypes, it is the different recovery rates for westward and eastward flight. In short, 'flight west is flight best'. This has been confirmed by authorities such as F. Halberg, J. Aschoff, and K.E. Klein and the considered opinion is that the endogenous system with its natural inclination towards a 25-hour day, is more able to adapt to the longer periodicity encountered in westward travel.

'For example, following a westbound flight from West Germany to the United States, 3 d [days] were required to reach 95% resynchronization of the psychomotor performance rhythm, whereas 8 d were required following return flights in the easterly direction. . . . Relative flight direction (homeward vs. outgoing) and time of flight departure (day vs. night) have relatively little effect on reentrainment.

(Winget *et al.* 1984: 1088)

The obvious application for air passengers is to allow extra time for the body to recover when they cross time-zones from west to east, and if their destination can be approached from either direction, to opt for the west. It should be noted that the time taken for resynchronization of the psychomotor performance rhythm is based on mean values which have also taken into account wide variations whereby 'about 25–30% of transmeridian travellers have no or only a few difficulties

76

adjusting to the sudden displacement of external time cues . . . [and] about the same percentage of travellers was estimated not to adjust at all' (Klein 1976: 226). Perhaps, therefore, a more expedient measure would be the one mentioned earlier, the allowance of a day per time-zone traversed for readjustment, which was proposed by Dr William Douglas (Douglas 1986), the flight surgeon to Project Mercury astronauts, and later confirmed by both Hubertus Strughold (Strughold 1971: 57) and Ross McFarland (McFarland 1974: 657). Of course, in view of the aphorism 'flight west is flight best', reduce the recovery time by at least a day in that direction.

And now for the entrée. The fact that international flights can cause loss of efficiency. Print that on the ticket! If that powerful figure, the American Secretary of State, could be humbled by dysrhythmia, his whole personality be telescoped into the single emotion of irascibility, and the result a conflagration that involved five nations, what chance does the president of a corporation stand to close a deal in top condition? Only in his case the cost of failure is not emblazoned in neon lights but paid in full by the company. In Conroy's study of business executives and time-zone transitions, it was shown that 50 per cent conducted negotiations before they had had a night's sleep in spite of the claim that only 20 per cent felt fit for the task (Conroy 1971: 69). But the reality is, as DeHart's textbook, *The Fundamentals of Aerospace Medicine*, observes: 'Politicians, statesmen, athletes, business persons and military personnel can all be affected by desynchronization, resulting in lower efficiency, poor decision making, and compromised negotiation ability' (DeHart 1985: 414).

In experiments to determine the decrements in performance experienced post-flight, Klein and co-workers found a decrease of between 8.1 and 10.2 per cent for westbound and eastbound travel respectively among young subjects – students and fighter pilots – compared to pre-flight rates (Klein 1976: 225). 'Simpler tasks (such as reaction time) recovered to baseline levels after 3 d, but decrements in complex tasks (like sensorimotor skills required to operate flight simulators) persisted for up to 5 d postflight' (Winget et al. 1984: 1089). In addition, a performance decrement of 9–10 per cent was more pronounced when eight time-zones rather than six were crossed. Of interest, too, is the fact that even a short stay of 24 hours in a new time-zone could result in what they termed a 'significant reduction in the overall performance level for at least 1 d after return to home base' (Klein 1976: 226). A similar result was reported by G.T. Hauty and T. Adams in their study of north–south flight where, although the effect was not as significant as in transmeridian flight, at least 24 hours were required for the normal rhythms to be restored (Hauty and Adams 1966: 1257–62).

Another study that involved young and healthy subjects, in this instance soldiers on transfer from Texas to West Germany, was undertaken by the US Army Research Institute of Environmental Medicine to determine the effects of translocation on performance and exercise capacity.

Following the flight, 50% of the personnel reported fatigue and sleep difficulty and 40% reported subjective weakness. These symptoms diminished significantly by the fifth day postflight. Postflight performance deterioration was found in dynamic arm strength (6.1–10.8%), elbow flexor strength (13.3%), sprint times (8.4–12%), a lift and carry task (9.5%), logical reasoning (15%), and encoding–decoding performance. The performance decline following transmeridian flight observed in this study may have been under-estimated since several individuals failed to complete the assigned tasks.

(Winget *et al*. 1984: 1089)

In view of the fact that these experiments were carried out on healthy, young subjects, as indeed is the requirement on ethical grounds, and the fact that air passengers do not necessarily conform to such an ideal category, a rider should be added to the effect that in general a greater deterioration in performance is to be expected from the public.

Evaluations of shift-work and sleep loss on the ground have also been undertaken to gain insight into levels of performance. Before illustrations are given it should be mentioned that according to Klein (1976: 223) our performance rhythms rise throughout the day to a maximum between 1200 and 2100 hours and decline at night to a minimum between 0300 and 0600 hours.

Wever found significant impairment in psychomotor performance following 6-h phase advances, but not after phase delays of the light–dark cycle. . . . Significant deterioration in vigilance, calculation proficiency and mood was observed in subjects whose sleep–wake period was advanced 2–4h. Female subjects advanced by 8 h exhibited a 17–38% deterioration in short-term memory, reaction time, and visual search performance. . . . Time shifts of 2–3 h can result in performance impairment in athletes and cosmonauts, and even the 1-h time change between standard and daylight savings time may result in performance deterioration. . . . However, significant performance deterioration occurs following 2–4 h advances in the sleep–wake cycle despite normal sleep duration. These results indicate that performance deterioration can directly result from circadian rhythm disturbance and not solely from sleep loss.

(Winget *et al*. 1984: 1089)

However, an additional factor, fatigue – which as has been demonstrated earlier could be induced by hypoxia, among other conditions – should be considered when performance is related to an aviation environment. Robin Dodge in a paper 'Circadian rhythms and fatigue: a discrimination of their effects on performance' (Dodge 1982: 1131) quotes the remarks made by J.R. Beljan who undertook a classified study for NASA on the subject which led to its subsequent redefinition. 'Fatigue and desynchronosis share only one similarity, both are a problem in aviation. Fatigue and desynchronosis are so entwined that each is essentially inextricable from the other.' So, it would appear that here is yet another constraint on our efficiency post-flight.

In the section of the review on pathology, the authors Winget *et al*. produce some surprises. They note, for instance, that there is a similarity between the symptoms of actue desynchronization and conditions such as fevers, migraines, hangovers, old age, mental disorders, sleep deprivation, and reactions to viruses or infection. Perhaps, they suggest, these conditions may be an expression of disrupted biological rhythms. Attention is drawn to the unusual effects of drugs. Although the use of hypnotics or sleeping pills is widespread, there is a recommendation that these should be avoided in an aerospace environment because they tend to prevent the rapid eye movement (REM) stage of sleep and take time to be eliminated from the body – they have a long half-life. Recent research on short-action hypnotics, e.g. triazolam, has demonstrated that they can cause memory loss for several hours. When this benzodiazepine, which has a half-life of 2.6 hours, was taken by three neuroscientists, they experienced episodes of anterograde amnesia (Morris III and Estes 1987: 945–6). Another complication is the actual time of administration. 'Both pharmaco-kinetic and pharmacodynamic effects of drugs may vary dramatically according to the time of day. This much neglected aspect of aerospace pharmacology could have serious implications in the treatment of space travellers and time-zone travellers' (Winget *et al.* 1984: 1090).

Whilst it would be apparent that there is sufficient evidence to demonstrate the adverse effects of desynchronosis on performance, the case for the remedies is not as conclusive. Perhaps the multiple variables, the complexity of the endogenous rhythms and the variations in individuals account for this. A challenge indeed! The lack, however, is compensated for by the fecundity of the remedial sphere and it would therefore be appropriate to deem jet lag a therapyfest. Drowsy sheep, perfumed baths, a diet of fasts and feasts, Pavlov's dogs, bright lights, and *Drosophila*, the genus of small fruit flies, are all featured in attempts to control our biological clocks. Ross McFarland relates in his review, 'Influence of changing time zones on air crews and passengers', that he visited Ivan Pavlov's laboratory outside Leningrad in 1935 to observe how adjustments in a dog's sleep could be varied by conditioned reflexes. The key to these experiments, however, was the presence of other dogs. It would suggest that the group factor could determine the result and this was later confirmed in human subjects, as Dr McFarland points out: 'the effects of crossing multiple time zones appear to be less because of the social and group influence' (McFarland 1974: 652). Perhaps the fact that Aeroflot crews are accommodated at Soviet embassies whenever they travel abroad and remain on Moscow time throughout may be based, in this rare case, not on political considerations, but on their compatriot's studies. The second implication, which is still relevant, is the use of sleep as a suitable antidote. It might appear to the reader to be inane or a facile suggestion, but for airline pilots on long-haul schedules this is essential in the absence of the ideal solution. Under pressure to maintain irregular hours, in addition to time-zone shifts and workload stresses, they are recommended to keep sleep deficits to a minimum and to maximize sleep credits. Group Captain Anthony N. Nicholson of the RAF IAM, a luminary of this unique field – indeed, he was awarded the Stewart Memorial Prize for his work – proposes a combination of dozes and long bouts of sleep in the management of the problem.

It is clear that naps, sleeps of 3–4 hours and very long periods of sleep are all attempts to adapt to irregularity of duty hours and time zone changes, and to ensure adequate rest before the next duty

period. It would be reasonable to assume that the natural requirements for sleep are met in this way – even though the timing and
duration of sleep periods are radically changed.

(Nicholson and Stone 1983: 307)

However, the mixture of long and short sleeps may not be practical
for passengers as they often need to be active post-flight.

A variation that substitutes rest periods for sleep periods, and also
borders on the obvious, is the ICAO (International Civil Aviation
Organization) or Buley formula. Dr L.E. Buley, an official of this UN
agency, developed an equation in 1966 that made allowance for flight
duration, departure and arrival times as well as time-zones traversed
(in excess of four). As will be demonstrated, it is not over-generous
in the allotment of recovery periods. For example, in a paper which
outlines the formula, he calculates that an executive would require
one rest day after a journey from Montreal to London, and nothing
in the reverse direction, 'to ensure maximum effectiveness of the officer
in executing his mission on arrival; of secondary importance is the
efficiency of his resumption of work on return' (Buley 1970: 680).

If there is an eccentric approach that could be compared to events
in *Alice in Wonderland* then for certain it is the attempt to eat your way
out of desynchronosis while your biological rhythms are in a perfect
state of synchronization. The achievement, which is through an
'amazing new 3-step program' (as it is described by one of the
originators), will also appeal to readers of that children's story for it
involves 4 days of alternate fasting and feasting. (What should be
explained is that, in this special case, 'fast' means limited portions.)
But you have to establish the breakfast time on the day of your arrival
at your destination before the pre-flight food plan can be initiated.
There are other hard bits, too, for you have to remember when you
can have caffeinated beverages – between 1500 and 1700 hours for
3 days and on the 4th only in the morning if westbound, or between
1800–2300 hours eastbound – and you cannot have alcohol on board
the aircraft. Also, if the flight is long, the passenger should sleep 'until
normal breakfast time at destination, but no later', so runs the advice
on an unnumbered page of the book, *Overcoming Jet Lag* (Ehret and
Scanlon 1983), but what is unclear is the procedure to follow should
the airline schedule not coincide with local breakfast time. I refer to
the Argonne Anti-Jet-Lag Diet developed by Dr Ehret and based on
earlier work by him, K.R. Groh and J.C. Meinert. Winget *et al.*

comment on the use of food constituents as synchronizers and the role of their diet plan: 'These investigators claim that high-protein breakfasts and low-protein high-carbohydrate dinners facilitate rephasal in rats and humans following advance phase shifts' (Winget *et al*. 1984: 1092).

Drugs, of course, could provide an answer and over the past decade several chronobiotics have been evaluated, without much success. If there is a measure of progress in this field, it is the restricted use, post-flight, of certain hypnotics – those free of residual effects in the daytime. In a *Lancet* editorial, 'Jet lag and its pharmocology', it is observed: 'Indeed, the judicious and occasional use of a low dose of hypnotic would appear, at least for the moment, to be the preferred approach, although adequate attention must always be given to sleep habits and day-to-day life (*Lancet* 1986: 494). What could be ideal in terms of a remedy is a pill that would enable us to resynchronize our biological rhythms with the local time at our destination much in the same way as we reset a clock or watch. Research has been undertaken in this direction by J. Arendt *et al*. who in the initial stages used sheep to test the pineal hormone, melatonin. Recent experiments with human subjects, reported in the *British Medical Journal*, have been favourable (Arendt *et al*. 1986: 1170). However, as the aforementioned editorial in the *Lancet* has stressed, acting upon such results should be tempered with caution.

> The claim that melatonin can shift circadian rhythms is premature. Its apparent usefulness in alleviating the effects of jet lag may be related to some ill-defined psychotropic activity, but such effects may be undesirable, particularly if they modify daytime function. Further, it does not appear to have had the benefit of detailed preclinical development, which is now rightfully demanded of drugs. Melatonin is a possible inhibitor of sexual development in rats and may initiate gonadal regression in voles. It also has endocrine effects in man. These effects cannot be dismissed lightly, and demand careful appraisal before this agent can be used freely by humans.
> (*Lancet* 1986: 494)

If the well-trodden route of drugs does not produce a solution in the long term there are several other areas open to exploration. The small fruit fly, much featured in genetic research due to its short life cycle – less than 2 weeks at room temperature – may yet provide a key to controlling our biological clocks. That at least is the hope of

Dr T. Bargiello *et al.* from Rockefeller University, New York, who appear to have identified a gene responsible for the circadian rhythms in the *Drosophila*. How this arose can only confirm Byron's observation that truth . . . is stranger than fiction. There is a fruit fly which does not have a 24-hour biological cycle and as a consequence its behaviour is random. Bargiello and his colleagues compared the DNA of the mutant with normal flies and were able to isolate the specific deficiency. Later, when the missing components were inserted into the mutant's genetic material, it reverted to circadian rhythms (Bargiello *et al.* 1984: 752-4).

Phototherapy with bright lights is also a field in its infancy now but which appears to hold promise for the future. In a single laboratory study with a subject who had been preselected, nine Harvard scientists (Czeisler *et al.* 1986: 667-71) demonstrated that exposure to artificial light, of an intensity equivalent to early morning daylight, can influence the human circadian oscillator. The procedure by which it was achieved was cumbersome at the least, for the subject, an elderly woman, had to sit in front of a bank of sixteen 4 ft, 40-watt fluorescent lamps for 4 hours each day, from 1940 to 2340 hours, over a week. At this stage, even if we were able to assume that conclusive proof could be offered in the future, the wisespread application of the idea to counter jet lag would seem impractical. How could one expect air passengers – that impatient group of people who pay to travel at the fastest speed – to wait for several hours in front of bright lights before departure and later at the destination to resynchronize themselves? And what if there was a flight delay?

Last but not least is aromatherapy. Although to some the word might pose a tongue twister, it is only the modern version of the use of plants, in this instance odoriferous, for the treatment of illness. It was coined in 1928 by R.M. Gattefosse. There appears to be an age-long tradition in man that wherever an antidote to an ailment occurs free in nature, the need for further investigation is obviated. Such is the belief of most natural practitioners and Daniele Ryman, who formulated the anti-jet-lag baths and showers, is no exception. No research beyond the rudimentary into the nature of the problem has been done to prove or disprove the remedy. However, it may have one virtue: its simplicity. Two aromatic baths are taken each day after arrival, one for sleep and the other to keep awake. If nothing else the passenger will be assured of cleanliness. As there is anecdotal evidence of its efficacy, I asked Dr Geoffrey Bennett of the CAA for an opinion. He smiled. 'Well, I would think it has a high placebo effect. I don't suppose it could do any harm because it is natural.' Here he shrugged his shoulders. 'If it works, fine. How it works, may not be relevant.'

Before any conclusion can be drawn on the jet syndrome, we must be reminded in the first place of the origin of our biological rhythms. They are derived from an astronomical event of gigantic proportions – the rotation of the Earth on its axis every 24 hours. How can one argue with a body which has a mass of 6,600 trillion tons, a continuous rotational speed of 620 m.p.h, and a constant gravitational force of 32 lb per ft/sec/sec, or even consider how to counter its effects? Perhaps we should therefore proceed with caution in our attempt to tinker with an intricate mechanism, more obscure than any watch, that has evolved as a result. A moderate line on corrective measures may be appropriate.

Charles Lindbergh on his transatlantic flight from New York to Paris in 1927 was the first to pace his diet. During the 34 hours in the air, he consumed one sandwich – out of the five he had in a brown paper bag – and that was just half an hour before he landed at Le Bourget. The logic behind the decision was recorded in his book *The Spirit of St. Louis* (Lindbergh 1953) and with hindsight can be seen to be sound. 'It's probably wise not to eat, anyway – easier to stay awake on an empty stomach' (ibid.: 201). Water was another matter. Although he had a gallon in reserve, he limited himself to the quart flask in the cockpit, to be used in the event of an emergency at sea. The correspondent of *The Times* who talked to him that day, 22 May, commented on this meagre fare. 'He did not quite finish his slender store of provisions, he drank nothing but water, and his chief sensation on arriving was that he was most amazingly thirsty' (Anon. 1927). The account would not be complete without mentioning that he tried to revive himself with smelling salts in the 27th hour (ibid.: 451) but had become too desensitized by the cold to obtain any benefit. Lots of water and a little food to reduce the need to sleep (as Wiley Post also noted later) appears to be good advice in the light of Lindbergh's tough trip – he flew without cabin pressurization, under the weather (i.e. 50–10,000ft), and he took five times as long to cross the four time-zones as we do today.

There, too, is the question of sleep. Air passengers can take a leaf out of the professionals' book and build credits in the sleep-store, either before departure or on board. Another technique is recorded by the authors of 'Time–zone effects': 'Pilots have reported many informal means of inducing sleep between flights, including moderate exercise (walking) and warm baths' (Siegel *et al.* 1969: 1254). This has an advantage because they 'avoid the necessity of taking traditional hypnotics, with consequent loss of REM . . . ' (ibid.: 1255). If there is a general recommendation, it would be to pace your body whenever you fly. But whatever the measures, we have to live with the fact that transmeridian air travel affects us for a short time. It slows us down, impairs our performance, and we lose control of our faculties. That at least is the situation until the perfect remedy is found. Yet, perhaps the ceaseless activity in this field is a sign that we seek to cure the incurable.

Chapter Eight

GUTS: THE FEAR OF FLYING

What an awesome experience to skirt the surface of the earth and to view it from the brow of an angel. To be privy to what only angels and the gods of the ancients were destined to see – the insignificance of everything. From a couple of miles up, all trace of humanity has vanished. The world we know has been replaced by bleak geometry, some of it man-made, some the work of wind and rain.

To be able to take the silver bird to almost any place on the planet, to have gained mastery over the skies above us, must rank with the other great technical advance, the discovery of the wheel. It should enable us, if we are to judge by the aerospace achievements of the past two decades alone, to make a quantum leap for *Homo sapiens*.

The question is, what about our psyche? For in that fragile vessel we have carried innumerable myths of monsters and gods who could transcend our terrestrial existence with ease; soar into the heavens at will and inhabit distant stars. What of this baggage that has accumulated in our collective unconscious for hundreds of thousands of years, or since that first occasion when we jumped from a height and crashed to the ground. No doubt that painful moment was etched for ever and perhaps provided the stimulus to fire our imaginations from a prehistoric age.

Now it would seem that all that is behind us. Or is it? How can we expect to thrust that long yesterday aside without a single repercussion? We may well ask what has happened in the dark recesses of our psyche. Have we become anaesthetized in an effort to come to terms with the revelatory event of flight or are we frozen in a catatonic posture through our inability to do so? It may be a simple case of time lag before such an event can be assimilated. But if you search for answers, I warn you, there are few. What is apparent, though, is that there are people who suffer from an anxiety about flight or the fear of flying, which is the popular term for the psychological disorder that originated in the Second World War and was limited to describing the effects of combat theatres. Whether the disorder is a vestige or only a visible part of the whole is matter for speculation, and if we are to gain any insight into the problem we have to return to the beginning of aviation.

There is a story that is told against 'primitive tribes' and concerns the arrival of an aircraft in their midst. The response is guaranteed to produce chuckles from us 'civilized folk'. For they bow before the flying machine and recognize the pilot as a god. An unusual variation of the tale appears in the book *Diamonds in the Sky* (Hudson and Pettifer 1979), and relates to the experiences of the pioneer aviator, Ian Grabowski, in New Guinea.

> They [the tribesmen] thought we were the dead returned and they admired us for coming. One man tied himself to the machine so that he could be taken up to see the other world. Another came to us and said 'You know, all my relatives are dead, let me go with you'.
>
> (Hudson and Pettifer 1979: 186)

But perhaps the last laugh is at the expense of the 'civilized folk' as that incident occurred in the 1930s when a similar reaction could be elicited from us. In fact, so marked were the spiritual implications of the innovation to the Americans that the first three decades of the twentieth century could be called the 'era of the winged gospel'. Indeed, there is an original study by J. Corn of the same title that illuminates those social aspects of aeronautics which it would appear we have forgotten without much trouble (Corn 1983).

To a generation that had been born in the latter half of the last century, like Wilbur and Orville Wright, it would not have been difficult to imagine that anything which could fly into the sky should be associated with heaven and the Creator. How else could the public assimilate what to them would seem incredible and inexplicable, and at a time when there was a lack of appropriate words, except for 'supernatural', 'inhuman', 'occult', to describe it. A witness who was present at what was then termed 'an aviation meet' in 1910 recorded his impressions.

Thirty-thousand eyes are on those rubber-tired wheels waiting for the miraculous moment – historical for him who has not experienced it. Suddenly something happens to those whirling wheels – they slacken their speed, yet the vehicle advances more rapidly. It is the moment of miracle.

(Corn 1983: 4)

Another account, published in a Christian weekly during the same year when a million people sighted an aircraft over Chicago, was more forthright and eloquent.

Toward what were they gazing? Was there a new sign in the heavens that told of a future scarcely dreamed of? . . . and those who gazed felt awestruck, as though they had torn aside the veil of the future and looked into the very Holy of Holies. . . . We bowed our heads before the mystery of it and then lifted our eyes with a new feeling in our souls that seemed to link us with the great dome of heaven, stretching above and over all, and hope sprang eternal for the great new future of the world.

(Corn 1983: 30)

To the writer, Mary M. Parker, the event was analogous to the appearance of the Star of Bethlehem which had signified the birth of Christ. Therefore, in her mind and in the minds of the majority of Americans, according to Corn, the aircraft became a mechanical messiah that would transform life, 'making human society like heaven' (Corn 1983: 32) – a notion that would persist until the Second World War. (What may surprise readers is that its use as a form of transport was a minor consideration.) Although no comparable study has been done on this side of the Atlantic, it would appear that similar sentiments were engendered in the British. Many of the poets present in *Wings*, an anthology of flight published at the beginning of the 1940s, exalt both the pilot and the machine. W.H. Auden in the *Airman's Alphabet* produces these lines under the heading of 'Flying':

> Habit of hawks
> and unholy hunting
> and ghostly journey
> (Auden 1986: 79)

If there was an apogee to this attitude, it could be the triumphant trip of Lindbergh, which would also account for his unprecedented popularity, unmatched by other aviators until the appearance of the astronauts. In the public at the time, there existed a strong desire to pay homage both to him and to the 'Spirit of St Louis'. Streets, schools, and babies were named after him. Memorabilia abounded, much in the same way as icons and other mementoes commemorate the lives of the saints and miracles of the Madonna. The clergy seized the opportunity to proclaim him a model of Christian virtue. He 'exemplified the self-control needed "to discipline the flesh" so as to lead the heroic adventure of Christian life. Another divine suggested that the flight offered "a practical lesson on mystical religion", for only the "true mystic" sets off into the unknown, trusting to God!' (Corn 1983: 23). But at the head of the adulation were ordinary people whose views were reflected by newspapers and magazines. A particular instance is the enormous output of poetry – more than for any other figure or event in the west's history – that appeared to mark the feat. Irrespective of the merit of the poems, a common theme emerged: the pilot or machine was a god while flight was a divine experience. Lindbergh was hailed under various guises: 'Son of the Sky', 'Lord of the Air', and 'god from a golden isle'. Without doubt he was America's homegrown saint.

What is remarkable about this religious response to flight is that it is still part of the psyche's legacy today. For most of us passengers in the pad end of the fuselage, it no longer remains on a conscious level. But for those in the sharp end, the airline or private pilots, its presence cannot be ignored albeit that it is called by another name. Joy. Ecstasy. Mastery. Whatever the expression, the emotions associated with it appear to be renewed on every trip. Take Captain Bill Wallace, a veteran of some 33 years who has spent the equivalent of 3 years aloft. I spoke to him a month before he retired from TWA. 'It's a high,' he said, 'launching here [London] tomorrow. I really look forward to take-off. Getting that huge beast airborne and having it soar up through the clouds and break out into the blue. And all the weight and power of the – engines, and as you say it's defying the laws of gravity. . . I think He smiles when we break out from the clouds and head for the heavenly realm' (Wallace 1985). Even with military flyers this is evident. There is a tradition in the US Air Force that whenever a pilot transfers from one assignment to another, he is given a memento, a plaque on which John Gillespie Magee Jnr's poem 'High flight' is inscribed. The key lies in the final line: 'Put out my hand, and touched the face of God' (Cassem 1989: 400–1).

If we seek roots to the joy and fear of flying, then perhaps they are here. Once we had breached the sacred domain of the gods and the Creator, in spite of the encomium we sent forth, retribution followed. Crashes. So many sons of Icarus were sacrificed in those flimsy machines. (As most of the aircraft were used to transport the mail at the time it was dubbed 'the period when death flew the mails' (Vidal 1985).) The second stage of this development occurred once air travel became safe and sophisticated. The winged gospel was exchanged for the secular doctrine of psychiatrists and psychologists. However, I am certain that the problem still exists but under another guise. No magic wand can banish overnight the primordial idea of a superior being in space, nor for that matter can the existence of a modern airliner make the fear of falling obsolete. Whether we are active or passive flyers, we are bound to be affected to a greater or lesser degree.

Before we embark on the modern interpretation of these concepts, I suggest we examine passengers' first encounters with heavier-than-air vehicles. Indeed, it was a basic and honest experience, for you knew what you were up against within seconds of take-off. You could smell the fumes from the exhaust. You were deafened by the roar of the engines and the drone of the propellers. Your whole body shook from the vibration of the fuselage, and above all, your stomach was all over the place because of the rough ride. If there was a common affliction, it was associated with the latter as the turbulence found at these low altitudes of flight produced vomiting or, as it was known, airsickness. Some aircraft, like the lightweight Fokker, were more prone to pitching and rolling in 'bumpy air' with the consequence that they had a higher proportion of ill passengers and had to be hosed out on a regular basis after landing. Even on a fair day, there were some who succumbed to this complaint. Therefore, it was standard procedure to have cardboard containers – 'burp or erp cups' – at every seat (Solberg 1979: 215). Later the airlines would adopt a preventive approach to the problem and issue all passengers with small packets of 'comfort'. Each packet would contain chewing gum to ease the pressure in the ears on ascent or descent, a piece of cotton wool to reduce the noise, and an ampoule of ammonia to smell at the onset of airsickness. It would be an oversight at this stage not to give the passive flyer a brief insight into what happens in the cockpit. In a classic book on the subject, Wolfgang Langewiesche refers to the three secrets of human flight. Two of these are of interest and involve new concepts that need to be assimilated. The first is that when flying an aircraft we have total freedom of movement and as a result can accomplish six types of motion at once:

> Speed forward, slip sidewise, climb or sink, roll over sidewise, pitch nose-up or nose-down, and yaw its nose to the right or left. But the pilot's own brain, his nerves, his body are at first still rooted to the ground.

(Langewiesche 1954: 18)

The second concerns the development of an air sense whereby we have to learn special ways of seeing, hearing, and touching. The medium through which we travel is invisible and therefore the eye cannot rely on perspective or middle ground. Speed has to be either heard as it hisses against the skin of the craft or 'felt' through muscle tension and the position of joints and tendons – kinaesthetic sensation as it is known. In all, it can be summed up like this: When the terrestrial man first goes aloft he is deaf, blind and dumb' (Langewiesche 1954: 22).

Now there occurred an event that would have as much impact on the future of civil aviation as would the subsequent introduction of the pressure cabin. In fact, it would do for the psyche what pressurization was to do for our physiology. Everyone at the time knew that the source of the principal discomfort of flying was the fear of falling, which was accentuated not only by air currents but by the type of acceleration identified as fore-and-aft pitch. If, however, this negative aspect could be countered, there might be a possibility of persuading the public that the miracle of flight was routine and not extraordinary. It seemed at best an outlandish proposition to consider but there was someone who did and he came up with a feasible solution.

In 1930, Steve Stimpson, who was the manager of United Airline's San Francisco office, got it into his head that a special crew member be put on board for the sole benefit of the passengers. Such a presence, he believed, would help them through the ordeal of air travel, in which at least half got airsick. What he had in mind at first was Philippino males, who because of their slender build would be at an advantage in the small cabin. But fate had other plans. When a pretty nurse, Ellen Church, stepped into his office to apply for a job, he knew that the only flaw in his original idea was that he had got the sex wrong. He soon learnt that she too was convinced that flight attendants should be hired and he was quick to recognize that the additional factor of health could strengthen his case. Stimpson now became more determined to get his suggestion accepted and sent a memo to his boss:

It strikes me that there would be a great psychological punch to having young women stewardesses or couriers or whatever you want to call them. I am certain that there are some mighty good ones available. I have in mind a couple of graduate nurses that would make exceptional stewardesses. Of course it would be distinctly understood that there would be no reference made to their hospital training or nursing experience, but it would be a mighty fine thing to have this available, sub rosa, if necessary for airsickness.

Imagine the psychology of having young women, as regular members of the crew. Imagine the national publicity we could get from it, and the tremendous effect it would have on the travelling public. Also, imagine the value they would be to us not only in the nearer and nicer method of serving food but looking out for the passengers' welfare.

(Solberg 1979: 211)

In spite of the persuasive tone, the request was rejected. But the assistant to the president, Pat Patterson, who had also received a copy of the memo, decided to authorize it. This is how the first stewardesses were introduced. Ellen Church was put in charge of a group of seven and drafted the job specification. All candidates should be nurses and should not be over the age of 25 years, the weight of 115 lb, or the height of 5ft 4in. The benefits of these criteria were obvious in United's fleet of Boeing 247s with their low ceilings and where space and weight were at a premium. Among the duties they had to perform were to carry the baggage aboard, to screw down seats if they were unfastened, and to serve meals – fruit salad, rolls, fried chicken, and coffee – from steam chests. What of the less apparent benefits, described by Stimpson as the 'psychological punch'? For instance, the sex appeal of the female attendants – an aspect that provoked an immediate response from the wives of pilots who were afraid they might lose their husbands. (They wrote letters of protest to the airline and one even insisted that she always met her husband when he landed.) On the other hand, a favourable impression was created among the men who would go to great lengths to disguise their fears or, if they were unable to contain their queasiness, they would retreat into the toilet to conceal their embarrassment. In short, their macho instincts served well as a prophylactic. However, there is little doubt that both sexes derived reassurance from the innovation as it met with success and forced the competitors to follow suit.

That could be a good end to the story of the rise and rise of the winged waitresses, or how the service industry in the sky came to be. However, to leave matters there would be unjust to Stimpson whose contribution to commercial aviation is greater than he is given credit for. What he achieved was no less than a psychological masterstroke for he introduced the distractive element into air travel. (Long may it thrive!) The passengers could now focus their attention on something other than the adverse conditions; it was not dissimilar to the diversion of a conjurer There was also a subtle aspect to this distraction because it provided people with an object on which they could project their fears and anxieties. Little has changed over the years in the dual role of the winged waitress or waiter, except that they now have to compete with other entertainments and their part as the object of compassion, which could be performed with ease by nurses, has now been transformed into the object-with-the-frozen-smile which any person can enact. To complete the picture, the interior of the pressurized, high-altitude jetliner no longer bears any resemblance to the rudimentary cabin of its predecessor that was in close contact with the elements, but rather to a padded coach such as one would expect to find in surface transport.

The question is, are distraction and insulation the best means to tackle the problem of the psyche in air travel?[1] There is no clear answer because, like most other areas that concern passengers and aviation medicine, it remains unresearched. On the other hand, we cannot ignore the fact that the distraction approach could be interpreted as an attempt to shelve the problem and avoid responsibility for it. However, in the absence of relevant information that is a moot point. Therefore we have to view it in a more general fashion. One aspect which I am sure that most people would admit to is their ambivalence towards flying. On the positive side, there is the association of glamour and excitement, which does not attach to other forms of transport, and this is topped by a sense of exhilaration when we can indulge in our dreams instantly. The downside, however, is the reality. No one who has flown will deny that the pre-flight environment can be fraught with frustration and despair. What description could be more apt than Sylvia Plath's: 'Panic with a dog-face, devil-face, hag-face, whore-face, panic in capital letters with no face at all – it's the same Johnny Panic, awake or asleep' (Plath 1968). The situation is recognized by both airlines and doctors. In an interview, a spokesperson from British Airways Medical Service had this to say:

'You start at home. You've got to get from your home to the airport – that's tiring in itself. Think of the airport environment – the distances, the queues, the check-ins, the whole caboodle. There's stress involved, there's anxiety. Most people are anxious when they fly. They're afraid they'll miss their flight. Or they're concerned. Or it may be a very emotional experience. If you don't speak the language very well, or you're deaf or blind, just consider how very disappointing that can be!' Dr Richard Fairhurst, an 'aeromedical evacuation specialist', goes a step further and hints at the treacherous nature of the pre-flight environment. 'In my standard lecture to general practitioners on problems of flying,' he states, 'no. 1 is fear. It's not hypoxia. Most people are actually still frightened of flying. It's an irrational fear. They don't understand why aeroplanes stay up in the air. You can see the obsessive behaviour in the departure lounge. So *that* can obviously produce medical problems.' He added that when an analysis was made of sudden deaths at Heathrow, the authorities were able to single out the typical case: a 40-year-old businessman, who had had an argument with his wife the previous night about the trip, was late for the flight the next day and, as a consequence, was 'rushing like the clappers' (Fairhurst 1987).

And what of the in-flight environment? In theory, the restricted and enclosed space of the cabin would be sufficient to turn most passengers into candidates for claustrophobia. But in practice the padded entertainment 'coach' would appear to alleviate this and other adverse effects. To what degree, is unknown, as indeed are the post-flight symptoms. Here is another area that should be investigated.

What we do know something about is the extent of the fear of flying for the general population (*Newsweek* 1977). Before any figures are given for surveys undertaken in the USA (Agras *et al*. 1969: 151–6) and in Sweden (Nordlund 1984: 45–60), I should emphasize that the term 'fear' is not equivalent to 'aerophobia', in which definite phobic symptoms are exhibited, but to a non-specific apprehension about flight. Fear varied from a high of between 25 per cent (Sweden) and 20 per cent (USA) for people who experienced a slight apprehension about flying to a low of between 15 per cent (Sweden) and 11 per cent (USA) for those with a greater or intense apprehension.

The Swedish study, which was based on 2,000 questionnaires, revealed that the peak of fear for those individuals who had experienced a slight apprehension was reached when the aircraft met either 'air pockets' or clear air turbulence (CAT) at cruising altitude. (See

Figure 8.1 Experience of apprehension during the various phases of an air trip

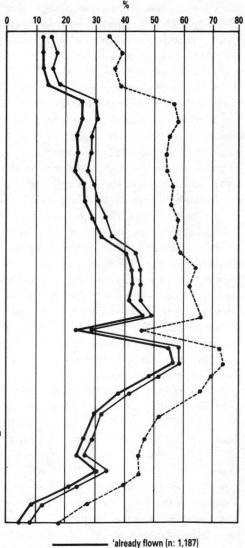

Figure 8.1 for a comprehensive view of various phases of fear and correlative percentages.) One of the anomalies to emerge was that 5 per cent attributed the cause of their fear to aerophobia, the dread of heights. Dr Nordlund was surprised by such a finding in view of the fact that dizziness was not experienced at normal flight altitudes, and suggested that it may be induced at take-off and landing when the ground is in sight. At the end of the survey the psychiatrist was left with a sufficiently strong conviction to express it as a personal opinion that the condition was more common than was first thought. Dr Nordlund went as far as to assert that some '50% of the population could be assumed to experience fear of flying if we define the term as a definite sense of apprehension during at least some short phase of the air trip or slight apprehension (more in the sense of being defensive) during most of the flight' (Nordlund 1984: 59–60). The basis for such a figure was to use a wider definition of the word, one which would include those who have never flown because of this dread – estimated to be at least 10 per cent of the Swedish population – and because of the low risk of air transport even to encompass those with mild states of fear. There would also have to be the acceptance of CAT as a normal occurrence of flight. Another factor that was cited in support of the opinion was the replies to what would appear to be a trick question. The respondents were asked whether a close relative or friend suffered from the fear of flying and whether either of them refused to fly. An affirmative result of 42 and 38 per cent respectively was obtained and the inference was 'that people had themselves in mind when they gave this answer'. The 'frequent flyer' sector, too, should be examined because when courses for 'fearful flyers' were run by airlines in the past, it was found that they were attended by seasoned passengers (Halbroth 1986). But it may be inevitable that when one is overexposed to an experience chockful of fear and anxiety, one will tend in due course to be undermined by it. Tony Good, a businessman who chalks up over 100,000 air miles a year, admits to such a view. 'The more I fly,' he says, 'the more daunting the prospect of the next trip becomes' (Good 1986). I read the strain in his features and it prompts the perennial thought: when will we know the long-term effects of air travel on this much prized and vulnerable group, in particular? Could it be cancer from the radiation that occurs at flight altitudes? Could it be circulatory disease from pre-flight panic and continuous but short exposures to cabin altitudes before the body has had a chance to acclimatize? Or could it be a factor such as the environmental tobacco smoke (ETS) present in pressurized cabins?

Perhaps we are now in a position to examine the face of Johnny Panic, and to attempt to penetrate the many guises. This is difficult, though, because the definition has undergone distinct changes since it was first conceived by a Royal Flying Corps flight surgeon, H.G. Anderson, in 1919. He summed it up as reluctance to fly, an aeroneurosis, as T.S. Strongin notes in a historical review of the subject (Strongin 1987: 264). The review demonstrates a divergence of opinion over the years that has resulted in a modern classification of disorders under the 'fear of flying' or, as the author wants to describe it, 'FOF'. Listed are anxiety problems, exhaustion, traumatic stress, psychosis, and motivational alterations. And to these may be added several physical symptoms including sweating, insomnia, diarrhoea, vomiting and faintness which in themselves could characterize other conditions encountered in air travel like the jet syndrome. Whether the disagreement is a sign of vigour in this section of aviation medicine or is due to the fact that the religious element has been excluded from the deliberations, is a matter for speculation.

At this stage I realized that it would be a suitable moment to approach a psychologist at the IAM for a basic explanation. I talked to Roger Green who, as it turned out, was ideal for, in his own words, he was a 'nuts-and-bolts' man (Green 1987). Everything about his office attested to the fact. His attitude towards smoking was clarified at the door where next to the designation Head of Flight Skills, was a 'No Smoke-Zone' sign in luminous red. If the offender had not got the message by the time the desk was reached, there was a reminder on it – a wooden plaque inscribed with the remark 'Thank you for not smoking'. In the short while I was alone, I took stock of my surroundings. There was no couch as would have befitted a Freudian and if there were any clues, I concluded, they might be found in the glass-fronted bookcase. The books appeared to be part of a static collection which included Riesman's *The Lonely Crowd* and Sartre's *Perception Learning*. Later, he would reveal, in a jocular manner which tempered most of his statements, that the favourite among these was Hamlyn's *Colour Guide to Psychology* for 12-year-olds. What did distinguish the bookcase, though, was a picture of a nude woman which was stuck to one of the glass partitions. On the wall was a photograph of a small aircraft which he had piloted, and on the otherwise uncluttered desk was something of which he was proud: a computer complete with printer. There was no mistake, here was a technician among psychologists.

When he appeared on that winter's day, he was dressed in a navy-blue guernsey and round his neck on a long silver chain was the plastic identity card. Was this gesture of independence in a military establishment similar to that of a co-pilot who sports an open-neck shirt in the presence of a captain who is conscious of rank? I wondered as one does in the company of any professional of the psyche. But I soon realized from his manner – he is a fun person to be with – that it may have just been a question of comfortable clothing. As principal psychologist at the IAM he has been involved over the past 17 years in a variety of projects on aeromedical human factors both for the military and civilians. Flight skills research today is a misnomer for it has extended beyond the original brief and is part of the Behavioural Sciences division, together with Vestibular Physiology and General Psychology.

The subject I had come to discuss, he intimated, did not present a problem because, as he put it, 'I'm not really a fear of flying bloke.' However, what he would do was 'to come up with the best guess'. The disavowal was an important step as the topic appears to engender, or rather embody, flights of fancy. For example, Sigmund Freud wrote a monograph on Leonardo da Vinci, a part of which was entitled 'The erotic roots of aviation' (Freud 1983). In it, he groups together motley facts: that storks bring children; that the colloquial expression in German, to bird (*vögeln*), means to have sexual intercourse; that the Italians call the male organ a bird (*l'uccello*), and that the phallus sometimes appears to be winged in ancient cultures. Therefore, he concludes the inevitable: that the wish to fly (in a dream) can be equated with the desire for sexual achievement. I do not propose to proceed along such a course as this would necessitate a book in itself, but rather provide a basic approach that Roger Green, in spite of his inherent modesty, could reinforce. He recalled a recent visit to Toronto when he 'went up this thing called the CM Tower. . . . It's 1,500 ft off the ground, and in aeroplanes I don't mind that at all. On the CM Tower my legs were like jelly.' He chuckled. 'I thought then, "Gosh, it must be like this for people who are frightened of flying." They spend 12 hours sitting in an aeroplane with their legs shaking, hating every second of it!

'Now, I knew that there wasn't any point in being frightened up there. There's been a million people . . . before me and there would

UAA CONSORTIUM LIBRARY

Please return the items on the
date below. For renewal before
the due date you may call
786-1871 during business hours
RESERVE MATERIALS MAY NOT BE
RENEWED OVER THE PHONE

Title: The curse of Icarus : the health fa
ctor in air travel
Item ID: 1001056900
Date due: 5/18/2006,23:59

Title: Human factors for pilots
Item ID: 1001290074
Date due: 5/18/2006,23:59

Title: Airline pilot age, health, and perf
ormance : scientific and medical considera
tions : report oStar SP21
Item ID: 1000314441
Date due: 5/18/2006,23:59

probably be a million people after me without anything going wrong. So the chances that I was going to fall off or the thing was going to break were pretty low. And I look at flying in the same way.'

Earlier in the conversation he had alluded to the fact that it was beneficial for us to express such a fear. The reason was sound.

'If, generally speaking, it's a bad thing for people to be high up off the ground then it is a good thing if people are frightened. High up off the ground, either stuck up a tree or on the edge of a cliff, is normally dangerous. So it's a good instinct for the species to have, not to be there.' The statement made a lot of sense because it demonstrated a priori that there was a real danger which resulted in a real fear. Perhaps we should accept that this is part of our instinctual knowledge and the manner in which we deal with the situation will determine whether we have a problem or not. The majority of air travellers would appear to have overcome the fear through reasoning. However, there is a group known as 'the white-knuckle brigade' who are unable without a great deal of effort to gloss over the facts or delude themselves about the risks and a percentage of these may be tipped over into the anxiety category. At the other extreme there would be another group with a predilection for danger who are inveterate risk-takers.

And what can be done to alleviate the fear? I was reassured by him 'that by comparison with other risks that people habitually take in life, flying [is] a reasonably good one. So it's not something that you need to get particularly upset about. The same as me', he added, 'going up the CM Tower. I think that, from the evidence, we have an irrational anxiety, which can be effectively dealt with by some form of desensitization. And if I personally were suffering from a flying phobia that's what I would want to set out to do.'

He began with a description of an extreme form of this relaxation treatment that was termed, with great aptness, flooding. 'If somebody is actually frightened of spiders, you put spiders on their hands and all over them. Once they realize they're covered with spiders and they have not come to any harm you know they are compelled not to mind!' Whilst I could appreciate that the arachnophobe might, with a measure of forbearance, be able to curb the fear, I had no illusions that the same was possible with a patient who had to be exposed to a dozen snakes. The better technique, he indicated, was to confront people with the unreasonableness of their fears. 'Establish it at a conscious level so that they do appreciate there is nothing to be frightened of.' To be specific, it would require them to examine the causes of this emotion – confined spaces, heights, expectation that the aircraft will crash, or the inability to control the flight – and at the same time to remain tranquil.

Roger Green explained how progressive desensitization, which was popularized by Joseph Wolpe, was undertaken. The essential element was to teach the patient to relax. Here he became empathic – a trait I had noticed throughout our talk – for he leant back in the chair, stretched his legs out in front and crossed them. 'You relax like this,' he said; 'concentrate on your feet. Make them feel heavy. Then when you have taught the patients a technique for relaxation, get them to think about the thing they find anxiety-provoking, like flying. That thought will increase their heart rate and at the same time you instruct them to relax. As both anxiety and relaxation are incompatible, they will resort to the latter. Now you gradually work them through the more traumatic aspects. First they're at the airport, next they're on the aeroplane, and then they're rushing down the runway ready for take-off. All along their relaxation technique can override their anxiety. You end up by being able to take them out to the airport and put them on an aeroplane. With a bit of luck, touch wood, you will have done them a bit of good' (Green 1987).

Although it is usual for desensitization to be implemented by a therapist, he indicated later that the method does lend itself to self-treatment. What you have to do is make yourself comfortable either in an armchair or on a bed; concentrate on your hands or legs until you sense a heaviness; and think through the situation step by step. What it amounted to was a rehearsal for the various states of anxiety that may be encountered, much in the same way as a simulator prepares a pilot to cope with flight problems in the air.

Another simple feature that should not be neglected in any treatment of the fear of flying is the control of over-breathing, or hyperventilation. It is apparent, as more evidence becomes available of the link between falls in carbon dioxide and the onset of panic attacks or phobic states, that the inspiration-rate (breathing rate) will play an important part in the future. (See Chapter 5, 'The great mimic'.)

There was one factor that had concerned me ever since I had heard of the numerous courses for the relief of aerophobia. What if in some cases, I had asked myself, the fear had a physiological basis which could be aggravated by cabin pressure? How could a therapist without any knowledge of aviation medicine – and the majority seemed to fit into this category – deal with such a situation? I put the question to Roger Green who, if anything, seemed surprised. 'You don't think that flying phobics are perfectly ordinary people who happen to have a phobia about flying?' However, he was prepared to concede that instinct could have a role in that it may conceal a biomedical cause or peripheral dysfunction. Later I found a couple of illustrations of this. The first was the mitral value prolapse (MVP). Researchers had observed that the condition was present in 66 per cent of a subject sample who had complained of anxiety. The second related to the dysfunction of the vestibular system whereby the sense of balance and the movement of the head are affected. Individuals with the complaint, which produces symptoms of headache, nausea, imbalance, and vertigo, are known to develop agoraphobia and anxiety. (Hallam 1985: 58). The answer to the second question was therefore obvious. Any unqualified person, whether clinical psychologist or psychiatrist, should demur from the treatment of people with a flying phobia unless an aviation medical specialist has ascertained that the flight environment will not put their health at risk. Not to adopt a cautious approach and to encourage the public to think of the condition as a 'stupid problem' – an attitude prevalent among the air travel industry who have vested interests – is to leave these practitioners open to litigation in the future.

There was no doubt that the 'nuts and bolts' that comprised Roger Green's method were sound. And I may add that I was not the first to gain such a positive impression, for it is not unusual for strangers to refer to him as Dr Green, as was the instance in a recent television programme, in spite of his protest – 'I am a humble psychologist.' In answer to his parting shot, 'At any rate, how are we doing?', 'Roger, fine.'

It would be inappropriate at the final stage not to mention a serious consequence of the disorder. The ruin of a career. That the hard core of flyers, the military pilots, could be afflicted came as a surprise. For they are volunteers and would not put aside their livelihood because of an irrational notion or 'stupid problem'. What also should be borne in mind is that each of them has undergone a rigorous selection process that, among other things, eliminates individuals with psychopathological conditions. Candidates with a high reactive anxiety let alone a free-floating anxiety would never pass muster. Therefore, it is of interest to note that they are prone, though not to the extent of the passive flyer, and to examine the causes.

In a judicious paper, Dr David Jones from the Aeropsychiatry

Branch of the USAF School of Aerospace Medicine considers the subject from a motivational viewpoint. He poses the question why experienced men with an accident-free record 'unexpectedly become unbearably anxious about flying' and highlights a basic element which is often ignored: that the occupation a priori is dangerous. And he has no truck with the argument that one can also be killed when one crosses a street or drives a car on the motorway. 'Flying', he emphasizes, 'is an additional risk, not an alternative risk!' (Jones 1986: 131). In time, most pilots come to terms with the realities of the dangers of flight through a mixture of rationalization, humour, and suppression or denial of their feelings. He indicates that the question which should be asked of flyers is not why some are afraid to fly but rather why all are not.

> The answer appears to me to lie in the amount of pure joy the flier derives from flying, the amount of anxiety mixed with the natural fear, the extent to which the flier's defenses have been challenged by circumstance, and on the adequacy and maturity of the flier's psychic defenses.
>
> (Jones 1986: 131)

In an unusual step, he equates joy with the other deep-seated emotions: love and fear. He develops the analogy with the observation that unless one has experienced the sensations – in particular, the sense of control over time and the freedom in space – it is useless to expect one to understand. However, it would appear that the level of ecstasy is on a par with a religious experience. It elevates the doers to the point where they feel that they have a power over death, and often the phrase 'cheated death again' is repeated after successful missions.

The roots of anxiety, Dr Jones states, may be found at the same 'primitive' depths as the roots of the joy of flying. He bases his reason on the belief that everyone is 'born with an instinctive fear of heights'. And as evidence he offers the fact that 'one of the first tests of the newborn infant's neurologic integrity is the presence of its Moro reflex, a grasping response to any stimulus which suggests falling' (Jones 1986: 132). As we master our environment, we learn that to fall can indeed be dangerous. If any seeds of anxiety can be planted then it may be at such a formative period. Whether they will develop into a neurosis later or will be overcome will depend on the individual. Dr Jones's definition of the fear of flying? 'A complex phenomenon, mixing elements of mental health and neurotic roots, childhood dreams and fears, real dangers and imaginary threats, and all the varieties of experiences which may befall a flier as he or she ages' (Jones 1986: 136). What is relevant, though, is the duality of joy and fear, which would appear to be entwined in our psyche. Therefore, if you manage to scale heights without injury or death, there is the thrill of achievement. A religious depiction can be found in Moses' ascent of Mt Sinai and the Ten Commandments he brought on his return. The modern equivalent without doubt is the commonplace trip of the flyer – combat or passenger – who streaks across the sky at high altitudes and comes back safe to Earth.

If there is a conclusion, perhaps on balance it is that more people are affected by the fear of flying than is recognized. Send a plane-load of people up in an uninsulated fuselage *sans* cabin crew, entertainment, and food, and a lot more sufferers will appear. For some who may argue that technology has provided an answer, I must point out that it has only concealed or repressed the condition. The cause will always remain as long as we inhabit a terrain that is not composed of an overall smooth flat surface and where the air above is not free of gravity.

In the meantime, we should heed the summation of flying of M. Passepartout – a companion of Jean Cocteau, who went on a round-the-world flight with him in the 1930s – when he exclaimed, 'Man has guts!' (Cocteau 1942: 204).

Chapter Nine

A DOSE OF CONCORDE: DANGERS OF HIGH-ALTITUDE FLIGHT

If ever there was a civilian aircraft built where the human factors were given precedence over the engineering, or at least placed on an equal footing, it was the supersonic transport (SST), the Concorde. As a result, a new aspect of physiology was unearthed and known problems of high-altitude flight had to be faced. Before its advent, human factors were considered in a higgledy-piggledy fashion by aircraft designers and lacked the benefit of a systematic and organized approach.

For some time, I had been intrigued by the low cabin pressure of the SST in comparison to the other popular subsonics like the B747. The recommended pressure was 5,000 ft despite the fact that Concorde cruised above 60,000 ft. Why had such an anomaly arisen, I had wondered, when it had been inculcated in at least two generations of aviation engineers that the heavier the aircraft, the higher the cost to operate? Not long after, I met one of the scientists, Dr David Denison. (An account of my interview with him appears in Chapter 4.) He had been the head of the Altitude Research Section at the RAF IAM, and he answered my question.

It had been known since the late 1920s that at a height of 20,000 ft the mental and motor functions deteriorated because of the lack of oxygen. However, it was only during the development of supersonic jets that the effect of mild hypoxia over a prolonged period was discovered. There is a detectable impairment in our night vision and an interference in our ability to learn. Both factors could pose problems for the crew on the flight deck where seconds rather than minutes count when decisions are made. 'If you give somebody a not very complicated task that's novel', Dr Denison elaborated, 'they will learn it less quickly at 8,000 or 5,000 ft than they will at ground-level. Once they've learnt it they can do it just as fast in either place, so it interferes with their ability to learn but not with their ability to perform an already learnt task' (Denison 1986).

What this could represent to the conscientious executive who likes to be busy on board is that the work accomplished might not be all that it appears to be. I had this vision of a high-powered businessman with a portable computer on his lap and I asked the doctor about this. 'If he is doing well-rehearsed calculations, there would be no interference at all. But if he is trying to work out something novel that involves complicated new thoughts then he is less likely to do them well on the aircraft.' These observations, published as a paper in 1966, were based on research with subjects in novel or emergency situations where they had to assimilate a lot of information that was unexpected. It was found that they would be at a disadvantage if under these conditions they breathed in cabin air at 8,000 ft. Therefore, this was one of the reasons for the recommendation that cabin pressure be pegged at 5,000 ft in the SST (Denison *et al.* 1966: 1013).

When the Concorde came into service in 1976 it struck a chord of cacophony throughout the world because the sonic boom brought in its wake raucous detractors. Now, after over a decade of flight, the clamour has passed, yet the aeromedical problems of its passengers still remain. These were overlooked by the protesters who were concerned with broader issues at the time. There are two problems, ozone (O_3) and radiation, and whenever you fly in Concorde you get a dose of each.

I had always associated ozone in my mind with the smell at the seaside that refreshes and invigorates and is encountered when seaweed decays. I had not known of its other property, its powerful oxidizing action that favours its use in bleaches and deodorants, until I heard what had happened to the passenger oxygen masks in the Comet. These, the standard drop-down masks on airlines, which were then made from natural rubber, were found to be corroded. That discovery indicated ozone contamination of the cabin.

This came to light when I spoke to Dr Geoffrey Bennett, the former Chairman of the British Committee of the Anglo-French Concorde Aeromedical Group and now Chief Medical Officer of the Civil Aviation Authority. 'There were other rubber components in the aircraft but the oxygen masks were more obvious because the foam actually crumbled' (Bennett 1986). What was apparent, however, was that the ozone would become a greater problem with the SST because it flew well above the tropopause. Further research also revealed that the concentration of ozone in the cabin would vary with latitude and season and significant contamination occurred for short periods (Harding and Mills 1983: 117). In a paper on the subject, Dr Bennett demonstrated that in the northern hemisphere the concentration was highest in March and April in high latitudes and lowest in September and October in low latitudes. At altitudes of over 60,000 ft, the ozone concentration would reach levels of 4–6 p.p.m.v. (parts per million by volume) (Bennett 1962: 969).

When I enquired what effect ozone had on the body, he gave the analogy of an incident where too much chlorine is let loose in a swimming pool and it irritates the nose, throat, chest, and eyes. Ozone too is a powerful irritant that causes an inflammatory reaction and has a similar degree of toxicity. But it was not difficult to restrict the entry of the gas into the cabin atmosphere.

This was achieved through the combination of the thermo-instability of ozone and a catalytic converter. A platinum filter that changes ozone into oxygen was installed in the air conditioning compressor circuit where the optimum temperature for its decomposition, 400 °C, was reached during ascent and cruising. The cabin concentration of ozone at these phases of flight should remain below 0.1 p.p.m.v. which is the maximum concentration set for industrial workers exposed to the gas over a 5-day, 40-hour week period. (See Chapter 10, 'Air travel, beware travel'.) However, this system is not wholly efficient as double the allowable dose of ozone can enter for 3 minutes on every Concorde trip. The contamination level can reach 0.25 p.p.m.v. when the engines are throttled back before descent and the compressor temperature falls to about 300 °C.

In the handbook on *The Medical Aspects of Supersonic Flight* which is a joint publication of Air France and British Airways, ozone is described as a 'strong oxidising agent and is toxic to man. Its biological effects are essentially respiratory' (Preston and Lavernhe – no date). An observation is also made that concentrations of 0.1 p.p.m.v. were found abroad subsonics like the B707 at altitudes of 39,000 ft and therefore the problem was not restricted to SSTs (Preston and Lavernhe – no date: 25).

Although radiation is a hazard with which we are familiar, it is unusual to link it to air travel. However, with the development of the Concorde, this area had to be investigated and a programme was initiated to measure the amounts of cosmic radiation present in the atmosphere at the flight levels of such aircraft. As Dr Bennett recalled, sensors were placed on military aircraft, and on balloons which the Meteorological Office released all over the place, and radiation detectors were also put on a collection of civil aircraft such as B707s that flew at lower altitudes. Extensive coverage of various atmospheric layers was undertaken to study both forms of cosmic radiation, the galactic and the solar.

Galactic radiation originates from our galaxy and produces an almost constant intensity of high-energy particles and heavy particles. The intensity is highest in the polar latitudes where the dose equivalent rate at 60,000 ft is in the region of 0.0155 milli-Sieverts (mSv or 1.55 millirems) per hour. Solar radiation, on the other hand, is sporadic and usually of lower energy with the result that it is less able to penetrate the atmosphere. Its production is dependent on solar flares that vary in intensity and are associated with sunspots which follow cycles of between 10 and 11 years. The highest intensity is again found in polar latitudes where the dose equivalent rate is about 1 mSv/hr (100 millirems/hr) but can increase to 2 mSv/hr and on rare occasions to 20 mSv/hr at 40,000 ft (Committee on Airliner Cabin Air Quality 1986: 130). This high level of radiation is an infrequent occurrence and 'can be damaging to passengers' (Bennett 1986).

The US National Oceanographic and Atmospheric Administration collects data on cosmic radiation throughout the world and can forecast the likelihood of solar activity within a 24-hour period. As Concorde is not shielded from these emissions due to the uneconomic weight penalties it would impose, a detection system has been fitted. It includes a detector unit in the passenger compartment and display instruments on the flight deck. Incorporated into the system is an audible and visual alarm that will be activated if the dose equivalent rate reaches two critical levels, 0.1 mSv/hr (10 millirems/hr) for the alert and 0.5 mSv (50 millirems/hr) for descent action. 'If one of these high intensity solar flares happened to blast out at the time the aeroplane was flying', Dr Bennett observed, 'it would descend to get more protection from the atmosphere above so as to cut down the radiation level to the occupants.'

The maximum permissible dose for air travellers or the public as recommended by the International Commission on Radiation Protection (ICRP) is 5 mSv (500 millirems) a year. It has been estimated that this would allow for some 60 return trips across the North Atlantic by Concorde every year if on each single flight passengers received a radiation dose of about 0.04 mSv (4 millirems). What should also be mentioned is that subsonic aircraft are not free of the effects of cosmic radiation. As Dr Bennett noted, 'If you take the 707 or 747 across the Atlantic, it doesn't fly as high and therefore the radiation per hour is less but, on the other hand, you spend twice as long getting there.'

In the case of the Concorde pilots who could do 160 return trips a year, it has been estimated that they could have a total annual dose of 13 mSv (1,300 millirems) (Harding and Mills 1983: 115). This is well within the limit of the maximum permissible dose of 50 mSv (5,000 millirems) a year recommended by the ICRP for radiation workers but the National Radiological Protection Board has suggested that a new limit of 15 mSv be set by 1991 (Wilkie 1988). However, in each of these groups, the exposures to radiation are monitored. With the aircrew, the cumulative exposure can be calculated because there is an instrument on board that records the total dose on each flight. At first they were alarmed by the situation and insisted that they not only wore radiation exposure film badges but had the opportunity to decide whether or not they should wear lead-lined underpants. In the end, they acquiesced. Their job was to fly aircraft and the SST offered the ultimate experience that no civilian pilot could afford to ignore, which was later attested to by the low rate of sickness among them. There was also the argument that aircrews of subsonic jets in the long term got about the same amount of radiation.

What is of concern is that the public is unaware of this radiation risk. And as Dr Bennett commented, 'The fact is, the more radiation you absorb the more risk there is to your person.' I once read of a businessman who had made over 570 trips in Concorde and on its tenth anniversary in 1986 hoped to have reached 600. What an achievement, I thought at the time and, indeed, Mr Fred Finn has gone into the record books. But now I look upon him as a brave man. Does he know that he has accumulated a dose of about 24 mSv (2,400 millirems) too? Would he have done it, had he known? And the most important question is, was his radiation exposure monitored?[1]

There is a further bombshell on this subject: a study among nuclear power workers has found that huge margins of error exist on the radiation safety limits recommended by the ICRP. The study, which was undertaken by the London School of Hygiene and Tropical Medicine, concluded that these limits have been underestimated by more than 15 times, in particular with regard to the cancer risk, and they should be set lower (Fraser *et al*. 1985: 435-9; Beral *et al*. 1985: 440-9).

I asked Dr Bennett to comment on this new development. 'The average dose of radiation from all quarters', he answered, 'may have been underestimated but certainly not as far as aircrew. We are talking about measured doses – we know what they are exposed to. Clearly, it isn't a problem, except that all radiation is potentially harmful. There is no threshold effect for it, so you don't expose people to any more than you have to.'

The question of how these levels were set by the ICRP also arose.

'The recommended dosage limitation for passengers is based on the level of risk which this international committee considered reasonable for the average population to absorb because of the possible genetic effects of radiation passing on to future generations. But, of course, the number of people who are actually doing Concorde flying, for example, is very low. So therefore the genetic load of the population at large because of a few people flying Concorde is very small. People who work in the nuclear industry are allowed to accumulate ten times more radiation dosage than this because there are so few of them.'

The solution to this problem appears to have been reached through containment. There is a risk to one's person that is proportional to the amount of radition absorbed. But, if confined to a minute percentage of the general public, like supersonic passengers, it is bearable, OK. What of those on the receiving end? Would they agree if they knew?

Pregnant women, including stewardesses, are particularly vulnerable. 'They would be likely to suffer considerably more from radiation exposure,' Dr Bennett said. 'In the first three months of pregnancy when all the organs are forming, they're more suscept-ible to damage from radiation or drugs or anything else for that matter. That's why we tell pregnant women not to take a whole variety of drugs in the early months of pregnancy because the little foetus is particularly sensitive to damage from these circumstances.' It was this very hazard, he concluded, that had prompted the Concorde Aeromedical Group to consider the effect of cosmic radiation more seriously in civilian aviation than had been done in military aircraft.

When the British and the French co-operated on the design of the Concorde, there were few dramas as both countries already had experience of the production of military aircraft that flew twice the speed of sound at high altitudes. If there were differences, it was a question of style. The French technique was to discuss the non-controversial subjects before lunch and to substitute champagne for coffee at the mid-morning break. This 'would get the English into a reasonable state of mind'. At noon they would serve a heavy lunch with generous amounts of wine, 'so by the afternoon and evening', Dr Bennett remarked, 'we'd agree to anything!'

If the technical problems were straightforward, there was one potential hazard that caused concern. It was the sudden loss of cabin pressure. At one stage, a design without windows was even contemplated to preclude such an event. In the previous generations of aircraft, windows were blown out or pressurization was lost at a rate of one incident every 25,000 hours. As the SST would fly at heights at which the body fluids, including blood, boil, this occurrence was to be avoided at all costs. But that aspect was secondary to the serious problem of explosive decompression at altitudes over 52,000 ft that results in unconsciousness within 15 seconds of exposure, irrespective of whether pure oxygen or air is breathed. Up to 40,000 ft the standard drop-down oxygen masks provide adequate protection for healthy young passengers.

However, if and when such an incident occurs, the flight deck crew are protected. They are provided with a supply of oxygen through a special mask in order to be ready for an immediate descent before their motor function or judgement is impaired. The mask, which is fitted with an inflatable harness, has to be donned with one hand within 5 seconds. It is an unusual task and has been described by Air Vice-Marshal P. Howard, former head of the RAF IAM, as 'similar to that faced by a one-armed theatre nurse attempting to put on a cloth surgical mask against the clock' (Engle and Lott 1979: 252).

In the end, the design of the Concorde cabin was 'over-engineered' to guard against this hazard. It included small windows only 6 inches in diameter and a reserve capacity of air supplies. Therefore, if a window is lost at 65,000 ft the passengers would be exposed to a maximum height of 36,000 ft for 30 seconds provided that it was followed by an emergency descent. It is estimated that they would spend about 6 minutes above 20,000 ft, of which 3 minutes would be at 30,000 ft. 'This dose of hypoxia', according to Air Vice-Marshal Howard, 'would, in a passenger totally unprotected by oxygen, lead to unconsciousness but it would be insufficient to cause lasting cerebral damage' (Engle and Lott 1979: 251).

However, despite the possibility of rapid decompression, there are quantifiable risks that passengers on supersonic flights have to consider. Ozone and radiation are among these.

Chapter Ten

AIR TRAVEL, BEWARE TRAVEL: MEDICAL HAZARDS OF FLYING

If a passenger were to appear in a spacesuit on a flight one day, there is little doubt that such a presence would be greeted with a mixture of mirth, perplexity, and downright amazement. After a short while, fellow passengers might come to the conclusion that it was a publicity stunt. But what if that was not the case? What if the person knew something they did not know? For example, the person may have seen a secret report on the subject of air safety and decided to act on their own initiative.

What may surprise many air travellers is that anyone dressed in this manner, and not in the loose, comfortable clothes that are often recommended, may be better equipped for the aircraft cabin. What may shock them, too, is that there is a report, though not classified, that would justify the action. Of course, the sealed and pressurized suit of the astronaut may be an extreme way to respond to the fact that air in the cabin is polluted, that the cabin is not well ventilated, and that there are health effects from reduced pressure and cosmic radiation.

Before we can understand the full impact of the situation, we have to get some perspective on the role of human factors in the design of pressure cabins. From the outset, I would like to disabuse readers of the notion that the role of human factors was an important one. The origin was economic and took the form of a far-sighted businessman like Howard Hughes who would demand of an aircraft manufacturer, 'We want the fastest high-altitude airplane in the world! What's it going to cost? Will it be cost effective?' Out would come the slide-rule (in those carefree unencumbered pre-computer days) and the direct cost per seat/mile would be calculated. However, on this occasion, a new variable was added to the formula. It would cause not inconsiderable excitement because from then on a substantial reduction in an airline's operating costs would be obtainable. There was a simple reason, something that Langewiesche would later call the thin-air trick (Langewiesche 1954).

High air is thin air and thin air offers less resistance than thick air at sea-level. In a nutshell, you can fly faster without too much extra power. To take his example:

Suppose you are running an airline. Your aeroplanes cruise at 200 m.p.h. with 1,000-horsepower engines. Each trip over your route takes six hours. Well, the same aeroplane redesigned for cruising at 40,000 ft needs 2,000-horsepower engines. But it cruises at 400, makes each trip in half the time, and runs twice-as-big engines for only half the time. It burns no extra fuel. You have grabbed speed out of thin air, free of charge! And speed is a highly saleable commodity: your passengers are willing to pay extra for it. It also pays you off indirectly: each aeroplane can make twice as many trips per week. You don't have to buy so many aeroplanes.

(Langewiesche 1954: 81)

But how could the idea be translated into reality? It had been known since the nineteenth century that when balloonists ascended to altitudes over 25,000 ft, they had to carry their oxygen supplies aloft in order to survive. If anything had changed by the late 1930s, it was that the gas was breathed in, not through a pipe-stem clenched between the teeth, but via a mask that fitted over the mouth and nose (Dille 1988: 1010). This then would be the first option – passengers would wear oxygen masks. The disadvantage, however, was threefold. The weight of each oxygen cylinder was such that for oxygen to be taken on board in sufficient quantities would be prohibitive. The mask was uncomfortable to the degree that it was described as a malevolent hand clamped over the face, and the storage of oxygen presented problems because it was very reactive.

There was the other option. It was untried but had great potential: an airtight cabin that could be pumped up to a pressure near enough to sea-level. All that was required was the installation of compressors adjacent to the engines and thin air would be converted into thick air. Although there was still the disadvantage of the weight of the equipment, it was insignificant compared to the advantages in terms of safety, comfort, and operational efficiency. For example, the unpressurized aircraft that leaked bobbed like a cork in currents of air, the

Table 10.1 Analysis of cabin pressurization based on safety, comfort, and operating efficiency

Advantages	Disadvantages
Safety	
1 Time in icing layers cut down by more rapid ascents and descents without influencing passengers	1 Possibility of forced descents to lower altitudes in bad weather or over mountainous areas in the event of a loss of pressure
2 Stronger fuselage providing greater safety in forced landings on land or water	2 Necessity for carrying emergency oxygen in the event of a sudden loss of pressure
3 Less fatigue in flight crews	3 Increased distortion of vision through thicker windowpanes
4 Leakproof windshields promoting greater efficiency in pilots	
5 Better birdproofing because of thicker windowpanes	
Comfort	
1 Constant and adequate supply of oxygen	1 Greater difficulty in the control of odours
2 No need for cumbersome masks	2 More limited rates of cabin ventilation
3 No interruption in sleep during rapid descents	3 Possible results of oxygen lack in case of cabin or compressor failure
4 Freedom of movement, conversation, and other activities without oxygen masks	4 Passenger window space reduced unless paid for in excessive weight penalties
5 Decrease in airsickness due to smoother over-the-weather flying	
6 More even cabin temperatures	
7 Less distress to middle ear during rapid rates of ascent and descent	
8 Conservation of moisture in recirculated air	
9 Lowered noise transmission because of thicker windows and heavier structures	
Operating efficiency	
1 Increased regularity of schedules because of over-the-weather flying	1 Weight penalties around bulkheads, doors, and windows
2 Increased speed at high altitudes due to lower density of air	2 Increased maintenance of supercharger and cabin pressure regulator
3 Per annum payloads increased because of greater regularity of service and use of direct routes	3 Greater maintenance involved in preventing air leaks around the sleeves and bellows for the controls leading in and out of pressurized sections
4 Aerodynamic cleanliness promoted; less drag and fewer leaks	4 Greater difficulty in cooling the cabin at low altitudes
5 Lowered fuel consumption because of less time spent in ascents and descents	5 Added weight of fuel to supply power for superchargers
6 Increased efficiency in temperature control because of heating the air during compression and better sealing of apertures	6 Disposal of water or waste in flight more difficult
7 No human limitations during rapid climbs to cruising altitudes and efficient descents	

Source: McFarland 1946: 71

aircraft whose service was irregular because of bad weather would be replaced by one with a stronger fuselage, in which the passengers could enjoy smoother, quieter, and safer flights clear of the weather. However, at the same time, an unprecedented dangerous factor had been introduced – the loss of cabin pressure at high altitude. (A reminder of the pros and cons at issue then are given in Table 10.1.)

It should be obvious to readers that the manufacturer of the prototype, Boeing, did not base the design on human physiology but rather on another aircraft, the famous B–17 'Flying Fortress' bomber. The reason was logical enough: Wellwood Beall, the production chief of the Seattle plant, happened to have turned out a lot of bombers. The fact in itself did not inspire him with confidence in the new project and if anything he felt 'awful scared' about it (Solberg 1979: 183). What troubled him was the greater risk involved. It was one thing to transport explosive devices for the military and another to take civilians into the upper air.

> We crawled around inside the plane looking for the windshield leaks with a paintbrush in one hand and a can of soap water in the other. Fast as we found them, we sealed them from inside with neoprene tape we got from du Pont. We beefed up the window frames; we tried double windows. I said to Bill Allen, all we have to do is blow a window and we're in the soup!
>
> I told Bill we needed to hold a symposium. We invited people from Air Research and Douglas and Lockheed to Seattle – also Randy Lovelace, the doctor who had been doing experiments at Mayo Clinic and at his clinic in New Mexico to get at the problem of oxygen want.
>
> (Solberg 1979: 183)

Nevertheless, his first task was to strengthen the fuselage to the extent that it could withstand the internal pressure. The way to go about that is to create a round shape because pressure, that pushes outwards from inside a hollow container, tends to turn it into the shape of a ball. (All corners disappear in the process.) Therefore, the cabin would take the form of a large-diameter circular section and would be equal to a pressure differential of 2.5 p.s.i. Thus, when the aircraft flew at 14,700 ft, the cabin altitude would be at 8,000 ft. Another important element was the compressor which Air Research had fitted with a regulator. Wellwood Beall recalled, 'we decided the maximum pressure[1] a passenger could tolerate would be 8,000 ft and no higher

– a pilot could set it lower if his flight plan permitted' (Solberg 1979: 183).

The net result was the Boeing 307 with a pressurized fuselage – not the first, as Lockheed had produced one a couple of years earlier in 1937, the experimental XC–35. The Stratoliner, as the B307 was designated, was a misnomer for it could not fly anywhere near the stratosphere, which can extend from about 33,000 ft. Nor for that matter could it cruise above the weather, at some 20,000 ft, because the cabin altitude would reach a critical level that would require passengers to wear oxygen masks. There, too, was the fact that the cabin would overheat on hot summer days due to the absence of a cooling system. Such limitations only served to consign the aircraft to the scrapheaps of aviation history and it was left to the Lockheed D49, the Constellation, to become the world's first pressurized high-altitude airliner, in 1944.

The element of intrigue remains. For who arrived at that magic figure of 8,000 ft – the acceptable degree of hypoxia in commercial flights – and on what physiological or psychological criteria was the decision based? There would appear to be no clear answer, and there is the chance that the limit was arbitrary. In a classic paper of the time, Harry G. Armstrong makes no mention of the figure, although he does state: 'It has been definitely shown that, for normal persons, accustomed to sea level conditions, an ascent of only 4,000 to 5,000 ft can be made before the onset of anoxemia [hypoxia] occurs . . .' (Armstrong 1936: 2–8). Another paper, presented 3 months later (in June 1936) by James C. Edgerton, an aeronautical expert with the US Bureau of Air Commerce, that was published in the *Journal of Aviation Medicine*, does mention the figure without any reference to its origin. 'The consensus of opinion at present is that the supercharging of a pressure-cabin must be started at a level in the neighborhood of 8,000 ft' (Edgerton 1936: 73–6). But both his statement and that of Harry G. Armstrong were unsubstantiated. What may be nearer the mark is a reported exchange between them the previous year at a Department of Commerce conference which is mentioned in Dr Robert Dille's column, 'Aviation medicine heritage' (Dille 1986: 816). Armstrong: 'I assume that pressure compartments will be kept at or near sea-level conditions.' He would have voiced this opinion with the conviction of a man who was aware of Paul Bert's seminal work and the admonition that any increase or decrease of oxygen tension would be harmful. Edgerton, on the other hand, who could be expected to have empathy with the airlines, had replied: 'It means more weight is necessary. Structurally speaking, you will probably hear comments to the effect that it will be impossible.' Perhaps, in an effort to mollify members of the Aero Medical Association, he suggested that they tell the engineers at what altitude pressure control should begin. To give them a clue to what a compromise between the impossible and the practicable would be, he proposed 8,000 ft.

If there was anyone who was privy to these decisions and could shed light on the question, it was Ross McFarland, who was later to become the Professor of Aerospace Health and Safety at Harvard. As a physiological psychologist, he had collaborated early in his career with Sir Joseph Barcroft and in 1935 had been a member of the International High Altitude Expedition that had gone to Peru to study the effects of oxygen want on acclimatized inhabitants. During the next few years he was able to demonstrate that altitudes of between 6,000 and 8,000 ft could reduce night vision and cause significant impairment of immediate memory. He wrote a book on human factors and air transport design in 1946 and gave a comprehensive review of 'Human factors in relation to the development of pressurized cabins' for the Sixth Armstrong Lecture in 1971 (McFarland 1971).

The book is remarkable inasmuch as it attempts to right the balance between man and the machine in aviation and as a consequence puts forward a cogent case for human requirements. Here, for the first time, the passenger has a voice, albeit shortlived as no comparable work has appeared since. Of interest are his comments on the reaction of average air travellers to high altitude which in essence is a

> complex psycho-physiological reaction influenced by many variables. As in the case of most organic functions, the adjustment to oxygen lack may vary from person to person, and in the same individual from day to day. The most important physical variables in air transportation are as follows: (1) height attained, (2) rate of ascent, (3) length of exposure, and (4) roughness of the air and movements of the plane. Each individual's response is determined by his (1) age; (2) tolerance gained from repeated flights or residence at high altitude; (3) clinical abnormalities such as cardiac disorders, anemia, asthma, tuberculosis, and intracranial abnormalities; (4) amount of physical exertion during flight; (5) amount of regular exercise and physical fitness; (6) degree of general fatigue; (7) number of hours of sleep the night before; (8) kinds of food ingested;

(9) amount of alcohol, tobacco, or sedatives and other drugs taken before the flight; (10) emotional adaptation, ie freedom from fear, worry, and mental conflicts; (11) degree of relaxation or nervous and muscular tension. Naturally, an airline cannot control the behaviour or physical fitness of its passengers. Therefore the only satisfactory solution is to maintain as near sea-level conditions as possible in order to prevent the aggravation of any pre-existing conditions.

(McFarland 1946: 55)

How refreshed one feels by these words because here at last was an instance when the health needs of the public were as real as those of the pilot. They still are! But it would appear that people of the same mettle as Ross McFarland are few and far between or extinct. On the set cabin altitude, little else is offered other than the consensus of authorities which is unsupported by any evidence. 'Equally competent physiologists and flight surgeons have recommended, on the one hand, that oxygen is necessary at 8,000 ft and above at all times and, on the other hand, that 12,000 ft is the critical level' (McFarland 1946: 55). McFarland does mention in the same chapter that the Bureau of Air Commerce commissioned him – well before the introduction of pressurized cabins – to investigate the effects of oxygen deprivation (high altitude) on the human organism. This was undertaken with over 200 subjects whose ages ranged from 18 to 72 years and involved altitudes and rates of ascent found on domestic flights. If there was a measure to gauge the results, it was based on levels of psychological and physiological comfort or discomfort experienced. Objective tests on physiological problems appear to have been ruled out. As an example, each subject was required to check a list of complaints and to give an account of their subjective responses when exposed to various altitudes from 10,000 to 16,000 ft. Among the complaints reported were headaches, dizziness, and altered respiration (which included shortness of breath, irregular breathing, or frequent sighing) and it is not unexpected that over 50 per cent of the participants suffered from these at 16,000 ft (McFarland 1946: 57).

In his Armstrong Lecture, Ross McFarland offers a less generalized explanation for the determination of the optimum cabin altitude, even though it does appear to be weak and is preceded by what amounts to an apology.

It is possible that considerations relating to increased weight may have been of more concern to the aircraft designers and operating airlines than the effects of high altitude on crews and passengers. Also how was the decision made to have the cabin altitude at 8,000 ft? One of the factors which led to the decision of 8,000 ft cabin altitude was the realisation that there are a number of airports in South America, and a major one such as at Mexico City, at approximately this altitude.

(McFarland 1971: 9)

I do not think we are expected to place too much emphasis, though, on such a statement because it is known that high-altitude inhabitants have acclimatized to the conditions. For example, they tend to have larger chests, and more capillaries per tissue, than people who live at sea-level, and their arterial blood is richer in oxygen (Hurtado 1971: 1–13).

But in the next sentence, he delivered the punch line to members of the Aerospace Medical Association at their annual meeting.

Currently there is increased interest in having cabin altitudes nearer sea level, or between 3,000 and 5,000 ft, rather than 6,000 or 8,000 ft. This is due to the fact that many airline passengers are in the older, or very young age ranges, with a certain percentage having a significant amount of illness. In addition, it is known that alcohol will accentuate the effects of altitude, and the carbon monoxide from cigarette smoking will lower one's ceiling. It is possible that some of the fatiguing effects of long flights and crossing time zones may be due to the interaction of these factors.

(McFarland 1971: 9)

The reason given for the downward trend in cabin altitude is sound, but should not a low level have been fixed at the start? Harry G. Armstrong also had second thoughts on the subject and expressed concern sometime after the initial conference:

it is becoming increasingly apparent that stratosphere, or even substratophere, flying can never be carried out as a practical routine procedure until there is a change in aircraft design which will maintain a more nearly normal pressure about the occupants.

(Heimbach and Sheffield 1985: 110)

John Ernsting is of a similar opinion and in a review on acceptable compromises for the prevention of hypoxia in 1978 concluded that 'up

119

to 5,000 ft is acceptable for both crew and passengers of combat and passenger aircraft' (Ernsting 1978). (It could be argued that the passengers, who comprise a cross-section of the population, are not comparable to the preselected aircrews of fighter aircraft who tend to be fitter and younger; if anything, the altitude for the passengers should be lower.)

One may ask why there has been a recent shift of position on cabin altitude without any major research to prompt it? Does it only indicate that there never was a sound scientific basis for the original figure; that in such matters, it was a consensus of expert opinion which set standards and a few individuals of conscience who later tried to reset them? To obtain any evidence, we have to return to those events of over 50 years ago. At the time, there were more than 500,000 passengers per year, some of whom suffered from ear conditions, and there had been one in-flight death (Dille 1986: 816). In particular, we should examine James Edgerton's paper in the *Journal of Aviation Medicine* for there lies the nub of the answer. But first, we have to pose the question: what motivated the doctors to agree to something that was so arbitrary – a figure plucked from thin air? On a basic level it could be described as the 'scare factor' and fear. As Mr Edgerton presented his case, the airline industry faced a serious problem because of rumours that altitude produced ill effects in large numbers of people. 'It is quite evident that those passengers', he wrote, 'who have experienced such effects, ranging through a zone from the psychological to the physiological, may cease to patronize the airlines. The inevitable dissemination of such information would unquestionably discourage potential passengers' (Edgerton 1936: 73). Here was the 'scare factor' which, if uncontrolled, could bring this new form of transport not to the brink of the next step – stratosphere flying – but to disaster. To press his point home and in the hope that the flight surgeons would come to a quick resolution, he added: 'This question is not academic, but reflects a very lively fear in the minds of those concerned with airline operation' (Edgerton 1936: 73).

So the precedent was fixed, and although passenger traffic has increased over a thousandfold worldwide, no proper investigation of the so-called optimum altitude, 8,000 ft, has ever been undertaken to determine the specific effects on our health. Of course, specialists in aviation medicine are aware that air travellers with cardiovascular, respiratory, neurological, and gastrointestinal diseases; central nervous system, metabolic, blood and psychiatric disorders; severe sinusitis and otitis media conditions; and advanced pregnancy or post-operative cases are at risk through hypoxia and pressure changes. But as their practice is limited, in the main, to a select and small group, the air-crew, they are unaware of other problems that may afflict the general population and escape their net of contraindications to flight. (A few onboard incidents that I came across recently included an ovarian cyst that ruptured, a gut that became twisted, a tonsilectomy that haemorrhaged, and an old myocardial infarction, not a recent one as is specified, that caused complications.)

What may surprise readers is that they can of their own accord increase cabin altitude. The simplest way is to smoke a cigarette or drink alcohol. A chief component of tobacco smoke is carbon monoxide which has 300 times greater the affinity for haemoglobin than oxygen and will displace it to form carboxyhaemoglobin. Therefore, whenever a smoker inhales, they deprive their blood of a small percentage of oxygen. Ross McFarland, who did research on the subject in 1944, estimated between 4 and 8 per cent which is equivalent, in physiological terms, to a cabin altitude of 6,000 to 8,000 ft. If such a person boarded an aircraft where the cabin pressure was 6,000 ft, they would be at the equivalent of 12,000 ft. The effects of carbon monoxide are additive (McFarland et al. 1944: 381–94).

Alcohol, in Dr McFarland's experience, would appear to have a similar effect. It is a depressant that exercises a

> primary physiological action by depressing oxidation in the cells. The impairment is believed to result from histotoxic influences, ie, 'the tissue cells are poisoned in such a manner that they cannot use the oxygen properly similar to narcotics which inhibit oxidation.' This interpretation explains (1) the striking effects of alcohol on the nervous system and (2) why alcohol and oxygen want produce more serious effects on the nervous tissue and consequently on behaviour if both are experienced simultaneously. Thus if a person ascends to moderate altitude with alcohol in his blood, he would be especially vulnerable to the effects.
>
> (McFarland 1971: 13)

The implication that there is an interactive effect between alcohol and hypoxia has not been confirmed by recent studies (Higgins et al. 1970; Collins et al. 1987). If anything, they would suggest that there is no clear definition of alcohol effects at altitude and under certain conditions these effects could be additive. However, in the absence of any firm evidence, McFarland's explanation does provide a feasible solution and could account for the fact that one drink in the air seems equal to two on the ground.

From a passenger's point of view, the most obvious sources of discomfort are not pressurization, carbon monoxide, or alcohol, but dehydration and environmental tobacco smoke (ETS). The reason for the low humidity is simple. The outside air to begin with is almost devoid of water vapour and remains in that state, for it passes through the engine compressor at a temperature of about 500 °C before being cooled and delivered into the cabin without humidification (Peffers 1980). To obtain an idea of the aridity, we have to use the term 'relative humidity', which denotes the maximum moisture present in an amount of air at a given temperature and pressure. For example, the average relative humidity outdoors in the UK is about 70–80 per cent (Thomson 1985), while indoors with central heating it may drop to 25 per cent. Inside an aircraft, the fresh air has a relative humidity of less than 1 per cent. Strange as it may seem, the only way to boost that level is to have people on board, because whenever they perspire or breathe out they introduce water into the atmosphere (Committee on Airliner Cabin Air Quality (CACAQ) 1986).[2] Even with such a natural device, that is dependent on several factors – the number of passengers, how hard the cabin crew work, the outside and inside temperature, and the duration of the trip – the relative humidity can fluctuate between about 25 and 3 per cent (CACAQ 1986). An excellent illustration is given by Captain Frank Hawkins who flew in a DC10 from Amsterdam to Anchorage with 265 passengers, and back with only 108. On the outward flight, the relative humidity varied between 10 and 20 per cent, whereas on the return there was a gradual decrease from some 20 per cent to a low of 2 per cent near the end of the 8-hour journey (Hawkins 1986: 286).

The symptoms of dehydration (a dryness of the eyes, nose, throat, and skin) can be prevented through an intake of fluids like water, while diuretics such as coffee and tea should be avoided. If this regime is not carried out, in the long term it may cause urinary gravel in frequent flyers. Wearers of contact lenses should also be aware that the lenses dry out on long flights (Wright 1983).

Sufficient concern about ETS has been shown over the past few years for airlines to designate special smoke-free zones on aircraft. However, it should be mentioned that carbon monoxide is nevertheless present and may have a very slight hypoxic effect on non-smokers.

It is not unusual for a committee to produce a ponderous report in an almost impenetrable style, and *The Airliner Cabin Environment*, subtitled *Air Quality and Safety* (the committee is chaired by Thomas C. Chalmers of the Mount Sinai Medical Center, New York), is no exception. However, its credentials are impressive as the study was commissioned from the National Academy of Sciences by the US Congress. The reason for the study was that a series of congressional hearings in 1983 and 1984 revealed that not only was there an absence of some standards for cabin air quality but the data available were contradictory. The fact that the report exists and makes a contribution in a field where there is a dearth of information is indeed commendable.

Although I was already aware of most of the aspects covered from various aviation medical sources, I must admit that I was somewhat unnerved by the report. The rub was not that the committee had proved specific health effects – on the contrary, except in a few instances this was difficult to do – but that they had laid bare the full extent of the problem. If you contrast the reality with the erroneous impression that air travel is innocuous, there is bound to be an element of shock. In essence, an aircraft is an environmental control system (ECS) not unlike a heating, ventilating, and air conditioning (HVAC) system found in modern, sealed buildings, and subject to similar contaminants and pollutants. However, there are important variations as well as additional factors involved.

Ozone and cosmic radiation (see Chapter 9, 'A Dose of Concorde') are greater at cruising altitudes than at sea-level. The ozonosphere that exists somewhere between 40,000 and 140,000 ft has concentrations of from 1 to 10 p.p.m.v. (parts per million by volume) of the triatomic gas (O_3 – ozone) (Preston and Denison 1983: 6.65). As a result, levels of over 0.8 p.p.m.v. have been detected in subsonic aircraft that fly near or within the lower limits. These are in excess of the FAA Code of Federal Regulations (1 January 1985) that confines ozone concentration to a maximum of 0.25 p.p.m.v. at any time above 32,000 ft. It may not exceed 0.1 p.p.m.v. for periods longer than 3 hours, but it can be reduced either through the installation of control equipment or through the avoidance of routes or altitudes where the gas is most prevalent (CACAQ 1986: 115–17). In a period when flights were monitored (1978–9), it was reported 'that 11% were in violation of FAA's ozone concentration limits' (CACAQ 1986: 119).

The Earth is irradiated from all directions and the rate is highest in the polar regions. The origins are of both a galactic and a solar nature and, as in the case of ozone, radiation increases with altitude. But because the subject is controversial, it is essential to establish a firm basis at the outset. E.T. Bramlitt refers to this in a paper entitled 'Commercial aviation crewmember radiation doses':

> Cosmic radiation dose is incurred normally when it is received in man's natural environment. It should not be considered a normal dose when received at high altitudes where man cannot live without artificial protection. This distinction for the manner in which cosmic radiation dose is received is necessary because natural radiation dose is excluded from federal dose limiting guidance (FRC 60a).
>
> (Bramlitt 1985)

What it represents in terms of exposure for passengers is given in the committee's report as follows:

> At altitudes typical of subsonic commercial aircraft, 9–12 km (29,500–39,400 ft), the cosmic-ray dose equivalent is approximately 100 times the rate at sea level. The newer, higher performance aircraft are certified to 46,000 ft 'where the cosmic-ray dose equivalent rate' is nearly twice the rate at 10 km (32,800 ft). A five-hour trans-Atlantic flight at midlatitude and an altitude of 12km (39,400 ft) might result in an equivalent whole-body dose of 2.5 mrems. If the same flight goes over the pole during a time of more intense solar activity, the dose equivalent might be 10 mrems.
>
> (CACAQ 1986: 122–3)

Frequent flyers who log at least 100,000 miles a year in the air should have their exposure doses monitored regularly.

Table 10.2 Comparison of transport radiation exposure

Type of aircraft	Cruise time (hours)*	Dose rate (mREM hr)[†]	Total dose (mREM)
Subsonic (707, 747, etc)	8.4	0.50	4.2
Supersonic (Concorde)	3.8	0.98	3.7

Source: DeHart 1985
Notes: *Cruise range equals 8000 km/2439 miles.
[†] Flight altitude equals 13,300/43,635 ft between 30° and 60° north latitude.

If there are passengers at risk, the most obvious group is that of pregnant women.

Both the National Council on Radiation Protection and Measurements and the International Commission on Radiological Protection (I.C.R.P) recommend that exposure of the fetus during the entire gestation period from occupational exposures of the expectant mother not exceed 0.5 rem. Stewart and co-workers, MacMahon, and MacMahon and Hutchinson have determined that fetuses are at high risk. They showed that all types of childhood cancer and leukemia are doubled by extremely small doses of radiation.

(CACAQ 1986: 129)

Among the many differences between the HVAC system on the ground and the ECS on board is an unusual one that concerns the distribution of air. The ventilation rate per occupant is not uniform and appears to be at least two to three times higher in the First and Business Classes than in the Economy Class (CACAQ 1986: 43). But what should not be forgotten is that the ECS is distinguished by a unique and critical factor, the low air pressure. It is this that places aviation on a different scale from forms of surface transport. The outside air is hostile and if there is a leak or, worse, should a window be lost, 'we're in the soup', to quote that pioneer of pressurization, Wellwood Beall (Solberg 1979: 183) The threat, of course, comes from the ever-present hypoxia which, if severe, can strike like an unseen assassin. For that reason, we cannot take air travel for granted.

Before I proceed further, I should disabuse some incredulous readers of the notion that such incidents do not occur. They do. In the USA, for example, there were 355 that involved depressurization in commercial aircraft over the period of 1974–83 (CACAQ 1986: 107), while the USAF reported 540 in a 6-year period. (Rayman and McNaughton 1983: 357). Of the former, 43 per cent were categorized as significant, i.e. 'cabin pressure decreased to an equivalent altitude above 14,000 ft, passenger masks were deployed, or an injury resulted'. But the figures alone are insufficient and to have any comprehension of what they represent we must look at actual cases.

There are three I propose to use. The first two illustrate what is meant by a slow decompression and the third is a classic case of a rapid decompression or, as it is also termed, explosive decompression. Both events as they are re-enacted resemble scenes from a silent movie in which comedians and straight men are featured. The first starts with the take-off of a jet aircraft from Bangkok in 1963 when it was still

125

proper to designate an airline Qantas Empire Airways, and when flight attendants were content to be called stewards and stewardesses. An explanation of emergency procedures is given and all the way through passengers, who are unaware of the realities of the situation, either yawn or feign interest.

The drama unfolds at 38,000 ft in the cockpit, on the commencement of descent into Singapore, when the captain and flight engineer notice a pressure effect on their ear-drums. The captain checks the instrument for cabin altitude to discover it has risen to 8,000 ft from 6,500 ft and continues to surge at 2,000 ft a minute. When the critical level of 10,000 ft is reached, the warning light flashes and the horn sounds. Within 3 to 5 seconds, the flight crew have donned their oxygen masks and the descent rate is increased to 4,000 ft a minute.

If we switch the scene, we find that at the same time antics have begun in the cabin. A mask drops from the ceiling of the forward toilet while it is occupied by a steward. He attempts to re-stow it. A second steward stares in wonderment as rows of masks pop out above seats in the Economy Class. But the incident does not trigger him into action. On the contrary, he is under the impression that they were actuated by a malfunction. When he scans passengers in the section for confirmation, no one appears upset or inconvenienced. (Among them is an 8-months-pregnant woman to whom he had just administered oxygen from a portable set.) So he returns to the galley to secure bottles of liquor that tilt due to the steep angle of the aircraft. What happens next is strange, for a third steward spots him as he lifts the ice bucket, inverts it and bites the bar key. Then he sits on the floor. His brain, however, interprets this behaviour in another way – he is conscious of his lack of co-ordination as he knocks over the ice bucket, and several bottles, and proceeds to look for the bar key. He feels nauseous too and while on the floor has the presence of mind to use the portable oxygen.

In the cockpit, the crisis is still on as the cabin altitude races up to 18,000 ft, at which point it coincides with the actual altitude. The captain reduces the rate of descent to 2,000 ft a minute, and still further to 800 ft a minute when 14,000 ft is reached.

The chief steward also has his moment, for when the cabin altitude reaches 18,000 ft, he relinquishes the oxygen mask and walks unaided in the thin air of the Economy Class. However, he does admit to a slight breathlessness and ear pressure just before the masks appeared.

And what of the antics of passengers, one may ask? The steward who had earlier misjudged the situation in the toilet reported that of those he checked in the First Class, a number were obstructive - '[they] told him they did not feel the need to use a mask and in fact did not do so'. (He himself took oxygen from spare masks as he passed through because 'he felt light headed and slightly breathless'.) Other than that, there is no reference to the passengers except in a general sense: 'Some were rather amused, others thought it an interesting experience.' Attitudes, no doubt, that would have provoked laughter from an audience for it is not dissimilar to the cartoon where someone sticks their head into the open jaws of a lion, unaware of the danger. But it is one thing for the cabin crew who have undergone high-altitude training - with lectures, films, and exposure in decompression chambers - to act in a desultory way and quite another for air travellers without a basic knowledge of aviation medicine. Until such time as this is rectified, they are always destined to play the role of stooges.

The example of the slow decompression I have given is based on an account by E.H. Anderson, Director of Medical Services of the airline concerned, and not by an independent aviation authority (Anderson 1964: 33-5). In addition, there are some essential facts that should be mentioned. The investigation failed to identify the cause of the loss of cabin pressure, but it is believed to be connected with an outflow valve. 'The total time spent above 14,000 ft was four minutes and above 10,000 ft eleven minutes.' (However, it is not clear whether the time spent above 10,000 ft is 15 or 11 minutes.) What this represents is that those passengers without masks were exposed to the compensatory as well as the disturbance phase of hypoxia (see Chapter 4, p. 29).

In essence, the decrease in partial pressure of oxygen and the fall in arterial blood saturation would force passengers' whole bodies to respond. As they sat in the seats, within minutes their breathing would become faster and deeper - a fact that was noted by the stewards. Both the circulation and pulse rates would have increased, because of the rise in volume of blood pumped by the heart, and there would be an increase in blood pressure. (According to Dhenin's textbook, the heart rate of a subject at rest increases by 10-15 per cent at 15,000 ft and 20-25 per cent at 20,000 ft while the increase in pulmonary ventilation increases by 20-50 per cent at 18,000 ft and 40-60 per cent at 22,000 ft (Dhenin 1978: 70-1). Therefore, it should be obvious to anyone with cardiovascular disease how such a situation would affect them.) But as we are aware, the cabin altitude reached a high of 18,000 ft and as a result the hypoxia progressed into its disturbance phase. Here, the compensatory measures no longer suffice to maintain an adequate supply of oxygen to the tissues, and the individual experiences sleepiness, fatigue, lassitude, dizziness, headache, breathlessness, and an unjustified sense of wellbeing that resembles alcohol intoxication. (The latter symptom was exhibited by some passengers who appeared to be amused by the event.) Also there is an impairment in the critical faculties and muscle co-ordination – attributes which the second steward demonstrated in an admirable fashion in his bar scene.

Although there is little doubt that these phases occurred, no reference is made to them in Anderson's account. When the effect on passengers is mentioned, it would appear to be somewhat modified. 'The only complaint or ill effect noted was mild ear discomfort. Several children cried, apparently with pain in the ears.' If a medical examination had been carried out on the passengers after the aircraft had landed, perhaps some useful information would have emerged.

In another incident of slow decompression, which involved a British Caledonian flight from Spain (Santiago) to the UK in 1978, an examination of the passengers was carried out at the captain's request. The case, I must explain, is unusual inasmuch as I have been able to collate details from several sources. It first came to my attention at a Royal Aeronautical Society symposium on aviation medicine training of aircrews on 27 June 1985 when Captain R.F. Jones of British Caledonian gave a talk on 'Lessons from a loss of cabin pressure in flight'.

There were 179 Spanish workers on board – the aircraft was a charter – and the first indication of a problem came when the chief steward opened the door onto the flight deck, some 2 to 3 minutes into the cruise at 31,000 ft. As he entered with glasses of water on a tray, he noticed that the red warning light flashed, and he withdrew. (In such circumstances, he felt that his presence would be superfluous.) No sooner had he closed the door and faced the cabin area, than he discovered a stewardess slumped in the gangway, unconscious. At that moment, a passenger, who had seen her fall and in a gallant gesture had come to the rescue, also collapsed after a few steps.

On the flight deck the co-pilot, who was at the controls, and the captain continued in their attempt to rectify the rise in cabin altitude which a short while previously had registered 12,000 ft. However, they had become so engrossed in the emergency that they had neglected to don their masks earlier; they did this now. It was just as well as the cabin altitude at some stage breached the critical level of hypoxia, 20,000 ft.

Among the cabin crew and passengers there were further repercussions. Dizziness and headaches were experienced and another stewardess lost consciousness. Oxygen, that instant remedy for hypoxia, was much in evidence, in the form of both portable bottles and overhead masks. And if there was no pandemonium, it was due to the euphoric atmosphere that accompanies such occasions, for signs of panic were present. Six people, who included trained cabin staff, suffered from enuresis or, as Captain Jones was to put it, 'urinated themselves'. Perhaps the Spanish passengers would have been more alarmed had they been better able to communicate with the crew or had a better education. (Monge and Monge, pioneers of high-altitude physiology, found that 'mental symptoms are usually mild and easier to detect in people of higher education' (Balfour Slonin 1974: 372).)

As the decompression occurred in a busy air corridor, the pilot could not start a descent until clearance was obtained from the air traffic control (ATC) in Madrid and in France. Once granted, the BAC 1–11 dropped altitude from 31,000 ft to 15,000 ft in 3 minutes 50 seconds, where it remained for 10 minutes. It was during this period that pressurization was reinstated. Thereafter, the aircraft climbed to 25,000 ft and continued to Gatwick Airport.

What Captain Jones did not elaborate on was the welfare of the passengers. There were the usual ear problems and that was about it. I, of course, wanted more information and at the same time was curious to know how such a reportable incident was processed by the system. So I drove down from London to the Civil Aviation Authority at Redhill, Surrey, to see what I could find at the Safety and Data Unit. I was given a photocopy of the supplementary report that had been extracted from the airline's Air Safety Review in November 1978.

There were two references to the subject, or rather terse summaries, one of the events on board and the other of those on the ground. 'Some cabin staff and passengers became anoxic but after using oxygen the cabin staff assisted passengers using the cabin oxygen ring-main plus portable oxygen bottles' (CAA 1978a) How easy it is to dismiss the episode which for at least six people will be remembered for the rest of their lives. (On the other hand, if the statement was taken at face value, it would appear that some individuals died because the use of 'anoxic' has that implication.) The second reference had promise. 'After landing the cabin staff reported to the medical centre and the passengers were checked and cleared for further travel by a nursing sister.' I was interested in particular in the condition of the three – no mention is made of others – who had been unconscious through acute hypoxia. In physiological terms, 'unconsciousness occurs as the result of a gross lowering of the alveolar oxygen tension' (Dhenin 1978: 74). About 20 per cent of individuals are exceptions as the 'immediate cause . . . is failure of cerebral blood flow due to a sudden gross fall of arterial blood pressure'. There are personal variations, too, as in some cases it can happen at altitudes as low as 16,000 ft or as high as 24,000 ft (Dhenin 1978: 78).

When I asked for further documents on the incident, which was now distinguished by a database, no. 78/02472B, I was handed the captain's report and the authority's supplementary report on pressurization failure. (Photocopies of these were not provided so I had to make my own notes.) It would appear that the main cause was an open discharge valve. And if there was any blame to be apportioned, it was to the flight crew who 'kept the aircraft at FL 310 [31,000 ft] while a period of trouble-shooting was carried out. Had an emergency descent been initiated at once the effects of the incident would have been minimised'(CAA 1978a). An unusual fact which emerged was that nicotine contamination was a causal factor of the malfunction.

If I had expected to find a detailed account of the medical examination of passengers, I would have been disappointed. The only source was the captain's report which comes second-hand.

My impression was that of (roughly) a third of the passengers who had been most affected, only two or three were still affected, 'still very whoozy' and were still being given the odd whiff of oxygen.

(CAA 1978b: para. 5)

Taxied in for stand 3, arriving approx 1315. No medical staff to meet us and I contacted Flight Watch again to chase. I was told that the sister arrived at 1345. I asked the steward to have sister see me before she left. . . . Sister said that she had been asked to come only about ten minutes ago, that she had checked all the passengers. She thought most of them had no residual effects, [though] two or three still retained some after-effects. All of them had said they had felt some pain and/or discomfort around the ears, but her own opinion was that they wouldn't have mentioned it if she hadn't asked, and that they were all fit and free to travel.

(CAA 1978b: para 6)

One gets the impression that the sister was a model of efficiency, but whether she could have discharged her duties in such a simple manner and so short a time, with an aviation medical specialist and Spanish interpreter present, is another matter.

If a slow decompression announces itself in silence then a rapid decompression makes its presence known with a bang. When that happens, we have the worst situation in aviation next to a crash because it denotes a fracture of the pressure vessel, the aircraft. Inside air rushes out, as it would from a deflated balloon, in an attempt to equalize the pressure with the hostile atmosphere outside. In the classic example that occurred on board a National Airline's DC10 at 39,000 ft near Albuquerque, New Mexico, on 3 November 1973, the depressurization sounded like a loud explosion and the passenger in seat 17H was ejected through a cabin window.

Before we examine the comprehensive National Transportation Safety Board report (NTSB 1975) on the accident, which prompted several behavioural studies on crew and naïve subjects under such conditions (Busby et al. 1976), we should take a brief look at some earlier work on the subject. There are not many cases to go on because the event is uncommon. But when it occurs, inadequate medical examinations are carried out on passengers and as a result medical problems are not reported. Those studies that do exist are from intrepid self-experimenters and military pilots. Dr T. Benzinger, who was one of the German scientists to do research for the Luftwaffe on high-altitude flights, conducted courses for pilots not only in the Alps where they skied to increase their altitude fitness, but in the decompression chamber. In an interview that was featured in *Man in Flight* (Engle and Lott 1979), he spoke of the first experiments in which he himself was the subject. The results

> provided the physiological scientific basis for pressurized cabins in military aircraft for use in combat, and for the development of the pressure suits. The explosive decompression of cockpits or suits is the most vital problem of space operations. No other problem kills instantly. The suit is the life of man in space.
>
> Explosive decompression kills in two ways – by lack of oxygen so super-acute that it is unparalled by any other causes of anoxia except cyanide poisoning; and by air embolism which occurs when the airways are not fully open during the explosive decompression.
>
> (Engle and Lott 1979: 71)

There were accidents at Rechlin in the Junkers altitude chamber due to lung over-expansions through closed vocal chords. These were not serious for his healthy colleagues but they were for those with 'old, inactive calcified remnants of tuberculosis'. Helmut Kind died while Dr Hornberger developed pulmonary tuberculosis and Dr Doring was crippled.

Other serious cases include strokes or apoplexy, and pneumomediastinum; a fatal one of widespread air embolism (where bubbles of air block the passage of blood), lung rupture, and pneumothorax occurred because the victim is believed to have held his breath (Gillies 1965: 202). There is also the unfortunate example of the balloonist who suffered permanent brain damage in an accident and died 4 months later (see p. 53).

In the National Airline's incident, which involved 112 passengers and 12 crew members, 5 people lost consciousness and 24 were treated for ear problems, minor abrasions, and smoke inhalation. At about 1640 hours on the day of the flight, fragments of an engine penetrated the fuselage and within 6 seconds after the explosion, the aircraft descended at the rate of 5,000 ft a minute from 39,000 ft. But in view of the large hole created by the open window, the cabin altitude surged to 34,000 ft in 26 seconds. The decompression profile devised later for the NTSB report showed that the

> occupants were exposed to altitudes above 30,000 ft for about one minute and to altitudes above 25,000 ft for more than two minutes. Though the average time of useful consciousness is about 60 sec at 30,000 ft for persons without supplemental oxygen and less than two minutes at 25,000 ft, the lack of physical activity could explain why more hypoxia symptoms were not encountered by more passengers.
>
> (NTSB 1975: 33)

Some 5 minutes later, the flight was cleared to descend to 8,000 ft, and at 1659 hours the aircraft landed.

As the critical phase of hypoxia was reached, a run-through of those 5 minutes – although my calculations, based on the same data, indicate at least 6 minutes – should be given. The first thing to happen after the bang was that a male passenger was sucked through the window with such force that the fastened seatbelt could not prevent the ejection. (His body was never found in spite of a computer analysis of the possible trajectories.) At the same time, blue–grey smoke appeared and collected near the back of the cabin. There was a delay of 3 minutes in the presentation of oxygen masks in both the forward and the rear sections, while some on the left side of the rear did not drop at all. Three of the oxygen generators fell from their mountings onto the seats and on operation they became so hot that they scorched the upholstery. The portable oxygen canisters also proved to be problematic because they took time to assemble.

If parts of the life-saving equipment failed to perform in the emergency, there is little excuse for the manufacturers; if the same could be said of the passengers, they had every excuse because they were confronted by a combination of trials: the shock of the explosive decompression, the presence of smoke, the oxygen lack which was announced by masks that popped from the ceiling and by people who fell unconscious, the steep angle of descent and, later, the instructions on the bracing position for an emergency landing. In the report, there is evidence of confusion:

> Some of the passengers reported that they did not know how to use the equipment. Some removed the mask from the compartment door, and leaned forward toward the mask, rather than pulling the masks toward them. This prevented the lanyard from being pulled, and consequently the unit was not activated. Other passengers stopped using the masks, either because they could not discern oxygen flow or the reservoir bags did not inflate, or both, which caused them to believe that the equipment was defective.
>
> (NTSB 1975: 13)

Such behavioural responses and the deficient oxygen equipment would have made a proportion of the passengers vulnerable to acute hypoxia for over 3 minutes. And what if 10 per cent of those already suffered from heart, lung, or circulatory diseases? When you turn to the report for answers, the first impression is that you will find them in the contents under either one of two headings: 1.2 'Injuries to persons', and 1.13 'Medical and pathological information'. The first consists of a table in which injuries to crew and passengers are listed. Four crew and twenty passengers incurred non-fatal injuries and, as is known, there was one fatality among the passengers. In the case of the second, it is best to quote the two paragraphs of which it is comprised for the facts speak for themselves.

> Five persons reported that they became unconscious after the decompression. Three of the five were standing and were active.

The remaining two were seated in the lower galley area and lost consciousness when they stood up to obtain supplemental oxygen.

Twenty passengers and four crewmembers were examined at the military hospital at Kirtland Air Force Base. Ten persons were treated for smoke inhalation, and ten were treated for barotrauma.

(NTSB 1975: 12)

And that would appear to be that. Why only 17 per cent of the passengers were examined; whether any aviation medical specialists were present and what medical information was obtained; or whether there were any follow-ups, are questions that seem to be irrelevant. Again, as is the custom, the human beings get short shrift in such reports – this one runs to fifty-five pages – while the experts focus on the aircraft. Precedence was given to the scrutiny of 'the electronic interrelationship between the auto-throttle system and the associated N_1 tachometers' at the public hearing, and not the determination of which passengers could have had adverse effects because of their case histories (NTSB 1975: 2).

But there is more than meets the eye in this rapid decompression. I learned from a separate source, which was published a decade later, that the worst outcome of hypoxia had occurred in one instance. Dr J. Robert Dille reports in DeHart's textbook that 'one attendant reportedly suffered permanent neurologic damage' (DeHart 1985: 751). It makes one wonder what other conditions developed post-flight among those unfortunate passengers and aircrew. (There are, of course, some effects that have not been mentioned here but are discussed in Chapters 4, 5, and 6.) Gas expansion can cause overextension of the lungs which may result in the tearing of tissue and gas bubble embolism. It can also produce pain in the middle ear, in the sinuses, and in the stomach and intestines. Decompression sickness is another hazard that can occur after prolonged exposure – more than 5–10 minutes as is stated in Dhenin (Dhenin 1978: 174) – to altitudes above 28,000 ft. And an aspect that can be overlooked in a depressurization is the cold air, in the region of -44.4 °C at 30,000 ft, that can enter the cabin.

So it would seem that to wear a spacesuit on a conventional flight is not at all a bad idea. If anything, it would offer the passengers some measure of protection for their health where up to now there has been none. The airlines are protected by the Warsaw Convention, inasmuch as there is an international air agreement for the carriage of people in pressurized cabins. The airline pilots, too, are protected through their biannual medical examinations without which they cannot hold a licence. It is only the public, in particular the frequent business and the unhealthy travellers, who are left in a vulnerable position as a consequence of a decision made over 50 years ago to protect the air transportation industry still in its infancy. A virtual ban on acknowledging problems encountered at high altitude or in stratosphere flying was imposed by the US Bureau of Air Commerce while flight surgeons conducted a 'quiet survey among the medical profession'. It would appear that no one ever lifted the restriction in spite of the BAC's demise, and it has since set a precedent. The time has come to take the initiative and one way is to gain a basic knowledge of aviation medicine.

Chapter Eleven

THE CURSE OF ICARUS: AVIATION OR AEROSPACE MEDICINE

Aviation, or aerospace, medicine is a curate's egg. The good part is the maintenance of high standards of performance in astronauts, military and airline pilots and, indeed, an impressive body of work on physiology, psychology, and health and clinical aspects has accumulated the past half century to fulfil the purpose. The bad part is that none of it has been applied to the hundreds of millions of air travellers, in spite of the fact that the need is just as great. A larger proportion of older people fly today than ever before – 9 per cent of passengers are over 65 in the USA – and the frequent flyers – some 5 per cent of US passengers take more than ten trips a year – tend to be businessmen whose vocations depend on such a mode of transport (CACAQ 1986: 24).

If we are to make a start here, we should at least establish the extent of the need. But this is difficult for it means we have to resort to data and figures which are in short supply. I have spent hours in public and specialist libraries and even contacted peripheral bodies such as the Institute of Alcohol Abuse (where, in turn, I was solicited for statistics) and each time came away with little. There was one occasion, however, at a disused airbase in a remote part of England, when the pursuit paid off. I was provided with information from two separate sources in a single day. No cloak-and-dagger work was involved; I attended a seminar on 27 June 1985 at RAF North Luffenham, Oakham, Leicestershire when some airline officials chose to enlighten their peers on such topics as 'the need and methods of aviation medicine training' in commercial operations. Both of the speakers, Dr R.B. Maclaren and Miss Jean Cowan, were from British Airways.

Dr Maclaren reported on the year 1984/5 in which 22 million passengers were carried by BA. The risk of medical incidents of any sort was 1 in every 13,000, while for notified invalids (a wide category that includes the handicapped as well as those with serious and chronic conditions) it increased to 1 in every 350. Fourteen deaths occurred on aircraft and included two people who failed to be roused after the movie. There were ten unscheduled landings and seven pressurization failures, of which three were severe enough to warrant the use of oxygen systems. Insights into the role of aviation medicine in airlines were given. In most cases, the specialism was equated with safety procedures, but in some cases it was defined either as first aid or as a prophylactic against aircraft diversions.

Miss Cowan's main contribution was to demonstrate how rigorous BA's training methods were. For example, new entrants received a mixture of video films, formal lessons, practice sessions, discussions, health education, and *tests*. (The emphasis derives from the transcript of her talk.) The audience was informed that role-playing was included aboard a mock-up of the fuselage; this did not present problems as most of the cabin crew were extroverts. (I was later to find out that only 2 days out of the 6-week course were allocated to first aid and basic medicine.) In terms of new data, it was revealed that approximately 3,000 medical incidents occurred on BA's aircraft each year. An observation was offered, too, on an important problem encountered in-flight. 'It's quite upsetting having a death on an aircraft, particularly on a jumbo. Where do you put the body?'

Here then are the bare bones of the lectures – tantamount to an official statement that all is not well in the airways albeit on a minor scale. We can conclude that, in the case of BA, there are some eight medical incidents a day, at least one death a month, and the medical certificate of fitness for air travel (MEDIF form) issued to invalids or unfit passengers by their GP or the airline medical services is no safeguard against illness in-flight – in fact the risk is greater. (I should mention that there appears to be a discrepancy between Miss Cowan's and Dr Maclaren's figures. He gives an attack rate of 1 in 13,000 passengers, which represents 1,692 incidents per annum or 4.6 a day.)

But how much significance can we place on the statistics? We already know (see Chapter 1, 'The Barrier of Silence') that there are deficiencies in the reporting systems. A recent review has shown that 40 per cent of a voyage report sample described administrative and equipment difficulties rather than passengers' illnesses (Harrex 1985: 19). Then there is the lack of data on flight incidents. It would appear that the collection of data is a burden to airlines, and in BA's example they cut the annual load of 65,000 notified invalid cases in the mid-1980s to a manageable 12,000 per annum and later to 10,000 per annum. 'In the old days, I think we interfered too much,' said Dr James Dunlop of the BA Medical Service (BAMS). 'I think our 65,000 cases was probably 40,000 too many because we were looking at people who didn't have a problem. . . . Now we clear something in the region of 12,000 but they are genuine medical cases' (Dunlop 1987). That may be a plausible reason, but does it take into account both the increase in passenger traffic since then and the growth in the leisure sector, which now comprises 80 per cent plus of air travellers? (Green 1986). Another peculiarity is demonstrated in the selection of statistics. There appears to be an inclination to exclude notified invalids (Fairhurst 1976: 230) and cabin crew (Harrex 1985: 28) from ordinary passengers when reporting in-flight incidents and the result is that lower figures are obtained.

Dr Geoffrey Bennett is the Chief Medical Officer at the CAA; as no one else has served the two mistresses of flying and aviation medicine in the UK as he has, I approached him for some answers. He was trained as a pilot in the RAF and as a doctor at Oxford. Later, he joined BOAC as a part-time doctor and part-time pilot. In 1964, he was invited to go to what was then the Ministry of Aviation. When the CAA was born, he had to decide whether to go there or to the Ministry of Defence. It was a simple decision. 'I was flying mostly civil aeroplanes at the time,' he explained, 'so I elected to come to the CAA and I stayed with them' (Bennett 1986).

What is apparent when you meet him is that he thinks things through to a coherent and balanced conclusion – an attribute one would associate with the study of Greats rather than with medicine. On one occasion when I pressed him for some details of his undergraduate life, he broke through his natural reserve and related the only anecdote he had. 'I had a pathology scholarship at Oxford and when I went to see my tutor after I got it, to thank him for his efforts, he said, "Don't think you were so good, Bennett, it's just that the others were so bloody awful"!'

We talked about the dual role of the flying doctor. How important it is for a proportion of doctors to fly themselves – to be exposed to the problems first-hand – and to be reminded that they are there as a supporting service like an engineer because quite often they have a degree of self-importance? 'Most of the problems in aviation now are people orientated rather than physiologically orientated. The physiological problems have been solved more or less; the problems that remain are mostly problems with people.'

The office in which we sat was in the round tower, the medical block of the CAA in Kingsway, London. It was large with ample light, because the windows reached from the floor to the ceiling, and there was a minimum of office furniture. Dr Bennett's desk was clear except for a plaque that read: 'THOSE WHO THINK YOU KNOW EVERYTHING ARE ANNOYING TO THOSE OF US WHO DO'. Appropriate perhaps, I thought, to what had been said. When I ran out of ink on my first visit, he produced a ballpoint fashioned out of a plastic clyster from an enema-apparatus.

Early in his career, he was involved in research on a pilot's reactions and performance after decompression (Bennett 1961: 134–6) and on ozone contamination of high-altitude aircraft cabins (Bennett 1962: 969). He headed the Aeromedical Group on the British side in the Anglo-French Concorde project, a participation that resulted in the paper, 'Human factors in the Concorde SST' (Bennett 1965: 1094).

At the end of the interview, I enquired about the general state of health of people who fly. 'A number of estimations have been made and something like 10 per cent of the average passenger load are not totally fit. And that's the extent of the problem!' Several months later when we talked again, on 17 June 1986, he elaborated on the matter. Surveys had been done by the airlines themselves, he told me, whenever there was an opportunity. 'They've either done a survey of passengers or when they were medically examined after an accident . . . in the medical department. It's that sort of survey which is opportunistic and which produced the figure I take of 10 per cent.' When I enquired of Professor Stanley R. Mohler of Wright State University and past President of Aerospace Medical Association about the USA, he confirmed that the same figure would apply (Mohler 1988).

In the light of the current lack of information on public health in the air, which can also be interpreted as there being no problem, such a statistic may come as a shock. The implication is that 2.2 million passengers out of 22 million per annum who flew with BA, for example, were unfit to some degree or other. If you study figures on population, you will find that the percentage of pensionable age (65 and over for males and 60 and over for females) is 17 per cent in the UK, 16 per cent in the EC, and 14 per cent in the USA (DHSS 1984), and if a cross-section of the population travels by air, the 10 per cent figure of those who are not fit would appear to be quite reasonable. Indeed, I have since come across other projections like that of *World Medicine* where it was stated that '12% of all airline passengers are unfit in one way or another' (Wright 1983: 31).

To show who is fit to fly in broad terms has never been a problem. For doctors, there have been the aviation and aerospace textbooks, the large number of papers in medical and specialist journals, and the guidelines issued by airline medical services. However, as such material is not available to passengers, two health checklists are included in Chapter 12 of this book. It should be emphasized that these are for general information only and any specific problems should be declared on a MEDIF or INCAD form by your GP before being submitted to the airline's medical services for assessment, and a second opinion should be got from an aviation medical specialist (a D.Av.Med.) as a medical certificate is no guarantee against the occurrence of an in-flight medical emergency. In fact, the risk is higher amongst notified passengers.

As we are at least aware of the degree and nature of unfitness to fly, we should also explore the terrain of the specialism. It extends into two environments, the air, or space, and the ground, and includes in-flight medical incidents as well as pre-flight and the unfamiliar post-flight problems.

We have all experienced the stressful confines of the airport where multiple stressors ensure a good flow of adrenalin, a stress hormone. If anything, its secretion is stimulated by the increase in crowdedness and it would appear that repeated exposure to such places or situations does not always reduce the adrenalin output (Mills 1985: 642–50). For some, it may result in hyperventilation, anxiety, or high blood pressure, and perhaps a visit to the medical unit. A few may even have a heart attack before take-off. In general, it is the older people who are vulnerable. Dr Robert Lidell, a flying doctor from Dan-Air, spoke to me about his experience. 'The reasons we have less problems on aeroplanes than we should is because they all get "preselected" in the terminals' (Liddell 1987). In a study that involved Minneapolis/St Paul International Airport which has an annual passenger turnover of some 9 million, 471 medical runs were carried out by the emergency medical services and six deaths resulted from the eight cardiac arrests (Jetzer *et al.* 1986: 459–61).

But what happens later in that pressure vessel, the aircraft? For the captain and co-pilot, their heart rate – a good indicator of mental and physical stress – reaches a high level on take-off and is highest on landing (Kakimoto *et al.* 1988: 511–16). With passive flyers, on the other hand, although the interior is a well-known feature, the medical incidents encountered are not. In part, this is due to the fact that the overall design obscures visibility and that the immobile passenger is preoccupied with distractions for the period of the flight. Another element, which cannot be ignored, is the general ignorance of the pressure environment that reduces the oxygen content and at the same time pumps up the body. When passengers feel queasy, dizzy, irritable, or odd, they attribute the symptoms to pre-flight circumstances. (They may have eaten something that upset them, for example.) It is only once the condition appears to be serious that they may report it to the flight attendant. (In such a context, stoicism may be equated with ignorance.)

The question remains, what if the dizziness and abdominal pain were symptoms of the heart's dysfunction? Little could be done in such a case. The cabin crew, the airline's representatives, are not in a position to diagnose and deal with serious illnesses. If there was a doctor on board, the chances are that he would be in the wrong specialty (a psychiatrist, for instance), or that it might be expedient for him not to act the Good Samaritan because of the prospect of a malpractice suit. On the other hand, if the doctor can help, he may find that the medical kit is inadequate – an upgraded first-aid box – or not comprehensive enough. And where is he to treat the patient? With the exception of Air Afrique and UTA, no airlines with long-haul operations have special medical compartments in their aircraft which provide space for isolation, resuscitation, and medical treatment (Harding and Mills 1983: 14). The ultimate alternative in an emergency is to divert to the nearest location with a hospital. It would be negligent, however, not to observe that aviation medicine is a preventive branch of medicine and as such encourages the avoidance of emergencies. The unfit should not travel by air in the first place.

Anecdotes about medical incidents in-flight may be appropriate because they may give some insight into the problem. A good source of these is the correspondence columns of medical journals. Oxygen is thought to be the universal panacea for all illnesses in the air. This is often true, but not always. Dr Richard Jolly recalls a trip on a full New York bound jumbo when an 'American film producer was hyperventilating furiously and the cabin crew worried because the oxygen was making him worse. The use of an airsickness bag in the classic manner provided relief for all concerned as his PCO_2 rose to normal again' (Jolly 1977: 637). A woman doctor, a consultant physician, who responded to a call for help on a BA flight from the Far East to London, 'found a semiconscious man, cold and still sitting upright, oxygen being administered and passengers smoking in the row behind. The crew proffered the doctor their first aid kit – aspirin and Elastoplast. . . . For 14 hours she was virtually on duty . . .' (Lawrie 1981: 320). Dr Hugh Cameron McLaren, a regular flyer, comments that he has spent a good deal of his time with sick passengers and has attended to two episodes of unexplained fainting, a coronary thrombosis, gross emphysema with dyspnoea, and a fishbone in the throat. 'On these occasions the equipment produced has been inadequate and twice there was no oxygen in the labelled cylinders' (Cameron McLaren 1977: 44).

There is an unusual incident that occurred on a flight from Tokyo to Seattle when a young man felt sick, took an antinauseant, 'collapsed, and then, like a zombie, sat upright. His skin was an alarming green but it was warm, there was no rash, his pulse was strong and regular at about 70/min. and his breathing was regular and easy'. The doctor, Howard S. Rubinstein, got him to lie flat and asked for a stethoscope and a blood-pressure cuff.

> To my surprise the flight attendant told me that airlines did not generally carry stethoscopes or cuffs. They did, however, have oxygen, and she wondered if that would do. I said 'no' . . . and wondered how many people who did not need oxygen have vomited into their oxygen masks and then aspirated.
>
> (Rubinstein 1985: 353)

With no history of allergy, heart disease, or diabetes, the patient's condition proved to be an enigma. When the aircraft landed, he was one of the first off and made clear his intention not to consult a doctor.

In the period that I carried out my research, I came across anecdotes, as no doubt readers have. Some of the medical incidents in-flight are a tonsillectomy that haemorrhaged (Rule 1986), a follicle cyst of an ovary that burst (MacGoldrick 1987), the breast implant that leaked (Ryman 1988), the gut that became twisted and gangrenous (Perry 1986), and the nervous breakdown that resulted from frequent jet lag (Perry 1986). There is also the familiar incident when an older passenger, or the one with arteriosclerosis, becomes confused, or 'goes doolally' in aircrew parlance, through cerebral hypoxia, and alcohol appears to potentiate such a condition.

A more general view of both incidents and emergencies is outlined in two surveys. The most recent, 'Inflight medical problems of airline passengers' by Wing Commander Warren K. Harrex of the Royal Australian Air Force, which was published as a thesis for an M.Sc. in Occupational Medicine, is based on BA in 1984/5 and was undertaken to 'evaluate the appropriateness of cabin crew training' (Harrex 1985). The other review, by Stanley R. Mohler, Arnauld Nicogossian, and Robert A. Margulies, appeared as a paper, 'Emergency medicine and the airline passenger' (Mohler *et al.* 1980: 918-22).

The spread of problems from the most to the least common includes gastrointestinal, an unclassified group, cardiovascular, central nervous system, respiratory, psychiatric, musculoskeletal, genito-urinary, eye/ear/nose/throat, endocrine, and skin/allergy (Harrex 1985: 39). The main symptoms that occur are fainting episodes ('in the earlier report [they] were classified as being stress and anxiety related, but in the present study were divided into cardiovascular, central nervous system and unclassified groups . . .' (Harrex 1985: 29), hyperventilation, and chest pains. Another indicator is the medical reasons for flight diversions. Out of the ten over the period of a year, three were infarcs, two collapses (who were given cardiopulmonary resuscitation), two suspected spontaneous pneumothorax, two neurological problems (a cerebral irritation and a case with alternate periods of incoherence and loss of consciousness), and a haemorrhage from a miscarriage (Harrex 1985: 20). There were also in that year ten medical incidents on board the Concorde but no details are given (Harrex 1985: 34).

In terms of in-flight emergencies (accidents are excluded), Stanley Mohler *et al.* record the gamut seen daily on US airlines. The main headings include obstructed airway (asthma), cardiac dysfunction, haemorrhage, hypoxia (decompression and chronic obstructive lung disease), pain (abdominal, barotitis, and barosinusitis), and miscellaneous. Among the latter is alcoholic intoxication, drug overdose, childbirth, miscarriage, motion sickness, insulin shock, diabetic coma, psychiatric problem, epilepsy, stroke, vomiting, anaphylactic shock, food poisoning, and acute infectious illness (Mohler *et al.* 1980: 919).

'Death in the clouds' is the title of an article by Richard Wakeford in which he recalls one of the most harrowing experiences of his life

(Wakeford 1986: 1642–3). It was when a passenger died on a Concorde flight to New York; because of the lack of equipment and the inexperience of the cabin staff, the resuscitation attempt was characterized by an atmosphere of utter helplessness. Mr Wakeford, a psychologist with some skills in cardiac arrest management, participated in the attempt.

> It was messy: the man is incontinent. . . . Unqualified to diagnose death and incompetent to do so, I have nevertheless to decide whether to continue – in which case we all go to some God forsaken spot in eastern Canada – or to stop. I remember the lectures and ward rounds, at which I have been a participant observer. Wasn't lack of pupillary reflex a key sign? There is no reflex, nor any other sign. We can detect no life. We stop. The aircraft bends towards New York.
>
> (Wakeford 1986: 1642–3)

Both the staff and the passengers are grateful, and coffee and brandy is served. 'You do not pay £1,400 to be diverted to Goose Bay.' Such events are not as rare as one would imagine for, in the instance of BA, there are about ten deaths a year. In a recent report, 'In-flight deaths during commercial air travel' by Richard O. Cummins *et al.*, it was concluded that more than half the deaths were due to cardiac problems, and physicians were not present. Some 66 per cent who died were men, aged on average 54 years, and an unusual aspect was that 69 per cent of the deaths occurred among passengers who appeared to be healthy on departure (Cummins *et al.* 1988: 1983–8).

If there is an area of aviation medicine that would appear to have the greatest potential for growth, it is the post-flight stage. Little is known about the after effects of flying because of few follow-ups on passengers. When a survey has been carried out, as was done by Peter Beighton and Peter Richards on cardiovascular patients in 1967, a good result has been obtained (see p. 3). Accessibility is important, and within hours of disembarkation medical examinations can be conducted at hospitals near airports or by family doctors when the passengers are home. As public awareness of the subject increases, passengers will become more alert to post-flight problems.

Two anecdotes that appeared in the *Lancet*'s correspondence columns in response to an editorial on emergencies in the air (*Lancet* 1985: 28) should be mentioned. (They may demonstrate that the long non-stop flights produce more medical problems for both young and old passengers, a fact which is also alluded to by Harrex on several occasions (Harrex 1985).) The first was from Doctors Y. Hart, D.J. Holdstock, and W.A. Lynn, of the Ashford Hospital on the perimeter of Heathrow Airport, who 'see a steady stream of illnesses which have been developed in flight' (Hart *et al*. 1985: 353–4). They remonstrated against the editorial's omission of the fact that 'major manifestation of the illness may not occur until after disembarkation'. Several patients with thromboembolism had presented in this way. There was one with a near-fatal outcome:

> A 39-year-old woman collapsed on leaving a 27 h flight from Kuala Lumpur, Malaysia. She had been previously well apart from symptoms suggestive of mild gastroenteritis immediately before and during the flight; she had no risk factors for coronary artery disease and was not taking oral contraceptives. She required resuscitation in the ambulance. On arrival in casualty she was unconscious and shortly afterwards arrested. After intensive cardiopulmonary resuscitation, she improved, though she was still acidotic; 48 h later she was clinically normal. Subsequent electrocardiographs showed subendocardial ischaemia and cardiac enzymes were elevated. 6 days later a ventilation-perfusion scan at St. Peter's Hospital, Chertsey (Dr. Patrick Robinson) showed evidence of multiple pulmonary emboli, and we assume the major event to have been a large pulmonary embolism.
>
> (Hart *et al*. 1985: 353–4)

When I later spoke to the consultant at the hospital, Dr Holdstock, he revealed that there had been other cases of pulmonary embolism among women after intercontinental flights (Holdstock 1986). One was only in her 20s while another was 45 years old. The latter was 'still taking oral contraceptive pills,' he added, 'which is a risk. She also smoked which doubled the risk of getting pulmonary embolism. She should have been advised by her doctor really before flying.' As passengers are given no advice on prevention, he and his colleagues suggested that they walk the aisles more often than required for calls of nature. Of interest too are recent thrombotic episodes that occurred to two men, a 48-year-old doctor and a surgeon aged 60. Both had no predisposing medical history but were vulnerable to deep vein thrombosis and pulmonary embolism. Post-flight symptoms may appear within hours or weeks of arrival (Cruickshank *et al*. 1988). The second of the anecdotes is one that could be anticipated; it

145

involved elderly air travellers from Finland who went to Sri Lanka on a fortnight's holiday. There were three incidents of cardiac problems and it was fortunate that doctors were on the same tour. A 65-year-old man who had suffered from a myocardial infarction 2 years earlier lost consciousness soon after take-off on the outward bound flight. It was clear to Dr A.H.W. van Assendelft who recounted the incidents that the patient's vasovagal syncope was initiated by mild hypoxia. On the return journey, he was given oxygen and was fine. But a 67-year-old woman had a myocardial infarction a week after her arrival in Sri Lanka. Contrary to the American Medical Association's advice – the condition is a contraindication to air travel within a period of 4 weeks – she returned home with the group. The hospital in Colombo had provided her with a medical kit that contained an infusion set, frusemide, hydrocortisone and adrenalin ampoules, and she had taken a nitroglycerin sublingual tablet before departure. Provision had been made for her to lie across three seats. Dr van Assendelft who attended her felt insecure because he had been informed that, in an event of an emergency, the aircraft would not be able to land because they would be over Soviet and Afghan territory. The patient was referred to a local hospital for a check-up on arrival.

However, the inevitable did happen to another woman of about the same age who had been on their flight. She had a cardiac arrest in the baggage reclaim area and in spite of intensive cardiopulmonary resuscitation – mouth-to-mouth, intubation, and defibrillation – she died. 'It was a depressing end to a vacation', Dr van Assendelft noted (van Assendelft 1985: 648).

An account of such post-flight problems would be incomplete without a mention of an analysis undertaken by a New Zealand doctor, L.F. Johnson, of 455 consultations given to visitors in Auckland, within 48 hours of either arrival or departure (Johnson 1985: 62–7). The majority were from long-haul flights, and it would appear that the serious or life-threatening illnesses, some 16 per cent, were considerable in comparison to the 1 per cent encountered in residential general practice.

Nearly 4% of consultations resulted in hospital admission and there were three deaths (0.65%): one in a hotel room, and two within 30 minutes of hospital admission. These cases were a ruptured aortic aneurysm, cholecystitis with common duct stone and septic shock, and a myocardial infarct in a patient who presented with back pain.

An incidence of one death in every 150 consultations would be rather alarming in general practice.

(Johnson 1985: 66)

The fact that people's lives are still cursed, so to speak, because of general ignorance of aviation medicine is indefensible. Indeed, if it is the case, as expert opinion has indicated, that 10 per cent of the passenger population is unfit to fly – a figure that can be represented in tens of millions on both sides of the Atlantic – then that is sufficient reason for action to be taken and for the specialism to become part of public health. The casualties pre-flight, in-flight, and post-flight have for too long been concealed in national mortality and morbidity statistics.

Chapter Twelve

ARE YOU FIT TO FLY?

HEALTH CHECKLIST 1: ALL PASSENGERS

Allergies (*see* **Colds**)

Aqualung diving (*see* **Scuba diving**)

Cervical smears (*see* **Surgery**)

Children   *Recommendations*: Infants, who have a higher body water content than adults and therefore are more vulnerable to dehydration, should be given small amounts of water at frequent intervals. To assist with pressure changes, infants should be offered a dummy or pacifier, and older children boiled sweets or chewing gum. Newborn infants should not travel before 10–12 days and neither should children with bad colds or problem ears and teeth.

Colds   Any infection that produces catarrh or inflammation in and around the eustachian tubes, the middle ear, or the sinuses can cause severe pain, headache, through the inability to equalize air pressure. The middle ear (otitis media) is most vulnerable and in certain instances can lead to a rupture of the ear-drum, subsequent infection, and possible deafness. Sinuses, too, because of their rigid walls, can present hazards and on occasion rupture. *Recommendations*: Use decongestant sprays or nose drops an hour before descent or a Valsalva manoeuvre during descent. But it is advisable to delay your flight until the condition has cleared.

Colitis   Gas expansion in the intestine and stomach may result in severe discomfort, nausea, or vomiting, when inflammation is present. *Recommendation*: Control through bland diet.

Concorde   All factors on these Health Checklists apply to supersonic aircraft. But because of the high-altitude flights, there are greater concentrations of ozone and levels of radiation. What has also to be taken into account is the seasonal variation in ozone concentrations peaking in the northern hemisphere from February to May and the cycles of sunspot maxima that occur every 11 years or so. *Recommendations*: Hold a handkerchief to your nose for 3 minutes when the aircraft throttles back to begin its descent because the drop in temperature renders the ozone protection system ineffective. Asthmatics may have an attack because of its presence. If you fly often on Concorde, check that your annual dose of radiation does not exceed the ICRP limit for the general public. Women should not fly within the first 3 months of pregnancy because of radiation exposure to the foetus, and never in the period of sunspot maxima.

Decompression   If you hear a loud bang and/or see masks drop from the ceiling, you will know it is an emergency. Breathe oxygen from the mask immediately because of the threat of severe hypoxia. Do not indulge in heroics for inaction may result in brain damage or death. *Recommendations*: Should no mask appear above you, find another over an unoccupied seat or ask a flight attendant for the portable oxygen canister. Untangle the tubing, draw the mask towards you, and place it over nose and mouth. If necessary, tug the lanyard to initiate the supply. Assist any children to do the same, once you have secured your own oxygen supply.

Deep cuts (*see* **Surgery**)

Dehydration   The low relative moisture content in an aircraft causes dryness of the eyes, throat, nose, and skin. Contact lenses tend to dry out. *Recommendations*: Drink about half a pint (240 ml) during the flight. Avoid alcohol, strong tea, or coffee as they produce further dehydration. Use moisturizer for the skin. Wearers of contact lenses should apply lens solution to keep their eyes moist.

Dilation and curettage (D&C)   (*see* **Surgery**)

149

Drugs (*see* **Medication**)

Fear of flying As flight is unnatural to man and few understand the physical principles involved, the fear of flying is inherent to a degree in most people. The first flight can induce apprehension – to be shut in, so far off the ground, is sufficient reason – but with experience such fear can disappear. However, there are some passengers who still tense on take-off and landing, and who may hyperventilate or faint in-flight. Others suffer from aerophobia and may panic at the thought of flying. *Recommendations*: Aerophobics may find desensitization helpful. But before considering any treatment, consult an aviation medical specialist to ensure that the flight environment will not put your health at risk since there may be a physical cause for your anxiety. (See Chapter 8, 'Guts: the fear of flying'.)

Frequent flyers Some passengers spend sufficient time in the air to warrant participation in a preventive medicine programme. Do not expect to work well on board as mild hypoxia affects your efficiency, especially in the assimilation of new tasks or information. Female passengers should anticipate irregularities in their menstrual cycles and exacerbated dysmenorrhea. *Recommendations*: Have an annual medical examination with an aviation medicine specialist. Do not forget to include a radiation exposure check and always drink lots of water to avoid urinary gravel.

Gastritis (*see* **Colitis**)

Hay fever (*see* **Colds**)

Hyperventilation (over-breathing) Most common on long-haul flights when passengers are anxious and the cabin is hot and stuffy. The condition can slowly develop into hypocarbia which in turn can make hypoxia worse. If it is not controlled the breathlessness can be followed by numbness, muscle spasms, and eventually unconsciousness. *Recommendations*: The simple antidote is to breathe into a paper bag or a disconnected oxygen mask. Do not take alcohol in an effort to relax as it only aggravates the hypocarbia.

Infectious diseases *Recommendation:* Out of consideration for other passengers do not travel if you have an infectious disease.

Jet lag (desynchronosis)   Whenever you cross several time-zones, you disrupt some fifty physiological and psychological rhythms in your body. This results in adverse effects on performance and wellbeing for the passenger is afflicted by irritability, stomach upsets, sleep disturbances, disorientation, aches of all sorts, nausea, changes in body temperature and menstrual cycles. *Recommendations*: Pace yourself because you need at least 1 day per time-zone crossed to recover. On board, eat little, drink a lot of water (non-gaseous), and avoid alcohol for the last 6–8 hours of a long-haul flight. Choose to arrive on a weekend if possible and fly west rather than east as recovery time is usually shorter. Although the use of sleeping pills is widespread, exercise caution in taking them during a flight because the cabin pressure can potentiate their effects. Recent research has shown that the fast-acting drug triazolam combined with alcohol may cause memory loss. Unusual remedies include the Argonne Anti-Jet-Lag Diet if you are diet-conscious or Daniele Ryman's After Flight Regulator if you are health-conscious. (See entry under 'Medication', and Chapter 7, 'The jet syndrome'.)

Medication   The effects of drugs may be heightened when you are exposed to the hypoxia of a pressurized cabin and when your biological rhythms are desynchronized through jet lag. In the case of some sleeping pills (hypnotics), there is also risk of amnesia when taken with alcohol. (See 'Jeg lag' entry.) *Recommendations*: Passengers under medication may wish to reduce the dosage in consultation with their doctor. Antihistamines which are found in proprietary medicines for cold cures, hay fever, or urticaria fall into this category and should be avoided during air travel because of their side-effects, e.g. fatigue, drowsiness, gastrointestinal disturbances, and a dry mouth. Epileptics are exceptions inasmuch as the dosage of the medication may have to be increased because hypoxia and over-fatigue can provoke an attack.

Plaster casts   The expansion of trapped gas in plaster may compress limbs. A case of gangrene possibly due to vascular compression and a degree of hypoxia has been recorded after a 7-hour flight. *Recommendations*: Avoid air travel 40 hours after application of plaster cast and consider splitting it for long flights.

Pregnancy   The aircraft cabin is far from an ideal delivery suite.

As its environment may induce labour, expectant mothers near to term should not fly. Complications with premature birth, childbirth, or the newborn infant could arise. There is also the risk of radiation exposure to the foetus which is most vulnerable in the first 3 months of pregnancy. *Recommendation*: Avoid flights up to the 12th week and then after the 34–35th weeks for long-haul and after the 36th for short-haul. It is important to consult your gynaecologist on the likelihood of a miscarriage.

Scuba diving If you have used an aqualung 2–3 hours before your intended departure, do not fly. Otherwise you may suffer from decompression sickness. *Recommendations*: Allow 12 hours between your last dive and your departure. When a depth of 30 ft has been exceeded, allow at least 24 hours.

Sickle-cell disease Hypoxia seems to provoke a crisis in people with sickle-cell haemoglobin C disease and sickle-cell beta-thalassaemia. *Recommendation*: Avoid air travel.

Sinusitis (*see* **Colds**)

Smoking As carbon monoxide in tobacco smoke combines with haemoglobin at the expense of oxygen, it reduces your oxygen intake and makes you more hypoxic. There is also the irritation to the eyes, nose, and throat that environmental tobacco smoke causes. *Recommendation*: For your own health and out of consideration for others, it is best not to smoke on board.

Stress in the flight environment
Airports The ground stress is significant for there are crowds, queues, check-ins, immigration controls, security checks, long distances, and delays. In addition to these stressors, most passengers are loaded with personal luggage. The unfortunate part is that one cannot become immune to such places because it would appear that adrenalin – the stress hormone – is often stimulated by an increase in crowdedness. *Recommendations*: Try to arrive early for your flight and take along some work or a book in order to be occupied if there is a delay. In the case of elderly passengers or those with serious conditions such as angina, notify airline staff of your disability so as to reduce stress of queues, etc. Also carry minimal

hand luggage and avoid static exercise, e.g. standing in queues.
Aircraft The cabin is a stressful area particularly on long international flights. This is due to two primary problems: hypoxia – a 25 per cent oxygen lack (to 8,000 ft) – and gas expansion – some 35 per cent increase in volume (to 8,000 ft). Also there is the presence of pollutants such as tobacco smoke, carbon dioxide, ozone, carbon monoxide and biologic aerosols, cosmic radiation, dehydration, and the fact that everyone is crowded in a confined space. *Recommendations*: Relax. Try to sleep. Do regular walks (hourly), leg exercises, and stand on your toes.

Surgery Whenever the skin is cut or scraped open, air is introduced into the wound. It needs time to be reabsorbed otherwise, if one flies too soon, trapped air will expand and cause a haemorrhage. Included in this category are appendicectomy, tonsillectomy, abortion, and other simple operations. *Recommendations*: Allow at least 10 days before air travel. For major operations, check with an aviation medicine specialist and the airline medical services department.

Swollen feet and ankles (the deckchair syndrome) If you suffer from cardiac insufficiency or have thrombotic or venous disease such as phlebitis or varicose veins, it is important to limit this postural swelling because of the risk of pulmonary embolism. *Recommendations*: To prevent the condition, rest your feet on your hand luggage so that the thighs are lifted from the edge of seat. If possible choose an aisle seat or one at the exit which has more leg-room. Walk around when you can. Wear support hose if you have varicose veins.

Teeth (aerodontalgia) Toothache may be caused on ascent by the expansion of trapped gas in defective fillings, decayed teeth, or apical abscesses. *Recommendation*: If you have any problems with your teeth, see your dentist before you fly.

Tonsilitis (*see* **Colds**)

Women If you are on the contraceptive pill, there is some risk of thrombosis or pulmonary embolism from the prolonged immobility of international flights. The risk could be doubled if you also smoke. Intra-uterine devices can become ectopic or displaced. *Recommendations*: Exercise your leg muscles frequently. Rest your feet on your hand luggage so that the thighs are lifted from the edge of the seat. Check with your gynaecologist that the IUD is still in place. (See entry under 'Frequent flyers'.)

HEALTH CHECKLIST 2: UNFIT PASSENGERS

Criteria In general, an unfit passenger is anyone who has a disease that impairs the heart's output, the lungs' ability to oxygenate the blood, the flow of blood through the circulatory system, the blood's oxygen-carrying capacity, or has blood that might clot readily.

HIGH-RISK CONDITIONS: CHECK WITH YOUR GP AND BE SURE TO TAKE A COPY OF THIS BOOK WITH YOU.

Cardiovascular disease   Angina pectoris. Cerebrovascular accident. Congenital heart disease (with poor climatic tolerances). Congestive failure. Hypertension (severe and pulmonary). Myocardial infarction (coronary thrombosis). Unstable cardiac arrhythmias. Valvular lesions.

Respiratory disease   Asthma. Bronchiectasis. Bronchitis (chronic). Bullous lung disease. Congenital pulmonary cysts. Cor pulmonale (pulmonary heart disease). Emphysema. Lobectomy. Pneumonia. Pneumonectomy. Tuberculosis.

Blood disorders   Anaemia. Haemophilia. Leukaemia. Sickle-cell disease.

Neuropsychiatric conditions   Apoplexy (stroke). Brain tumour. Cerebral infarction (thrombotic or haemorrhagic). Epilepsy. Mental illness. Psychosis. Skull fracture.

Progressive kidney or liver failure.

Gastrointestinal disease   Acute diverticulitis. Acute gastroenteritis. Acute oesophageal varices. Peptic ulcer. Ulcerative colitis.

Recent surgery   Abdominal. Chest. Ear. Facial (wired mandibular fractures).

Pneumothorax   (air in chest) and *pneumoperitoneum* (air in abdomen).

154

Unstabilized convalescent, post-operative, and handicapped people.

Severe diabetes mellitus.

Contagious disease.

Colostomy and ileostomy.

Large unsupported hernia.

Alcoholics (with a delirium tremens history or Korsakoff's syndrome).

Recommendations have not been given because when you suffer from such a condition or disease you should think twice before flying. However, if there is an emergency and you must go by air you should ask your GP to submit a MEDIF or INCAD form to the airline for approval and obtain a second opinion from an aviation medicine specialist as notified passengers tend to have a high attack rate. (Applicants should not be intimidated by the reference to invalid or incapacitation on the form as the restrictive term is used by most airlines.)

Chapter Thirteen

WHAT IS TO BE DONE?
THE HEALTH IN THE AIR
CAMPAIGN

What is to be done? The question is raised not to reveal culprits, to apportion blame, or to inflame passions, but to find a practical solution. Before we proceed, though, we should review the key elements. The first is the public who know little or nothing about aviation medicine or the side-effects of air travel. The second is the travel industry, who because of their vested interests are inclined to maintain the status quo. The third is the medical establishment who have made several attempts to break the silence, albeit within the profession. It is the interrelationship of these elements that will determine the success or failure of the resolution.

To begin, we shall have to assume that the travel industry will not make a positive contribution. Two incidents appear to confirm this. First, the introduction of medical kits aboard US airlines in August 1986 resulted from a successful lawsuit brought by doctors and the Public Citizen Health Research of the Aviation Consumer Action Project against the FAA (Medical News 1986: 290). The other involves Dr Richard Fairhurst of Europ Assistance who was invited to address delegates of the Association of British Travel Agents (ABTA) at their 1979 conference on medical problems in air travel. 'At the 99th hour,' he said later when I talked to him, 'I was banned on the grounds that talking about these things was counterproductive and it put holidays in a bad light. You see again the conspiracy in the travel industry to say there is no problem' (Fairhurst 1987). Perhaps, therefore, it is best to exclude this group from the initial discussions.

The fortunate aspect of the specialism is that it is a preventive form of medicine and dramatic results could be obtained if the public were to become aware of the medical risks of air travel. Should the dissemination of information be successful, at a stroke a large proportion of the critical 10 per cent of the passenger load would no longer want to be exposed to such hazards – this in turn might be reflected in a decrease in the morbidity and mortality statistics. But we are a long way yet from the course prescribed.

What then should be the interaction between the medical profession and the public? Experience has demonstrated that pressure within the profession is insufficient to bring about changes (see Chapter 1, 'The barrier of silence'). However, if the pressure was brought to bear from the outside, there might be another outcome. To start with, a demand has to be stimulated from the grass-roots and a book is one way to achieve it. I spoke to Stephen Lock, the editor of the *British Medical Journal*, about this and he agreed that 'the whole thing will be to raise the height of consciousness on everybody's ground, fiistly the travelling public' (Lock 1986). Once a consciousness has been created, the level can be raised through the development of a campaign. The name I would suggest is Health in the Air Campaign (HITAC). The composition of a committee is important; it should include members of the public as well as aviation medical specialists. The aims of HITAC, which could be run as a charity, would be twofold: education and data collection about pre-flight, in-flight, and post-flight medical problems.

The question of education is not simple. Whom does one educate? The majority of people I interviewed indicated that it should begin with the GP. For as Dr Geoffrey Bennett observed, 'Anyone who has anything the matter with them should consult their doctor before they go flying!' (Bennett 1986). To facilitate this, the British Medical Association might consider issuing similar guidelines to those the American Medical Association have issued in their 1982 paper, 'Medical aspects of transportation aboard commercial aircraft' (AMA CEMS 1982: 1007–11). There are other means to implement the policy, for example seminars, a series of lectures at postgraduate medical centres, and the reissue of Harding and Mills's collected articles on *Aviation Medicine* (Harding and Mills 1983). A significant result of the education would be a change in the profession's view of holidays, in particular of air travel. An instance of such a change is given by Dr Sandra Mooney of the BA Medical Service. 'I was in general practice and my patients often came to me and said, "My daughter wants me to go and visit her in Australia – what do you think?" And almost without batting an eyelid I'd tend to say, "What a good idea! It'll do you a power of good." Or "How lovely for you to see her", and such like comments. And I honestly believe that I didn't even twig to the fact that the flight environment may not be a wonderfully good thing or certain precautions should be taken for that individual – um, I plead guilty. It's only because I'm working in an airline now that I am much more alert . . . to these kinds of problems' (Mooney 1986).

But the most obvious solution is for doctors to obtain the Diploma in Aviation Medicine, as Dr Mooney has herself done. At present, the small number who do hold the D.Av.Med. carry out biannual medical examinations on licensed airline pilots. Perhaps, with an increased demand from patients, in particular the frequent flyers, more doctors will enter the specialism.

The education of the public appears to be an easier task. HITAC could serve as a centre for consumer advice, a focal point for publicity, and a link with the medical profession in order that combined programmes might be undertaken on occasion. In the long term, it could also act as a representative body for passengers in negotiations with the travel industry and other institutions. Such a role could become essential as there are areas in civil aviation where medical incidents can go unreported because no agency has responsibility for them.

What could present difficulties, though, is the initiation of a research programme. Not only could the exercise be expensive but the results could be inconclusive. Mr John Firth, a consultant neurosurgeon at the University Hospital, Nottingham, and President of the Commission Internationale Médico-Physiologique at the Fédération Aéronautique Internationale (FAI), may have an answer. When we talked, he suggested that 'the quickest way to get valuable information' is to set up a confidential reporting system for passengers. Several nations have already introduced a similar scheme for aircrew through the FAI. At most, it would require a reasonable computer, and where 'money would be helpful is to make time available for a number of people to sift through the results and to pass on cases, where appropriate, to either Ernsting, Chapman, Joy, or old Firth and his gang in Nottingham for assessment. The curse about this', he added, 'is that in the first year there would be about 40,000 passengers complaining and the majority of the reports would go straight into the wastepaper basket. But a half a dozen useful cases might come out of it. The alternative is to design research and say, we have got 40 doctors in 40 planes and keep them there for 40 years until we get 40,000 answers. You then immediately distort what's happening and by the time you get your answers, the ground rules have changed anyway.' In essence, the confidential reporting system for passengers seems an attractive solution because a simple message can be put to the public. 'Dear passenger, if you have had a medical problem following your flight, which you think may be related, contact us.' The ideal medium, he suggests, is the back of an airline ticket (Firth 1987).

Another method for research is to analyse admissions to hospitals near airports in order to identify passengers with post-flight problems. From the medical point of view, it would appear in the initial stages to be the most direct route to obtain useful information. Such analysis could extend the work of Beighton, Richards, and others, and provide a sound platform for the practice of aviation medicine in the public sector.

Once a general awareness of aviation medicine has been established, it would be an opportune moment to involve the travel industry. At least doctors and members of the public would now be in possession of the relevant facts and could make informed decisions about the situation. The principal role that airlines and travel agents could be expected to assume is to give advice on the hazards of air travel, on a similar basis as is done at present on immunization and the prevention of malaria. Indeed, under ABTA's code of conduct, it is part of their responsibility. 'Travel agents shall inform their clients of health requirements which are necessary for the journey to be undertaken and of which they have been officially notified . . .' (ABTA 1987). However, such an attitude has taken some time to evolve, as Dr Jean Lawrie observes: 'Many travel agents now give advice about prophylaxis for malaria – formerly the agents resisted this as being likely to deter travellers; this has not happened' (Lawrie 1986). There are airlines too that go some way to accommodate this aspect of travellers' health. British Airways, for example, provides an immunization service at centres in London and plans to establish travel clinics throughout the UK.

But airlines in general are a different kettle of fish. They are principals in international air transport and their operations are governed by a body of legislation called Air Law. The cornerstone of the legislation was laid in 1929 through Article 17 of the Warsaw Convention which defined the basic liability of carriers by air. The carrier's duties, that appear not to include the explicit provision of any information on health and the pressurized environment, are otherwise specific: '(1) to take and use all reasonable care and skill to provide an aircraft which is fit for the journey and the carriage of the passengers in question, and (2) to take and use reasonable care to carry the passengers safely' (Shawcross and Beaumont 1985: VII (80), VII 75a). In America where a higher standard of care is required of a carrier of passengers than of a private carrier, unlike in England, there was a case which is a good illustration of an airline's responsibilty to the public on in-flight incidents. It was demonstrated in Sprayregen *v.* American Airlines when 'duty did not oblige [the] carrier to warn that passengers with head colds might suffer hearing loss through pressurisation changes' (Shawcross and Beaumont 1985: VII (84),[2] VII 79).

What is apparent from both the judgement and the definition of a carrier's duties is the underlying assumption that the public are familiar with the pressure environment of an aircraft, and therefore, if there is a chance they could be affected by it, the onus is on them to take precautions accordingly. When I went to see Peter Martin, a partner in Frere Cholmeley at Lincoln's Inn Fields, London, and an editor of Shawcross and Beaumont's *Air Law* (Shawcross and Beaumont 1985), he confirmed the position. 'I think there are many common misapprehensions. I don't think the airline is an insurer of the life of its clients. He doesn't say, "Look I guarantee to deliver you alive, fit, and well." He says, "I'll carry you from place to place and if you have an accident, I'll compensate you."

'Now the word accident is generally defined . . . as a fortuitous external event which affects a person or the aircraft. . . . They [the airlines] rely very happily on those words of the Convention, Article 17, which says "arising out of an accident during the course of the carriage by air" and they say it has got to be met. And if it isn't and the poor chap comes on board and he's got some unidentified disability which bursts, so to speak, then the carrier cries "too bad" ' (Martin 1987).

The obverse side of the argument has also been determined. Should, for example, too many people burst in such a fashion, the airline has some freedom to refuse to accept passengers suffering from the disabilities in question when they present themselves for a flight if for no other reason than to avoid any embarrassment in the future (Shawcross and Beaumont 1985: VII (79.1), VII 75). 'In the standard conditions of carriage,' he explained, 'what we call the booklet conditions of all airlines prepared by IATA and adopted by most of them, there is a standard form article, usually Article 8, called the Refusal of Carriage. This says, "Carrier will refuse carriage or onward carriage or will cancel the reservation etc. if the carrier decides that such action is necessary for reasons of safety; [that such] action is necessary to prevent violation of any applicable laws; or that the conduct, age or mental or physical state of the passenger is such as to require special assistance of the carrier or cause discomfort or make himself objectionable to other passengers or involved in any hazard or risk to himself or other persons or to property.'' In other words, the carrier does regulate his conduct by his conditions of carriage in relation to a passenger who may be sick, in his view, by saying, ''I reserve the right to deny you carriage'' ' (Martin 1987).

The MEDIF form, which appears to have developed from this exclusion clause, can be used as an instrument in the rejection of passengers because it provides the medical basis for the decision. However, such an instrument can cut both ways. Take the case of someone with a disease who is cleared to fly by the medical services of an airline through the MEDIF and then dies on board.

I put the question to Peter Martin. 'The chances are that the airlines would be liable but not probably in the context of carriage by air. It would probably be liable for having given negligent advice. In other words, I think probably that you wouldn't sue in those circumstances. You'd probably say that it would be outwith the Convention – this is outside the Convention system. What I would say would be that doctors, the medical officer of the airlines, might have given negligent medical advice, namely, ''I've looked at your notes. I'm sure you'll be all right, old chap. You come along with us. You'll be fine.'' Something goes wrong – the chap was simply not fit to fly.

'There was no accident [however]. The airline performed quite normally and to optimum standards. The chap just pegs out because he can't take it. I think the airline would probably be liable outside the Convention system for having given negligent advice. But there is a difficulty here because the Convention system is supposed to be all-embracing and there is supposed to be no claim outside the Convention system for personal injury, death, or loss of baggage. It's either an accident or it's outside the Convention and you can't claim. But I think that these are very special circumstances unexplored by the lawyers yet' (Martin 1987).

The area he was certain of in terms of Air Law was a decompression because such an incident would arise either through pilot error or through the malfunction of equipment and therefore could qualify as an accident. (As has been demonstrated in Chapters 4 and 10.

There can also be dire consequences to the passengers.) 'If there was an explosive decompression, or a decompression which caused a person injury or death, that would be actionable.'

However, there is little likelihood of litigation because of the lack of opportunity to obtain evidence to support it. No system is in operation to detect the nature and the extent of medical incidents caused by a decompression. If such an event occurs, the operator or commander of a public transport aircraft is required (under the CAA's CAP 382 – the mandatory reporting scheme) to report only serious injury or death of passengers or flight crew. There is no onus on them to undertake an investigation into the passengers' health as is compulsory with the aircraft. This is a gross oversight and would appear to be biased in the airline's favour.

From the brief survey of some essential clauses in Air Law, it is apparent how comprehensive the Convention system is; if there are any problems, they will have to be resolved at an international level. Take the issue of printing warnings about the health hazards of air travel on airline tickets. Should the main or national carrier of a country be pressurized towards such action, there could be a protest about unfair competition because foreign carriers may not be bound by it. However, if the government was to legislate that warnings had to be printed on all literature and advertising produced by airlines that operate in the UK, as has been the case with the tobacco industry in the campaign against smoking, there would be no inequity and the matter would be settled at one stroke.

On the other hand, if HITAC was a great success, the airlines, for ever aware of market trends in the big push for profits, would be keen to exploit the health element in air travel. Some would want to be the first to recruit nurses as flight attendants (see Chapter 8, 'Guts: the fear of flying'), offer doctors free tickets, serve light meals and lots of water, carry a comprehensive medical kit on board, and even decrease the cabin altitude to about 5,000 ft on flights for retired passengers. (It should be mentioned that BA published their own *Travel Health Guide* until 1980 – edited by Dr A.S.R. Peffers – which not only listed some medical conditions that could cause problems but actually advised against the consumption of alcohol and cigarettes, to the detriment of their duty free sales (Peffers 1980: 17–18).)

The key question is, if the public is to be represented on medico-legal issues in negotiations with a body like the International Air Transport Association, who should be responsible? In *The Airliner Cabin*

Environment report (see pp. 16, 123–5), the National Research Council Committee indicated that a federal agency should be given the responsibility to oversee the health effects of air travel. The US Department of Transport through the FAA argued that they had the authority to do so and recommended the 'retention of the present system of health responsibilities' (FAA 1987). The opinion was offered in spite of the fact that at the hearing the FAA Director of Airworthiness made a public statement about the satisfactory condition of the cabin environment which later proved to be without foundation. Furthermore, his statement was reaffirmed by a senior executive of the Air Transport Association. It is obvious that if there is such close co-operation between these organizations – a situation that is only to be expected when a high standard of safety is to be maintained in air transport – there would be little room left for a third party, passengers' health.

Perhaps the answer lies in the creation of an Aerohealth Institute (AI) which in the long term would supersede HITAC. The main aim of AI would be to ensure that the government passed legislation to the effect that warnings about the health risks of air travel be printed on airline literature and advertisements. (Later, AI could be structured on a worldwide basis to facilitate negotiations with the airlines' international representatives, IATA and ICAO.) Although the framework would be medico-legal, the consumer element would provide a cutting edge to the activities. For example, a regular aviation health newsletter could be published, checks on medical facilities of airlines and airports undertaken and compared, the legal rights of passengers clarified, and where necessary changes in the law proposed.

In essence, what has to happen is for the air transport industry to emerge from the shadows – where it has been left to its own devices – into the daylight and come under public scrutiny. At last, the industry will have to be accountable for the health factor in the air.

NOTES

CHAPTER 1 THE BARRIER OF SILENCE:
UNSUCCESSFUL ATTEMPTS AT DISCLOSURE

1   Air Commodore J. Ernsting disavows any connection between the *British Medical Journal*'s editorial and the RCP's working party.

CHAPTER 4 LOW ON HIGH, HIGH ON LOW:
HYPOXIA, OR LACK OF OXYGEN

1   On separate occasions both Dr Mills and Dr Glaister have commented that in the case of mountain sickness there are exceptions. Suddenly member of a group who was acclimatizing slowly, for no reason all, gets cerebral or pulmonary edema (Mills and Glaister 1988).

2   This was not the first experiment on strangulation but it was the first carried out by a self-experimenter. The first was done in a US prison during the early 1940s, and involved 11 schizophrenic patients and 126 normal young male subjects (Rossen *et al.* 1943).

3   Definitions of such terms are complex and Air Commodore Ernsting comments as follows: 'This is not the definition of hypoxia – hypoxia can occur at any atmospheric pressure. Hypoxia due to breathing air at high altitude is hypoxic hypoxia, just as breathing a low PO_2 gas mixture at 10 m depth of sea water! Anoxia was widely used in the literature for what is now termed hypoxia up to about 40 years ago! Hypobaric hypoxia is one example of hypoxic hypoxia. Hypoxia is usually classified by physiologists as hypoxic, anaemic, stagnant and histotoxic.' (See Ernsting and King 1988.)

4   TUC at high altitude. Air Commodore J. Ernsting points out that similar studies had been carried out by Luft and others on this problem.

5   I kept the note which recorded my debarment from the library. It was handwritten on an MOD Form 4A, dated 5 June, 10.33, and headed 'Visit to IAM Library'.

> Dear Mr Kahn,
> I am sorry to have to *refuse* you entry but senior management has

directed that because entry means full time escort inside the wire. (As stringent security regulations of the RAE are applied over this side of the airfield too, as the access to the RAE is feasible once inside the common fence.) I am sorry I could not call you back to prevent the unnecessary journey.

W/C. S. Marshall

6   Professor David Denison comments on the original experiments carried out between 1960 and 1965: 'Some of the early work produced the opposite results but more recent ones confirmed them.'

CHAPTER EIGHT   GUTS: THE FEAR OF FLYING

1   It is of course a legal requirement to carry cabin crew for safety reasons.

CHAPTER NINE   A DOSE OF CONCORDE: DANGERS OF HIGH ALTITUDE FLIGHT

1   Was Mr Fred Finn's radiation exposure monitored? Dr G. Bennett comments as follows:

Yes it was. The exposure dose on each flight was recorded. He wasn't told of course but in fact there have been no abnormally high exposures.
(Bennett 1986)

CHAPTER TEN   AIR TRAVEL, BEWARE TRAVEL: MEDICAL HAZARDS OF FLYING

1   Perhaps, to make any sense, it should read either maximum cabin altitude or minimum pressure.
2   Most aircraft have no humidification equipment.

REFERENCES

PREFACE

CACAQ (Committee on Airliner Cabin Air Quality) (1986) *The airliner cabin environment: air quality and safety*, Washington: National Academy Press.

Edgerton, J.C. (1936) 'Problems in stratosphere flying', *Journal of Aviation Medicine*, June: 73–6.

CHAPTER ONE   THE BARRIER OF SILENCE

AMACEMS (American Medical Association Commission on Emergency Medical Services) (1982) 'Medical aspects of transportation aboard commercial aircraft', *Journal of American Medical Association* 247, 7: 1007–11.

Anon. (1975) 'Illness in the clouds', *British Medical Journal* i: 295.

Anon. (1987) 'Air quality aboard airliners bad: NRC', *Aviation, Space and Environmental Medicine* January: 92.

Association of Flight Attendants (1982) Exhibit A (passenger comments and flight attendant symptoms, 01/77–01/82). In the US Senate, Committee on Commerce, Science, and Transportation, Subcommittee on Aviation (97th Congress, 2nd Session). Airliner Cabin Safety and Health Standards: Hearing on S.1770, May 20, 1982. Washington, DC: US Government Printing Office, 1982 P.L. 98–466, Senate Report No. 98–468, pp. 3167–70

Beighton, P.H. and Richards, P.R. (1968) 'Cardiovascular disease in air travellers', *British Heart Journal* 30: 367–72.

CACAQ (Committee on Airliner Cabin Air Quality (1986) *The airliner cabin environment: air quality and safety*, Washington: National Academy Press.

CMCAMA (Committee on Medical Criteria of Aerospace Medical Association) (1961) 'Medical criteria for passenger flying', *Journal of Aviation Medicine* 32: 369–82.

Collins, R.E.C., Field, S., and Castleden, W.M. (1979) 'Thrombosis of leg arteries after prolonged travel', *British Medical Journal* 2: 1478.

Edgerton, J.C. (1936) 'Problems in stratosphere flying', *Journal of Aviation Medicine* I: 73–6.

El-Ansary, E.H. (1983) 'Aviation medicine', *British Medical Journal* 286: 1744.

Elliott, H. (1987) 'Passengers cheer jet's mercy diversion', *The Times*, 29 April: back page.

Fairhurst, R.J. (1975) 'Illness in the clouds', *British Medical Journal* 5 April: 40.

Harding, R.M. and Mills, F.J. (1983) *Aviation Medicine: articles from the British Medical Journal*, London: British Medical Association.

Inouye, D.K. (1983) U.S. Bill S.197. 'Cabin Air Quality', Senate Hearing 98–600 November 9, 1983, 98–1 Washington, DC: US Government Printing Office, 1983. Abstract 1983, S.261–18 1–4.

Klemes, M.A. (1982) 'Medical emergencies in flight', *Journal of American Medical Association* 248, 6: 648.

Lawrie, J. (1981) 'Medical responsibilities of airlines', *British Medical Journal* 282: 320.

Lee, N.C. (1975) 'Illness in the clouds', *British Medical Journal* 31 May: 505.

Mills, F.J. (1986) Personal communication, 8 May.

Mohler, S.R. (1987) Personal communication, 27 October.

Rais, G. (1987) 'Jumbo's RAF landing saves girl', *Daily Telegraph*, 29 April: 3.

Richards, P.R. (1970) MD thesis, University of London.

Richards, P.R. (1973) 'The effects of air travel on passengers with cardiovascular and respiratory disease', *Practitioner* 210: 232–41.

Roper, D.L. (1982) 'Air transportation after eye surgery', *Journal of American Medical Association* 247, 24: 3315.

Whaley, W.H. (1982) 'Medical considerations regarding flight crews', *Journal of American Medical Association* 248, 15: 1834–5.

WPCFAP (Working Party on Cardiovascular Fitness for Airline Pilots) (1975) 'Cardiovascular problems and flying', *British Medical Journal* 15 November: 416.

Wright, M. (1983) 'Am I fit to fly, doctor?', *World Medicine* 20 August: 31.

Yeager, C. and Janos, L. (1985) *Yeager*, London: Century.

CHAPTER TWO   DAEDALUS AND ICARUS

Breasted, James (1926) *The Conquest of Civilization*, New York: Harper Bros.

Graves, Robert (1974) *The Greek Myths*, 2 vols, Harmondsworth: Penguin Books.

Ovid (1982) *The Erotic Poems*, trans. P. Green, Harmondsworth: Penguin Books.

Ovid (1986) *Metamorphoses*, Book 8, trans. M.M. Innes, Harmondsworth: Penguin Books.

CHAPTER THREE   THE HOSTILE NOTHINGNESS

Bert, P. (1943) *Barometric Pressure: Researches in Experimental Physiology*, trans. M.A. Hitchcock and F.A. Hitchcock, Columbus, Ohio: College Book Company.

DeHart, R. (ed.) (1985) *Fundamentals of Aerospace Medicine*, Philadelphia: Lea & Febiger.

Eckstein, G. (1970) *The Body has a Head*, New York: Harper & Row.
Glaister, D.H. (1969) 'Lung collapse in aviation medicine', *British Journal of Hospital Medicine* February: 635–42.
Weisberg, J. (1981) *Meteorology*, Boston: Houghton Mifflin.
Yeager, C. and Janos, L. (1985) *Yeager*, London: Century.

CHAPTER FOUR LOW ON HIGH, HIGH ON LOW

Barcroft, J. (1920) 'Presidential address on anoxaemia of the Physiological Section of the British Association at a conference held at Cardiff', *Nature* 106: 125.
Bert, P. (1943) *Barometric Pressure: Researches in Experimental Physiology*, trans. M.A. and F.A. Hitchcock, Columbus, Ohio: College Book Company.
Blagbrough, A.E. and Nicholson, A.N. (1975) 'Subatmospheric decompression: neurological and behavioural studies', *Acta Astronautica* 2: 197–206.
Boyle, R. (1660) *New Experiments Physico-mechanical, Touching the Spring of the Air, and its Effects*, Oxford: Oxford University Press.
Chisholm, D.M., Billings, C.E., and Bason, R. (1974) 'Behaviour of naïve subjects during decompression: an evaluation of automatically presented passenger oxygen equipment', *Aviation, Space and Environmental Medicine* 45,2: 126.
Cumming, G., Scadding, G., and Thurlbeck, W.M. (eds) (1981) *The Scientific Basis of Respiratory Medicine*, London: Heinemann Medical.
DeHart, R. (ed.) (1985) *Fundamentals of Aerospace Medicine*, Philadelphia: Lea & Febiger.
Denison, D. (1981) 'High altitudes and hypoxia', in O.G. Edholm and J.S. Weiner (eds), *Principles and Practice of Human Physiology*, London: Academic Press.
Denison, D. (1986) Personal communication, 19 May.
Denison, D., Ledwith, F., and Poulton, E.C. (1966) 'Complex reaction times at simulated cabin altitudes of 5,000 ft and 8,000 ft', *Aerospace Medicine* October: 1010–13.
Dhenin, G. (editor-in-chief) and Ernsting, J. (ed.) (1978) *Aviation Medicine*, London: Tri-Med Books.
Dickinson, J. (1986) 'High altitude', in R. Dawood (ed.) *Travellers' Health*, Oxford: Oxford University Press.
Eckstein, G. (1970) *The Body has a Head*, New York: Harper & Row. [pp. 163–4]
Edholm, O.G. and Weiner, J.S. (eds) (1981) *Principles and Practice of Human Physiology*, London: Academic Press.
Engle, E. and Lott, A.S. (1979) *Man in Flight*, Annapolis, MD: Leeward Publications.
Ernsting, J. (1978) 'Prevention of hypoxia–acceptable compromises', *Aviation, Space and Environmental Medicine* 49, 3: 497–8.
Ernsting, J. (1984) 'Mild hypoxia and the use of oxygen in flight', *Aviation, Space and Environmental Medicine*, May: 407.
Ernsting, J. (1986) Personal communication, 7 August.
Ernsting, J. and King, P. (1988) *Aviation Medicine*, 2nd edn, London: Butterworths.

Fulton, J. (1948) *Aviation Medicine in its Preventive Aspects*, Oxford: Oxford University Press.

Gibson, T.M. and Harrison, M.H. (1984) *Into Thin Air*, London: Hale. [p. 124]

Gillies, J.A. (1965) *Aviation Medicine*, Oxford: Pergamon Press.

Horace (1927) *Odes and Epodes*, trans. C.E. Bennett, Cambridge: Loeb Classical Library.

Horace (1960) *The Odes and Epodes of Horace*, trans. J.P. Clancy, Chicago: University of Chicago Press.

Horace (1976) *Complete Odes and Epodes*, trans. J. Michie, Harmondsworth: Penguin Books.

Houston, C.S. (1984) 'Altitude sickness in travellers', *Travel and Traffic Medicine* 2. 2: 75.

Licht, H. (1933) *Sexual life in Ancient Greece*, trans. J.H. Freese, ed. L.H. Dawson, London: Routledge.

McFarland, R.A. (1946) *Human Factors in Air Transport Design*, New York: McGraw-Hill.

Messmer, R. (1979) *Everest: Expedition to the Ultimate*, London: Kaye & Ward.

Milledge, J.S. (1985) 'The great oxygen secretion controversy', *Lancet* December 21/8: 1409.

Mills, F.J. and Glaister, D.H. (1988) Personal communication.

Perry, I.C. (1983) 'Air travel fatigue', *Travel and Traffic Medicine* 1, 1: 18–21.

RAF IAM (Royal Air Force Institute of Aviation Medicine) (1983), MODPR and COI.

Rossen, R., Kabat, H., and Anderson, J.P. (1943) 'Acute arrest of cerebral circulation in man', *Archives of Neurology and Psychiatry* 50: 510–28.

Rule, K. (1986) Personal communication.

Solberg, C. (1979) *Conquest of the Skies*, Boston: Little Brown.

Stedman's *Medical Dictionary* (24th edn, 1982), Baltimore, MD: Williams & Wilkins.

Taylor, M.J. and Mondey, D. (1983), *Milestones of Flight*, London: Jane's.

West, J.B. (1981) *High Altitude Physiology*, Stroudsburg, PA: Hutchinson Ross.

CHAPTER FIVE THE GREAT MIMIC: HYPERVENTILATION, OR OVER-BREATHING

AMACEMS (American Medical Association Commission on Emergency Medical Services) (1982) 'Medical aspects of transportation aboard commercial aircraft', *Journal of American Medical Association* 247, 7: 1010.

DeHart, R. (ed.) (1985) *Fundamentals of Aerospace Medicine*, Philadelphia, PA: Lea & Febiger.

Denison, D. (1989) Personal communication, 3 August.

Gibson, T.M. (1984) 'Hyperventilation in flight', *Aviation, Space and Environmental Medicine* May: 411–12

Harrex, W.K. (1985) 'In-flight medical problems of airline passengers', unpublished M.Sc. thesis, University of London June 1985.

Lum, L.C. (1981) 'Hyperventilation and the anxiety state', *Journal of the Royal Society of Medicine* 74, January: 1.

CHAPTER SIX   THE BODY AS A BALLOON: GAS EXPANSION

Armstrong, H.G. (1961) *Aerospace Medicine*, Baltimore: Williams & Wilkins.
DeHart, R.L. (ed.) (1985) *Fundamentals of Aerospace Medicine*, Philadelphia, PA: Lea & Febiger.
Denison, D.M. and Preston, F. (1983) 'Aviation Medicine', in D.J. Weatherall., J.G.G. Ledingham, and D.A. Warrell (eds) (1983) *Oxford Textbook of Medicine*, Oxford: Oxford University Press.
Dhenin, G. (editor-in-chief) and Ernsting, J. (ed.) (1978) *Aviation Medicine*, London: Tri-Med Books.
'Minerva' (1982) column in *BMJ*, 6 March, *British Medical Journal* 284: 749.
Parsons, C.J. and Bobechko, W.P. (1982) 'Aeromedical transport: its hidden problems' *Canadian Medical Association Journal* 126, February 1: 237.
Vidal, G. (1985) 'Love of flying', *New York Review of Books*, January 17: 14.

CHAPTER SEVEN   THE JET SYNDROME

Anon. (1927) 'New York–Paris flight', *The Times*, 22 May: 15.
Arendt, J., Aldhous, M., and Marks, V. (1986) 'Alleviation of jet lag by melatonin: preliminary results of controlled double blind', *British Medical Journal* 292: 1170.
Bargiello, T.A., Jackson, F.R., and Young, M.W. (1984) 'Restoration of circadian behavioural rhythms by gene transfer in Drosophila', *Nature* 312: 752–4.
Buley, L.E. (1970) 'Experience with a physiologically based formula for determining rest periods on long-distance air travel', *Aerospace Medicine* June: 680.
Conroy, R.T.W.L. (1971) 'Time zone transitions and business executives', *Transactions of the Society of Occupational Medicine* 21: 69–71.
Czeisler, C.A., Allan, J.S., Strogatz, S.H., Ronda, J.M., Sanchez, R., Rios, C., Freitag, W.D., Richardson, G.S., and Kronauer, R.E. (1986) 'Bright light resets the human circadian pacemaker independent of the timing of the sleep-wake cycle', *Science* 233: 667–72.
DeHart, R. (ed.) (1985) *Fundamentals of Aerospace Medicine*, Philadelphia, PA: Lea & Febiger.
Dodge, R. (1982) 'Circadian rhythms and fatigue: a discrimination of their effects on performance', *Aviation, Space and Environmental Medicine* 53(11): 1131–6.
Douglas, W. (1986) Personal communication, 28 October.
Ehret, C.E. and Scanlon, L.W. (1983) *Overcoming Jet Lag*, New York: Berkeley Books.
Eliot, T.S. (1949) 'Burnt Norton', *Collected Poems 1909–1935*, London: Faber & Faber.
Engle, E. and Lott, A. (1979) *Man in Flight*, Annapolis, MD: Leeward Publications.
Hauty, G.T. and Adams, T. (1966) 'Phase shifts of the human circadian system and performance deficit during the periods of transition III North-South

flight', *Aerospace Medicine* 73: 1257–62.

Klein, K.E. (1976) 'Air operations and circadian performance rhythms', *Aviation, Space and Environmental Medicine* 3: 221–30.

Kowet, D. (1984) *The Jet Lag Book*, London: Futura.

Lancet (1986) 'Jet lag and its pharmacology', (unsigned editorial) *Lancet* 30 August: 494.

Lindbergh, C.A. (1953) *The Spirit of St Louis*, London: John Murray.

McFarland, R.A. (1974) 'Influence of changing time zones on air crews and passengers', *Aerospace Medicine* June: 648–58.

Morris, III, H.H. and Estes, M.L. (1987) 'Traveller's amnesia', *Journal of American Medical Association* 258(7): 945–6.

Nicholson, A.N. and Stone, B.M. (1983) 'Circadian rhythms and disturbed sleep: its relevance to operations', *International Journal of Aviation Safety* 1: 301–9.

Post, W. and Gatty, H. (1931) *Around the World in Eight Days*, London: Hamish Hamilton.

Siegel, P.V., Gerathewohl, S.J., and Mohler, S.R. (1969) 'Time zone effects', *Science* 164: 1249–55.

Singer, I.B. (1986) 'Disguised', *New Yorker*, 22 September: 35.

Strughold, H. (1952) 'Physiological day-night cycle in global flights', *Aviation Medicine* 19 October: 464–5.

Strughold, H. (1971) *Your Body Clock*, London: Angus & Robertson.

Winget, C.M., Deroshia, C.W., Markley, C.L., and Holley, D.C. (1984) 'A review of human physiology and performance changes associated with desynchronosis of biological rhythms', *Aviation, Space and Environmental Medicine* 55, 12: 1085–96.

CHAPTER EIGHT   GUTS: THE FEAR OF FLYING

Agras, S., Sylvester, D., and Oliveau, D. (1969) 'The epidemiology of common fears and phobias', *Comparative Psychiatry* 10: 151–6.

Auden, W.H. (1986) 'Journal of an Airman: Airman's Alphabet', in E. Mendelson (ed.) *The English Auden*, London: Faber & Faber Ltd.

Cassem, N. (1989) '2nd Lieutenant Ned O'Brien: Memorial Tribute', *Aviation, Space and Environmental Medicine* 60, 5: 400–1.

Cocteau, J. (1942) in H.G. Bryden, *Wings: An Anthology of Flight*, London: Faber & Faber Ltd.

Corn, J. (1983) *The Winged Gospel*, Oxford: Oxford University Press.

Fairhurst, R. (1987) Personal communication, 5 February.

Freud, S. (1983) 'The erotic roots of aviation', in J. Thorn (ed.) *The Armchair Aviator*, New York: Charles Scribner's Sons.

Good, T. (1986) Personal communication.

Green, R. (1987) Personal communication, 22 January.

Halbroth, R. (1986) Personal communication.

Hallam, R.S. (1985) *Anxiety: Psychological Perspectives on Panic and Agoraphobia*, London: Academic Press.

Hudson, K. and Pettifer, J. (1979) *Diamonds in the Sky*, London: Bodley Head/BBC.

Jones, D.R. (1986) 'Flying and danger, joy and fear', *Aviation, Space and Environmental Medicine*: 131–6.

Langewiesche, W. (1954) *A Flier's World*, London: Hodder & Stoughton.

Newsweek (1977) 'Boeing Survey', *Newsweek*, April 23: 41.

Nordlund, C.L. (1984) 'Fear of flying', *Institute of Air Transport Magazine* 12: 45–60.

Plath, S. (1968) 'Johnny Panic', *Atlantic Monthly* September: 54–6.

Solberg, C. (1979) *Conquest of the Skies*, Boston: Little Brown.

Strongin, T.S. (1987) 'A historical review of fear of flying among aircrew men', *Aviation, Space and Environmental Medicine* 58(3): 263–7.

Thorn, J. (ed.) (1983) *The Armchair Aviator*, New York: Charles Scribner's Sons.

Vidal, G. (1985) 'Love of Flying', *New York Review of Books* January 17: 14–20.

Wallace, W. (1985) Personal communication, 5 May.

CHAPTER NINE A DOSE OF CONCORDE

Bennett, G. (1962) 'Ozone contamination of high altitude aircraft cabins', *Aerospace Medicine* 8: 969–73.

Bennett, G. (1986) Personal communication, 17 March.

Beral, V., Inskip, H., Fraser, P., Booth, M., Coleman, D., and Rose, G. (1985) 'Mortality of employees of the UK Atomic Energy Authority, 1946–79', *British Medical Journal* 291.17.8: 440–9.

CACAQ (Committee on Airliner Cabin Air Quality) (1986) *The airliner cabin environment: air quality and safety*, Washington: National Academy Press.

Denison, D. (1986) Personal communication, 19 May.

Denison, D., Ledwith, F., and Poulton, E.C. (1966) 'Complex reaction times at simulated cabin altitudes of 5,000 and 8,000 feet', *Aerospace Medicine* October: 1010–13.

Engle, E. and Lott, A. (1979) *Man in Flight*, Annapolis, MD: Leeward Publications.

Fraser, P., Booth, M., Beral, V., Inskip, H., Firsht, S., and Speak, S. (1985) 'Collection and validation of data in the UK Atomic Energy Authority Mortality study', *British Medical Journal* 291.17.8: 435–9.

Harding, R.M. and Mills, F.J. (1983) *Aviation Medicine: articles from the British Medical Journal*, London: British Medical Association.

Preston, F. and Lavernhe, J. (no date) 'Medical aspects of supersonic flight', booklet published jointly by British Airways and Air France.

Wilkie, T. (1988) 'Sellafield radiation cash may be offered', National Radiological Protection Board's new limit reported in the *Independent* 17 November: 2.

CHAPTER TEN AIR TRAVEL, BEWARE TRAVEL

Anderson, E.H. (1964) 'A decompression incident in a civil aircraft', *Aerospace Medicine* 1 January: 33–5.

Armstrong, H. (1936) 'The medical problems of sealed high-altitude aircraft compartments', *Journal of Aviation Medicine* I: 2–8.

Balfour Slonin, N. (ed.) (1974) *Environmental Physiology*, St Louis: Mosby.

Bramlitt, E.T. (1985) 'Commercial aviation crewmember radiation doses', *Health Physics* 49: 945–8.

Busby, D.E., Higgins, E.A., and Funkhauser, G.E. (1976) 'Effect of physical activity of airline flight attendants on their time of useful consciousness in a rapid decompression', *Aviation, Space and Environmental Medicine* 2: 117–20.

CAA (Civil Aviation Authority) (1978a) Supplementary report extracted from British Caledonian Air Safety Review, November 1978, 'Pressurisation loss', 11–2 78/02472B, Redhill, Surrey: CAA.

CAA (Civil Aviation Authority) (1978b) Captain Keatley's report to the CAA, occurrence 26.6.78, 78/02472B, Redhill, Surey: CAA.

CACAQ (Committee on Airliner Cabin Air Quality) (1986) *The airliner cabin environment: air quality and safety*, Washington: National Academy Press.

Collins, W.E., Mertens, H.W., and Higgins, E.A. (1987) 'Some effects of alcohol and simulated altitude on complex performance scores and breathalyzer readings', *Aviation, Space and Environmental Medicine* 58: 328–32.

DeHart, R. (ed.) (1985) *Fundamentals of Aerospace Medicine*, Philadelphia: Lea & Febiger.

Dhenin, G. (editor-in-chief) and Ernsting, J. (ed.) (1978) *Aviation Medicine*, London: Tri-Med Books.

Dille, J.R. (1986) Aviation medicine heritage column, *Aviation, Space and Environmental Medicine* 8: 816.

Dille, J.R. (1988) 'Aviation medicine heritage', *Aviation, Space and Environmental Medicine* 10, 59: 1010.

Edgerton, J.C. (1936) 'Problems in stratosphere flying', *Journal of Aviation Medicine* June: 73–6.

Engle, E. and Lott, A. (1979) *Man in Flight*, Annapolis, MD: Leeward Publications.

Ernsting, J. (1978) 'Prevention of hypoxia-acceptable compromises', *Aviation, Space and Environmental Medicine* 3: 495.

Gillies, J.A. (1965) *Aviation Medicine*, Oxford: Pergamon Press.

Hawkins, F. (1986) *Human Factors in Flight*, London: Gower Technical Press.

Heimbach, R.D. and Sheffield, P.J. (1985) 'Protection in the pressure environment', in R. DeHart (ed.) *Fundamentals of Aerospace Medicine*, Philadelphia: Lea and Febiger.

Higgins, E.A., Davis, A.W., Vaughn, J.A., Calerston, E.M., and Funkhauser, G.E. (1970) Report nos FAA-AM-68-18/70–5, Washington: FAA Office of Aviation Medicine.

Hurtado, A. (1971) 'Influence on physiology' in *High Altitude Physiology*, London: CIBA Foundation, Churchill Livingstone.

Langewiesche, W. (1954) *A Flier's World*, London: Hodder & Stoughton.

McFarland, R.A. (1946) *Human Factors in Air Transport Design*, New York: McGraw-Hill.

McFarland, R.A. (1971) Armstrong Lecture, presented 28 April at 42nd Annual Meeting of AMA, Houston, Texas: 9, transcript presented to the Royal Aeronautical Library.

McFarland, R.A., Roughton, F.J.W., Halpern, M., and Niven, J.I. (1944) 'Effects of CO and altitude on visual thresholds', *Journal of Aviation Medicine* 15(6): 381–94.

NTSB (1975) Report No. NTSB-AAR-75-2, Washington: NTSB.

Peffers, A.S.R. (ed.) (1980) *British Airways Travel Health Guide*, London: Johnston & Bacon.

Preston, F.S. and Denison, D. (1983) 'Aviation medicine', in D.J. Weatherall, J.G.G. Ledingham, and D.A. Warrell (eds) *Oxford Textbook of Medicine*, Oxford: Oxford University Press.

Rayman, R.B. and McNaughton, G.B. (1983) 'Hypoxia: USAF experience 1970–80', *Aviation, Space and Environmental Medicine* April: 357–9.

Solberg, C. (1979) *Conquest of the Skies*, Boston: Little Brown.

Thomson, W.A.R. (ed.) (1985) *Black's Medical Dictionary*, London: Adam & Charles Black.

Wright, M. (1983) 'Am I fit to fly, doctor?', *World Medicine* 8: 31.

CHAPTER ELEVEN   THE CURSE OF ICARUS

Bennett, G. (1961) 'Reactions and performance of airline pilots following decompression', *Aerospace Medicine* 32: 134–6.

Bennett, G. (1962) 'Ozone contamination of high altitude aircraft cabins', *Aerospace Medicine* 33: 969.

Bennett, G. (1965) 'Human factors in the Concorde SST', *Aerospace Medicine* 36: 1094.

Bennett, G. (1986) Personal communication, 17 June.

CACAQ (1986) *The airliner cabin environment: air quality and safety*, Washington: National Academy Press.

Cameron McLaren, H. (1977) 'Medical hazards of air travel' (letter), *British Medical Journal* July: 44.

Cruickshank, J.M., Gorlin, R., and Jennet, B. (1988) 'Air travel and thrombotic episodes', *Lancet* 27 August: 497–8.

Cummins, R.O., Chapman, P.J.C., Chamberlain, D.A., Schubach, J.A., and Litwin, P.E. (1988) 'In-flight deaths during commercial air travel', *Journal of the American Medical Association* 259: 1983–8.

DHSS (1984) *On the State of the Public Health for the Year 1984*, London: HMSO.

Dunlop, J. (1987) Personal communication, 5 February.

Fairhurst, R.J. (1976) 'The invalid passenger and air transport', *Practitioner* 8: 230.

Green, R.L. (1986) Personal communication, 16 November.

Harding, R. and Mills, F.J. (1983) *Aviation Medicine: articles from the British Medical Journal*, London: British Medical Association.

Harrex, W.K. (1985) 'In-flight medical problems of airline passengers', unpublished M.Sc. thesis, University of London, June 1985.

Hart, Y., Holdstock, D.J., and Lynn, W.A. (1985) 'Medical emergencies in the air' (letter), *Lancet* 2: 353–4.

Holdstock, D.J. (1986) Personal communication, 17 June.

Jetzer, T.C., Dicharry, C., Glumack, R., Zanick, D.C., and Webb, A.G.

(1986) 'Airport emergency medical services', *Aviation, Space and Environmental Medicine* 5: 459–61.

Johnson, L.F. (1985) 'The role of the hotel doctor', *Travel Medicine International* 3.2: 62–7.

Jolly, R. (1977) 'Medical hazards of air travel' (letter), *British Medical Journal* 3 September: 637.

Kakimoto, Y., Nakamura, A., Tarui, H., Nagasawa, Y., and Yagura, S. (1988) 'Crew workload in JASDF C-1 transport flights 1. Change in heart rate and salivary cortisol', *Aviation, Space and Environmental Medicine* 6: 511–16.

Lancet (1985) 'Emergencies in the air' (editorial), *Lancet* 2.

Lawrie, J. (1981) 'Medical responsibilities of airlines' (letter), *British Medical Journal* 282: 320.

Liddell, R. (1987) Personal communication, 9 February.

MacGoldrick, M. (1987) Personal communication, 23 February.

Mills, F.J. (1985) 'The endocrinology of stress', *Aviation, Space and Environmental Medicine* 7: 642–50.

Mohler, S.R. (1988) Personal communication, 24 April.

Mohler, S.R., Nicogossian, A., and Margulies, R.A. (1980) 'Emergency medicine and the airline passenger', *Aviation, Space and Environmental Medicine* 9: 918–22.

Perry. I. (1986) Personal communication, 7 August.

Rubinstein, H.S. (1985) 'Stethoscopes on aircraft' (letter), *Lancet* 2, 9 February: 353.

Rule, K. (1986) Personal communication, 10 September.

Ryman, D. (1988) Personal communication, 14 February.

van Assendelft, A.H.W. (1985) 'Elderly people flying to the tropics' (letter), *Lancet* 3: 648.

Wakeford, R. (1986) 'Death in the clouds', *British Medical Journal* 293: 1642–3.

Wright, M. (1983) 'Am I fit to fly, doctor?', *World Medicine* 8: 31.

CHAPTER TWELVE ARE YOU FIT TO FLY?

Health checklist 1: all passengers

Air France and British Airways (undated) *Medical Aspects of Supersonic Flight* (booklet).

AMACEMS (American Medical Association Commission on Emergency Medical Services) (1982) 'Medical aspects of transporation aboard commercial aircraft', *Journal of American Medical Association* 247, 7: 1007–11.

Anon. (1961) 'Medical criteria for passenger flying', *Aerospace Medicine* 32, 5: 369–82.

Bennett, G. (1987) Personal communication, 7 June.

British Airline Pilots' Association (1980) *Fit to Fly: A Medical Handbook for Pilots*, London: Granada Publishing.

British Airways (1980) *Travel Health Guide*, ed. A.S.R. Peffers, London: Johnston & Bacon.

REFERENCES

British Airways Medical Services (undated) *Your Patient and Air Travel*, a yellow guide for doctors.

Chapman, P. (undated) Notes for the Guidance of Practitioners, British Caledonian Airways.

Chisholm, D.M., Billings, C.E., and Bason, R. (1974) 'Behaviour of naïve subjects during decompression: an evaluation of automatically presented passenger oxygen equipment', *Aerospace, Space and Environmental Medicine* 45, 2: 123-7.

Dawood, R. (1986) *Travellers' Health*, Oxford: Oxford University Press.

Ernsting, J. (1989) Personal communication, 16 June.

Fairhurst, R.J. (1976) 'The invalid passenger and air transport', *Practitioner* 217: 229-34.

Green, R.L. (1972) 'Special article: the selection of patients for air travel', *Modern Medicine* February: 112-18.

Green, R.L., Huntsman, R.G., and Sarjeant, G.R. (1971) 'Sickle-cell and altitude', *British Medical Journal* 4: 593-5.

Greist, J.H. and Greist, G. (1981) *Fearless Flying*, Chicago, IL: Nelson Hall.

Harding, R.M. and Mills, F.J. (1983) *Aviation Medicine: articles from the British Medical Journal*, London: British Medical Association.

Hoffler, G.W., Turner, H.S., Wick, Jr., R.L., and Billings, C.E. (1974) 'Behaviour of naive subjects during decompression from 8,000 to 30,000 feet', *Aerospace Medicine* 45, 2: 117-22.

Inglesias, R., Terres, A., and Chavarria, A. (1980) 'Menstruation: disorders of the menstrual cycle in airline stewardesses', *Aviation, Space and Environmental Medicine* May: 518-20.

Johnson, L.F. (1984) 'Aviation medicine, part 2: fitness to fly and the role of doctor travellers', *New Zealand Medical Journal* 97, 763: 602-5.

Lavernhe, J., Lafontaine, E., and Laplane, R. (1978) 'Concorde and cosmic rays', *Aviation, Space and Environmental Medicine* February: 419-21.

Morris, III, H.A. and Estes, M.L. (1987) 'Traveller's amnesia. Transient global amnesia secondary to triazolam', *Journal of American Medical Association* 258, 7: 945-6.

Preston, F.S. (1975) 'Medical aspects of supersonic travel', *Aviation, Space and Environmental Medicine* August: 1074-8.

Preston, F.S. and Denison, D.M. (1983) 'Aviation medicine', in D.J. Weatherall, J.G.G. Ledingham, and D.A. Warrell (eds) *Oxford Textbook of Medicine*, Oxford: Oxford University Press.

Turner, A.C. (1982) 'Is this person fit to fly?' *Medicine in Practice* 1, 10: 258-60.

Wachtel, T.J. (1983) 'Medical hazards of air travel for older people', *Geriatrics* 38, 6: 78-82.

Weatherall, D. and Sleight, P. (1988) Personal communication, 19 July.

Wright, M. (1983) 'Am I fit to fly, doctor?', *World Medicine* August: 31.

Health checklist 2: unfit passengers

AMACEMS (American Medical Association Commission on Emergency Medical Services) (1982) 'Medical aspects of transportation aboard commercial aircraft', *Journal of American Medical Association* 247, 7: 1007–11.

Anon. (1961) 'Medical criteria for passenger flying', *Aerospace Medicine* 32, 5: 369–82.

British Airline Pilots' Association (1980) *Fit to Fly: A Medical Handbook for Pilots*, London: Granada Publishing.

British Airways (1980) *Travel Health Guide*, ed. A.S.R. Peffers, London: Johnston & Bacon.

British Airways Medical Services (undated) *Your Patient and Air Travel*, a yellow guide for doctors.

British Caledonian Airways (undated) *Notes for the Guidance of Practitioners*, Dr Peter Chapman.

Dawood, R. (1986) *Travellers' Health*, Oxford: Oxford University Press.

Denison, D. (1989) Personal communication, 3 August.

Ernsting, J. (1989) Personal communication, 16 June.

Fairhurst, R.J. (1976) 'The invalid passenger and air transport', *Practitioner* 217: 229–34.

Green, R.L. (1972) 'Special article: the selection of patients for air travel', *Modern Medicine* February: 112–18.

Green, R.L., Huntsman, R.G., and Sarjeant, G.R. (1971) 'Sickle-cell and altitude', *British Medical Journal* 4: 593–5.

Greist, J.H. and Greist, G. (1981) *Fearless Flying*, Chicago, IL: Nelson Hall.

Harding, R.M. and Mills, F.J. (1983) *Aviation Medicine: articles from the British Medical Journal*, London: British Medical Association.

Inglesias, R., Terres, A., and Chavarria, A. (1980) 'Menstruation: disorders of the menstrual cycle in airline stewardesses', *Aviation, Space and Environmental Medicine* May: 518–20.

Johnson, L.F. (1984) 'Aviation medicine, part 2: fitness to fly and the role of doctor travellers', *New Zealand Medical Journal* 97, 763: 602–5.

Preston, F.S. and Denison, D.M. (1983) 'Aviation medicine', in D.J. Weatherall, D.A. Warrell, and J.G.G. Ledingham (eds) *Oxford Textbook of Medicine*, Oxford: Oxford University Press.

Turner, A.C. (1982) 'Is this person fit to fly?', *Medicine in Practice* 1, 10: 258–60.

Wachtel, T.J. (1983) 'Medical hazards of air travel for older people', *Geriatrics* 38, 6: 78–82.

Weatherall, D. and Sleight, P. (1988) Personal communication, 19 July.

Wright, M. (1983) 'Am I fit to fly, doctor?', *World Medicine* August: 31.

CHAPTER THIRTEEN   WHAT IS TO BE DONE?

ABTA (1987) Code of conduct No. 1: 2.9(i), London: Association of British Travel Agents.

AMACEMS (American Medical Association Commission on Emergency Medical Services) (1982) 'Medical aspects of transportation aboard commercial aircraft', *Journal of the American Medical Association* 247, 7: 1007–11.

Bennett, G. (1986) Personal communication, 17 March.

Civil Aviation Authority (1986) CAP 382 Mandatory Occurrence Reporting Scheme, Cheltenham: CAA.

REFERENCES

Dunlop, J. (1986) Personal communication, 23 June.

FAA (1987) Airline cabin air quality: comments on 21 recommendations in National Research Council report, United States Department of Transport, Summary: iii.

Fairhurst, R. (1987) Personal communication, 5 February.

Firth, J. (1987) Personal communication, 8 March.

Harding, R.M. and Mills, F.J. (1983) *Aviation Medicine: articles from the British Medical Journal*, London: British Medical Association.

Lawrie, J. (1986) Personal communication, 2 October.

Lock, S. (1986) Personal communication, 27 May.

Martin, P. (1987) Personal communication, 10 February.

Medical news (1986) 'FAA adopts rule to require medical kits on airliners', *Aviation, Space and Environmental Medicine* 3(7): 290.

Mooney, S. (1986) Personal communication, 9 May.

Peffers, A.S.R. (1980) (ed.) *British Airways Travel Health Guide*, London: Johnston & Bacon.

Shawcross, C.N. and Beaumont, K.M. (1985) *Air Law* edited by P. Martin, J.D. McClean, and E. de M. Martin, London: Butterworths.

INDEX

179